GABRIEL GARCÍA MÁRQUEZ

Recent Titles in Greenwood Biographies

Sitting Bull: A Biography
Edward J. Rielly

Eleanor Roosevelt: A Biography
Cynthia M. Harris

Jesse Owens: A Biography
Jacqueline Edmondson

The Notorious B.I.G.: A Biography
Holly Lang

Hillary Clinton: A Biography
Dena B. Levy and Nicole R. Krassas

Johnny Depp: A Biography
Michael Blitz

Judy Blume: A Biography
Kathleen Tracy

Nelson Mandela: A Biography
Peter Limb

LeBron James: A Biography
Lew Freedman

Tecumseh: A Biography
Amy H. Sturgis

Diana, Princess of Wales: A Biography
Martin Gitlin

Nancy Pelosi: A Biography
Elaine S. Povich

Barack Obama: A Biography
JoAnn F. Price

GABRIEL GARCÍA MÁRQUEZ

A Biography

Rubén Pelayo

GREENWOOD BIOGRAPHIES

GREENWOOD PRESS
WESTPORT, CONNECTICUT • LONDON

LONDON BOROUGH OF REDBRIDGE	
CL	
HJ	02-Mar-2009
863.64	£19.95

Library of Congress Cataloging-in-Publication Data

Pelayo, Rubén, 1954–
 Gabriel García Márquez : a biography / Rubén Pelayo.
   p. cm. — (Greenwood biographies. ISSN 1540–4900)
 Includes bibliographical references and index.
 ISBN 978–0–313–34630–9 (alk. paper)
 1. García Márquez, Gabriel, 1928– 2. Authors, Colombian—20th century—Biography. I. Title.
  PQ8180.17.A73Z826 2009
  863'.64—dc22
  [B]   2008036706

British Library Cataloguing in Publication Data is available.

Copyright © 2009 by Rubén Pelayo

All rights reserved. No portion of this book may be reproduced, by any process or technique, without the express written consent of the publisher.

Library of Congress Catalog Card Number: 2008036706
ISBN: 978–0–313–34630–9
ISSN: 1540–4900

First published in 2009

Greenwood Press, 88 Post Road West, Westport, CT 06881
An imprint of Greenwood Publishing Group, Inc.
www.greenwood.com

Printed in the United States of America

∞

The paper used in this book complies with the Permanent Paper Standard issued by the National Information Standards Organization (Z39.48–1984).

10 9 8 7 6 5 4 3 2 1

*I dedicate this book to both Gerald A. Lamb,
my adoptive father, and the memory of my mother.*

CONTENTS

Series Foreword		ix
Acknowledgments		xi
Introduction		xiii
Timeline: Events in the Life of Gabriel García Márquez		xvii
Chapter 1	Origins: Aracataca-Macondo	1
Chapter 2	"Bogotazo" and the Barranquilla Group	15
Chapter 3	Cinema, Europe, and Marriage	31
Chapter 4	New York, Mexico City, and Making Films	49
Chapter 5	The Myth of *One Hundred Years of Solitude*	63
Chapter 6	World Famous, September 11, 1973	81
Chapter 7	The Nobel Prize, Television, and Movies	99
Chapter 8	Journalism, Pilgrims, and Demons	115
Chapter 9	The New Millennium	129
Chapter 10	The Readings and the Friendships	141
Selected Bibliography		151
Index		157

Photo essay follows page 80

SERIES FOREWORD

In response to high school and public library needs, Greenwood developed this distinguished series of full-length biographies specifically for student use. Prepared by field experts and professionals, these engaging biographies are tailored for high school students who need challenging yet accessible biographies. Ideal for secondary school assignments, the length, format, and subject areas are designed to meet educators' requirements and students' interests.

Greenwood offers an extensive selection of biographies spanning all curriculum-related subject areas, including social studies, the sciences, literature and the arts, history and politics, as well as popular culture, covering public figures and famous personalities from all time periods and backgrounds, both historic and contemporary, who have made an impact on American and/or world culture. Greenwood biographies were chosen based on comprehensive feedback from librarians and educators. Consideration was given to both curriculum relevance and inherent interest. The result is an intriguing mix of the well known and the unexpected, the saints and sinners from long-ago history and contemporary pop culture. Readers will find a wide array of subject choices from fascinating crime figures like Al Capone to inspiring pioneers like Margaret Mead, from the greatest minds of our time like Stephen Hawking to the most amazing success stories of our day like J. K. Rowling.

While the emphasis is on fact, not glorification, the books are meant to be fun to read. Each volume provides in-depth information about the subject's life from birth through childhood, the teen years, and adulthood.

A thorough account relates family background and education, traces personal and professional influences, and explores struggles, accomplishments, and contributions. A timeline highlights the most significant life events against a historical perspective. Bibliographies supplement the reference value of each volume.

ACKNOWLEDGMENTS

I am everlastingly grateful to Anne Small and Thomas M. McManus, to Sister Maria-Ines Aparicio and Pastor Hans-Fredrik Gustafson, PhD; and Jonathan J. Beauchamp for their microscopic readings, interest, and editing of the entire manuscript. For my trip to Gabriel García Márquez's birthplace, I am indebted to John Redden, Fidel Vargas Salcedo, and Rafael Darío Jiménez Padilla, Director of the García Márquez Casa-Museo Foundation in Aracataca. I am also grateful to Sandra Torres Ordóñez and Frank Capellan for collecting data and John D. Garges for his contributions to Chapter 1.

INTRODUCTION

Gabriel García Márquez is one of the world's greatest storytellers in any language. He is a journalist, a short-story writer, a novelist, an international best-selling author, a master of "magic realism." In October 1982, then 55 years old, already world-famous, he was recognized by the Swedish Nobel Foundation as the winner of the Nobel Prize for Literature. The Spanish-speaking world was jubilant, thrilled. The Mexican government, on the same day the news of the Nobel Prize was announced, bestowed on García Márquez the Aztec Eagle Medal, the highest honor given to a foreign national. The Cuban administration gave him the Felix Varela Medal, the highest honor for intellectual achievement. The Colombian government, which, the year before, had sought his arrest, wanted the prodigious Colombian son back in his native country.

From all corners of the world, "the telegrapher's son from Aracataca" received laudatory calls, whether from friends such as French president François Mitterrand and Fidel Castro in Cuba, or fellow writers, and friends in general. On December 10, 1982, when the Nobel Prize for Literature was bestowed on him, faithful to his roots and his superstitions, he carried a yellow rose for good luck and wore a white *liqui liqui*, an informal peasant outfit, typical of northern Colombia. He was the fourth Latin American to win the Nobel Prize for Literature.

The chapters of this book are divided into decades, up to 2007. Each period covers the life, works, and greatest moments of Gabriel García Márquez, as well as what was happening around him. The coda that closes each chapter provides a broad outlook on major world events, with special attention to Latin America and its people. The coda enhances the understanding of the social and historical context of the time period, so the reader can see Gabriel García Márquez within the flow of nations and world affairs. The last chapter, without being comprehensive, is devoted to some of his friends and a number of his readings. His writing, more than any other Latin American author's, has allowed millions of readers around the globe to incorporate a literary concept of Latin America.

García Márquez invented his own make-believe universe and immortalized it as Macondo, rather as William Faulkner did with his imaginary Yoknapatawpha County and its inhabitants. In *One Hundred Years of Solitude*, and the work prior to it, García Márquez portrayed the life of Macondo, its peoples, and the saga of the Buendía family, mainly from his place of birth: the small town of Aracataca, near the Colombian Caribbean coastline. But he also sketched from the history of the country and the past of the continent at large, from its discovery to colonial times and the wars of independence. The reader of this book may find that nearly everything he has written is interconnected with García Márquez's own life. The memories of his childhood helped him create his masterpiece, *One Hundred Years of Solitude*. Raised by his maternal grandparents, he learned the art of storytelling and the importance of words from them. His first book was a present from his grandfather: a dictionary. Like William Faulkner and John Steinbeck in the United States, García Márquez has written about the land and the people who belong to it.

As a 20-year-old, García Márquez began publishing short stories. Like many authors before him, he began working as a newspaper reporter. One of the most widely read writers today, he continues to write journalistic articles. He has continued to publish literature since 1948, but his first major work, *Leaf Storm*, was rejected for publication in 1952 when he first sent it to Losada publishing house in Argentina. This novella, on the other hand, can be seen as the seed of what was going to become *One Hundred Years of Solitude*. *Leaf Storm* set the stage for both themes and techniques observed thereafter in his writing, culminating in *One Hundred Years of Solitude*. With *Leaf Storm*, he had found his voice as an author, but not a life as an artist. He would have to wait until 1967, with the overnight international success of *One Hundred Years of Solitude*, to be able to live as an artist who did not have to do anything other than write. In October of 1967, to escape from the crowds and the spotlight, he and his family moved to Barcelona.

Since 1958, he has been married to Mercedes Raquel Barcha Pardo, the "sacred crocodile," as Plinio Apuleyo calls her. Theirs was a love at first sight, which has lasted through the years. They have lived in New York City, Mexico City, Barcelona, Cartagena, and Bogotá, and traveled together around the world. His wife, however, has always kept out of the limelight. The same can be said of their two sons, Rodrigo and Gonzalo.

A college dropout, García Márquez got his education from the friends he made along the way and from his prodigious reading of literature from many nations. Now a wealthy and respected octogenarian, he counts as part of his wealth the number of friends he has kept. Some of these friends are cast in his writing, albeit not as central characters. Critics and biographers alike (as is the case in this book) refer to his writing influences, which range from Kafka and Sophocles to Modernist writers of the American Lost Generation and certain Latin American names. (All these influences are dealt with in Chapter 10 of this biography.) There are obvious influences from, or perhaps simply similarities to, such authors. As critics have pointed out, after all, there is no such a thing as an orphan book: all books are interrelated somehow. Gabriel García Márquez's writing style, however, is all his own. His words have touched millions of readers around the world, in more than 30 languages. His writing skill has allowed millions of people to imagine not only Latin America, but to experience most human conditions, as if in literary therapy, that they otherwise would never have experienced.

TIMELINE: EVENTS IN THE LIFE OF GABRIEL GARCÍA MÁRQUEZ

1927 Gabriel José García Márquez is born on March 6 in Aracataca, northern Colombia. Lives with his maternal grandparents, Colonel Nicolás Márquez Iguarán and Tranquilina Iguarán Cotes (cousins).

1933 Receives First Communion and is an altar boy.

1935 Teacher Rosa Elena Fergusson inspires in him his love for poetry.

1936 His most influential male figure, his grandfather, dies. His family moves to Sucre.

1946 He graduates from high school at Liceo Nacional de Zipaquirá boarding school.

1947 Registers in law school at the National University in Bogotá. Publishes his first two short stories: "The Third Resignation" on September 13 and "Eva Is inside Her Cat" on October 25, in *El Espectador,* Bogotá's premier newspaper.

1948 On April 9, Jorge Eliécer Gaitán, Liberal political leader, is killed. The violence that erupts will last for over two decades. The National University is closed. García Márquez moves to Cartagena. On May 21, starts working as journalist for the local newspaper, *El Universal.* Publishes his third short story, "The Other Side of Death," on July 25.

1949 Drops out of college in Cartagena. Moves to Barranquilla, where he befriends the members of the Barranquilla Group. Writes for the Barranquilla newspaper, *El Heraldo,* but continues to publish in Bogotá's *El Espectador:* "Dialogue with the Mirror" and "Bitterness for Three Sleepwalkers."

1950	While still working for *El Heraldo*, starts the tabloid magazine *La Crónica* with members of the Barranquilla Group.
1952	The manuscript for *Leaf Storm* is rejected by Losada publishing house, but his short story "Winter Time" is published in *El Heraldo*. The story will later be known as "Monologue of Isabel Watching it Rain in Macondo."
1953	General Gustavo Rojas Pinilla seizes power by coup d'état, and becomes president of Colombia. García Márquez sells encyclopedias alongside the Magdalena River and the Guajira Peninsula.
1954	On Monday, February 22, starts writing a weekly film column, the first of its kind, for *El Espectador*.
1955	Travels to Europe for the first time, to cover the "Big Four" Geneva Summit for *El Espectador*. In Bogotá, *Leaf Storm* is published. In Rome, he attends the Centro Sperimentale di Cinematografia. By wintertime, he has moved to Paris, where he lives, unemployed. He travels to Czechoslovakia.
1956	*El Espectador* shuts down to protest the dictatorship of Rojas Pinilla. From Paris, García Márquez writes for the weekly *Elite* in Venezuela. Works on the manuscripts for *No One Writes to the Colonel*, *In Evil Hour*, and the short stories for *Big Mama's Funeral*.
1957	Finishes *No One Writes to the Colonel*. Rojas Pinilla is overthrown. García Márquez travels through then-Communist countries from June to September with Plinio Apuleyo Mendoza. His account of the trip is published as *90 Days behind the Iron Curtain*.
1958	On Friday, March 21, marries Mercedes Raquel Barcha Pardo. Works in Venezuela, for magazines *Momento* and *Venezuela Gráfica*. *No One Writes to the Colonel* is published in Bogotá. Dictator Marcos Pérez Jiménez flees Venezuela.
1959	First son Rodrigo is born in Bogotá on August 24. Fulgencio Batista flees into exile; Fidel Castro takes over the government of Cuba. Plinio Apuleyo Mendoza opens an agency of the Cuban Latin Press in Bogotá, and invites García Márquez to participate.
1961	Moves to Mexico City after a short stay in New York City, where he works for Cuba's Latin Press news agency. The trip to Mexico with his wife and son is by bus. He wants to see the American South to better understand Faulkner's writing. The manuscript for *In Evil Hour* wins the Esso Literary Prize. Works as Chief Director for two magazines in Mexico City: *Sucesos* and *La Familia*.
1962	Second son, Gonzalo, is born in Mexico City on April 16. García Márquez does not authorize the Madrid publication of *In Evil*

TIMELINE

Hour. No One Writes to the Colonel is published in Colombia, and *Big Mama's Funeral* in Mexico.

1963 Writes movie scripts for the Mexican cinema. One of them is *The Golden Cock*, based on a story by Juan Rulfo.

1964 Writes the movie script for *A Time to Die*. The script is published in *Revista de bellas artes*.

1965 Starts writing *One Hundred Years of Solitude* in Mexico City. A film adaptation of "There Are No Thieves in This Town" is released.

1967 In June, *One Hundred Years of Solitude* is published in Argentina and becomes a best seller in Spanish. The book wins the *Primera Plana* prize in Argentina on June 20. In July, meets Mario Vargas Llosa, and in October, García Márquez and his family move to Barcelona.

1969 *One Hundred Years of Solitude* wins the Chianchiano Award in Italy and the prize for Best Foreign Book in France.

1970 *One Hundred Years of Solitude* is published in English. The 1955 journalism article, "Diary of a Shipwrecked Sailor," is published in book form.

1971 Columbia University awards him an honorary doctoral degree. The Padilla Affair causes division among some of the "Boom" Latin American writers. García Márquez is in the eye of the storm on both accounts.

1972 Wins the Rómulo Gallegos literature prize in Venezuela and the Neustadt International Prize for Literature in the United States, awarded by the University of Oklahoma and *World Literature Today*.

1973 *Innocent Eréndira and Other Stories* is published in English.

1974 Founds *Alternativa* magazine.

1975 *The Autumn of the Patriarch* is published. Moves back to Mexico City after eight years in Barcelona.

1976 *The Autumn of the Patriarch* is translated into English.

1978 Writes the short stories "Light Is Like Water" and "I Only Came to Use the Phone."

1979 "I Only Came to Use the Phone" is turned into a screenplay. Writes the short story "Maria Dos Prazeres." "Montiel's Widow" is published.

1981 *Chronicle of a Death Foretold* is published. García Márquez requests political asylum in Mexico. He is awarded the French Legion of Honor.

1982 Wins the Nobel Prize for Literature on December 10. Mexico awards him the Mexican Order of the Aguila Azteca prize, and

	Cuba the Félix Varela Medal. He is invited to be a member of the International Cannes Film Festival.
1983	*Chronicle of a Death Foretold* is published in English. The film *Eréndira* is released.
1985	*Love in the Time of Cholera* is published. The Association of Colombian Journalists awards him the 40 Años prize. A new film adaptation of *A Time to Die* is released.
1986	Works with Chilean Miguel Littín in the production of a TV series to depict the repression under Pinochet's dictatorship. *Clandestine in Chile: The Adventures of Miguel Littín* is published.
1987	Film adaptation of the novel *Chronicle of a Death Foretold*.
1988	Finishes *Love's Diatribe against a Seated Man*, his only play. Produces six TV shows for the Spanish National Television under the title *Dangerous Loves*.
1989	TV miniseries *Miracle in Rome* wins the prestigious Golden Nymph Award at the Monte Carlo TV Festival in Monaco. *The General in His Labyrinth* is published.
1990	Attends a Latin American Film Festival in Japan. Co-writes the TV script *The Two-Way Mirror* with Mexican Susana Cato. The opening play at the Latino Theatre Festival in New York is *Chronicle of a Death Foretold*.
1992	Has lung surgery to remove a tumor. *Strange Pilgrims* is published. The Repertorio Español Theater in New York adapts *Eréndira*.
1993	He is awarded an honorary degree from the Autonomous University of Santo Domingo in the Dominican Republic.
1993	*News of a Kidnapping* is published.
1994	Creates the Foundation for New Iberian-American Journalism, a non-profit organization in Cartagena. The University of Cadiz, Spain, awards him an honorary doctorate degree. *Of Love and Other Demons* is published. Short story "Eyes of a Blue Dog" is turned into a film.
1996	Screenplay collaboration for Sophocles' *Oedipus the King* is released as *Edipo Alcalde*.
1997	Opening speech for the First International Congress of the Spanish Language, celebrated in Zacatecas, Mexico. Meets with President Bill Clinton at the White House.
1998	Becomes one of the owners and Chair of the Colombian magazine *Cambio* (*Change*).
1999	*No Ones Writes to the Colonel* is turned into a film. García Márquez is diagnosed with lymphatic cancer.
2002	*Living to Tell the Tale* is published in Spanish.

2003 *Living to Tell the Tale* is published in English.
2004 *Memories of My Melancholy Whores* is published in Spanish.
2004 Film adaptation of *In Evil Hour* is released.
2005 *Memories of My Melancholy Whores* is published in English. A film adaptation of "A Very Old Man with Enormous Wings" is released.
2006 Teamed with Fernando Birri to release the documentary *ZA 05. The Old and the New*.
2007 Fortieth Anniversary Edition of *One Hundred Years of Solitude* is published. IV International Congress of the Spanish Language in Colombia is dedicated to Gabriel García Márquez to celebrate his 80th birthday and 25th anniversary as Nobel Laureate. He visits his birthplace, on May 30, with wife, Mercedes. In November, attends the opening ceremony of the 21st International Book Fair in Guadalajara, Mexico. The film adaptation for *Love in the Time of Cholera* is released on November 16. On December 5th, attends the 29th New Latin American Film Festival in Havana, Cuba.

Chapter 1
ORIGINS: ARACATACA-MACONDO

> My mother asked me to go with her to sell the house. [...] She did not have to tell me which one, or where, because for us only one existed in the world: my grandparents' old house in Aracataca.
>
> —*Gabriel García Márquez*, Living to Tell the Tale, 3

Long before his birth, Gabriel García Márquez's family history planted the seeds for his fertile imagination. His creative literary genius was formed by his unusual childhood, his vivid memory, and the perceptions sharpened by being the only child in a household of senior adults until he was six years old. Even the actual date of his birth is uncertain, whether due to inaccessible birth and baptismal records, or to deliberate obfuscation by his maternal grandparents, who raised him from birth to age seven. Gabriel García Márquez's life, however, is not an ordinary chain of events. Joy, love, longing, isolation, and solitude precede his life as a child, as a teenager, as a young adult, and well into his thirties.

Gabriel García Márquez was the firstborn of Eligio García and Luisa Santiaga Márquez Iguarán. His mother was the youngest daughter of Colonel Nicolás Ricardo Márquez Mejía and Tranquilina Iguarán Cotes. His maternal grandfather was a third-generation Colombian of Spanish ancestry. Like his father and his grandfather before him, the Colonel was also a jeweler of sorts. He dropped out of school as a young man to join a Liberal army to fight in the Thousand Days War (1899–1902) under the command of war hero General Rafael Uribe. When the war was over, he was discharged with the rank of colonel and settled in Aracataca. Although the Liberals lost the conflict against the Conservative Party, the colonel enjoyed a high reputation in liberal Aracataca.

Like the character José Arcadio Buendía, founder of Macondo in *One Hundred Years of Solitude,* his maternal grandfather married his cousin, killed a friend in a duel, fathered many children as he went along, and was a jeweler. The fictional Arcadio Buendía also fights in the Thousand Days War, and also becomes a colonel. But the Thousand Days War was a factual Colombian civil war between the Liberal and Conservative parties. From this war, literally a blood bath for the country, and its serious economic consequences, Panama gained its independence from Colombia in 1903.

García Márquez's maternal grandparents had a large house in Aracataca. It was a sizeable wooden home with a zinc roof, two unpaved blocks from the plaza. His grandfather, an important person in Aracataca, held office as the town's rent collector. Wherever the old man went in the township, he would take his grandson, Gabito, with him. In the late 1920s, when Gabriel García Márquez was a child, Aracataca was already an impoverished town of merchants, small shop owners, few professionals, and one movie house without a roof. The economy of the town was hit hard by the departure of the United Fruit Company (UFC). At the turn of the twentieth century, the UFC employed over 80 percent of the town's population. Few people in the town had cars, and those who did were mostly Americans who worked for the UFC. It must have been a sight to see cars then, some with their tops down, and with English-speaking people driving. But with the collapse of the New York stock market and the Great Depression of 1929, the UFC closed and left town. Once the UFC left, Aracataca began to decay.

García Márquez's maternal grandparents were considered to be among the town's aristocracy, if there ever was one. They had been among the earliest settlers, arriving before the wave of foreigners who came to Aracataca with the banana-bonanza, attracted by the UFC.

The love story of García Márquez's parents reflected a common theme of social disparity, with the bride's family's concomitant struggles to prevent the marriage. His father, Gabriel Eligio García, bore the double stigma of being born to a single mother and being a newcomer to the town. He carried only his mother's family name, García. She, Argemira García Paternina, had children by three different men. While that fact might have been unknown to his future in-laws, that Gabriel Eligio García was an outsider was not. He was an obvious stranger in town, one of the many who came to Aracataca looking for a better way of life during the UFC's banana-bonanza. Unlike many, he did not gain wealth, but found love instead. His being an outsider was too strong a strike against a bachelor who fell in love at first sight, out of his league.

He was, however, the town's telegrapher. This was a rather prestigious job for the town and the historical circumstances, but it was not good enough for his future in-laws, the Márquez-Iguaráns. With their illustrious ancestors' status to uphold, they did not want to allow their daughter to marry a stranger.

The young telegrapher had fallen in love with Luisa Santiaga Márquez Iguarán. Luisa was the youngest daughter of her rather socially prominent, if not wealthy, family. As one of the town's most respectable families, they looked down at those who came from afar. They would do whatever they could to stop their daughter from having anything to do with this man, Gabriel Eligio García—the telegrapher, the stranger. As a writer, Gabriel García Marquez explores this theme, the stranger in town, in many of his short stories and novels.

Their efforts were futile. Luisa Santiaga was hardheaded and determined to love the telegrapher, the outsider, a member of the group the townspeople called rubbish. These people, attracted to Aracataca by the banana-bonanza, were seen as "fallen leaves," an analogy for *La hojarasca*, the title of Gabriel García Márquez's first novel, known in English as *Leaf Storm*. The telegrapher and the prettiest girl in town were madly in love with each other. He would not let anything come between them. Against the bride's parents' wishes, against all odds, the love shared by Gabriel Eligio García and Luisa Santiaga Márquez Iguarán survived any and all oppositions—as the lovers in *Love in the Time of Cholera* do. They got married on June 11, 1926, but the young couple had to leave town. They settled in Riohacha (Ax River), a port city in the north, on the Atlantic coast in the Department of La Guajira. But the pregnant Luisa Santiaga soon came back to Aracataca by herself, a few days short of the ninth month after their marriage. She came back to give birth to her firstborn, only to leave him behind soon thereafter. The newborn stayed in the house of his maternal grandparents, in Aracataca, and his mother went back to Riohacha. (The town of Riohacha would later appear in *One Hundred Years of Solitude* and *Chronicle of a Death Foretold*.)

Gabriel García Márquez's biography may start with his birth, right here, March 6, 1927. His writing, however, encodes the life of his parents, his grandparents, and, to a great extent, some of the history of Colombia. From this conflicted beginning and unusual early childhood came the indelible impressions that shaped his writing. The facts of his ancestors' lives rivaled the most imaginative fiction, as when his grandmother claimed there were ghosts in two locked rooms in their house because people had died in them, leading the poor child to fear the dark and the presence of spirits of the dead.

Could the grandparents Márquez-Iguarán or the baby's own parents have forgotten, for some time, the birth date of the newborn? For decades, readers of Gabriel García Márquez were led to believe he was born in 1928, not 1927.

The boy was baptized in Aracataca, Colombia, as Gabriel José García Márquez. Unlike his father, the baby would carry two last names: García, from his father's lineage, and Márquez, from the maternal side. Let us remember that in some instances, Latin Americans and Spaniards use two last names. The first is the father's family name, and the second refers to the mother's lineage. Not all Latin Americans observe this tradition. Most Latin American writers, in fact, use only their father's last name. Think, for example, of Carlos Fuentes and Octavio Paz; Pablo Neruda and Julio Cortázar; Isabel Allende and Rosario Ferré. However, there are others, such as Federico García Lorca and Mario Vargas Llosa, who carry both parents' last names. The most important figure in Spanish literature uses this tradition. We often refer to him as Cervantes, as we do with Shakespeare or Dante, but his full name is Miguel de Cervantes Saavedra, the novelist, playwright, poet, and creator of *Don Quixote*. From his birth on, however, Gabriel García Márquez has been called either Gabo or Gabito—nicknames for Gabriel.

García Márquez remembers discovering soccer in 1931 at four years old. He also recalls the experience of going to Catholic Mass. As a five-year-old, he sees a dead man for the first time (death will be a recurring theme in his writing, particularly in the first short stories), and enjoys Caribbean and tango music, and singing. At this tender age, he shows a prodigy's talent for drawing.

One of his greatest memories is his first contact with the written word at five years old. His grandfather gave him a dictionary as a result of a disagreement with a bystander while at a circus tent in town, over the difference between a camel and a dromedary. Gabito, looking at a dromedary, had asked his grandfather what "that animal" was. A camel, responded his grandfather, only to be corrected by the onlooker. "This book [his grandfather told him] not only knows everything, but it is also the only one that is never wrong."[1]

If the images of death and the stories of ghosts marked his future writing, from listening to all the women who inhabited the house in Aracataca, getting a dictionary from his Grandpa was definitely a moment that would stay etched in his mind and his future life. He was destined to become a magician with words, a wordsmith. It looks as if, thereafter, nothing else was ever more important than the written word, reading, and writing.

He later recalled, vaguely, that as a young child in 1932 he heard people chanting, "Long live Colombia, down with Peru." The dispute was over the Colombian-Peruvian boundaries to gain access to the Amazon River. This led to a war over the territory of Leticia, which Colombia lost.

In 1933, now six years old, García Márquez was an altar boy and received his First Communion. Readers of Gabriel García Márquez may notice a marked tendency to deal with religious iconography, names, and liturgical celebrations alongside miracles, priests, and the Church. This is due to his upbringing at home and his schooling up until high school. One of his four sisters, Aida Rosa, became a nun, but changed her mind and left her religious vows of chastity, poverty, and obedience after 22 years of religious life.

When he was six years old, his parents moved back to Aracataca with two more children: his brother, Luis Enrique, a year younger than him, and his sister, Margot. Gabito, however, remained his grandfather's favorite. By then he was used to going almost everywhere in town with him. His beloved maternal grandfather was García Márquez's most influential father figure, more so than his own father. In his childhood, he would call him Papalelo, a compound word Gabito made, fusing Papá and Abuelo. (*Abuelo* is Spanish for grandfather.) This was nothing out of the ordinary; all small children, in all languages, are linguists to this extent. His grandmother, Tranquilina, was called Mina.

His passion for telling stories started around this time. Upon returning home from the movies, in the company of his grandfather, at the dining table he would recount the films they had seen together in the town's movie theater. He had it in him: he was already a *raconteur*.

The first two years of school, where he learned to read, were spent at the Montessori elementary school in Aracataca. By 1935, the eight-year-old had started to read under the direction of teacher Rosa Elena Fergusson, who instilled in him his love for poetry. Poetry, in fact, was his passion until he enrolled in college. Poetry was foremost in Latin American letters until the second half of the twentieth century. The Montessorian teaching method, highly popular at the start of the twentieth century, encourages children to be independent without neglecting a sense of responsibility. The method allows children to come in touch with their senses, and special attention is given to the individual student as opposed to the class as a whole.

García Márquez's sense of independence, observed throughout his life, can be traced as far back as these early years. Not many children learn to live without a mother from almost their moment of birth. One can easily hypothesize that his constant usage of the theme of solitude goes back to these very early years of abandonment. He meets his mother for the first time at the age of five, and his father at the age of seven. If a writer does indeed write about his own experiences, in his case it becomes obvious why solitude is one of the themes that permeate his oeuvre. Most of his characters start as prototypes in his early writings and evolve to full characters in *One Hundred Years of Solitude;* all of them are based on real people. His thematic issues are all based on real incidents as well.

García Márquez remembers 1936 quite well, not because General Anastasio Somoza took over as dictator of Nicaragua, nor because General Francisco Franco led the start of the Spanish Civil War, but because in 1936, the most influential male figure in his life died. With the death of his chubby, sanguineous, one-eyed grandfather, the García Márquez family moved out of Aracataca. The mansion of Gabriel García Márquez's golden years of innocence was left behind, empty. The family literally locked up and left. They came back to Aracataca 14 years later, but only to try to sell the house. García Márquez was 22 years old then. This is, precisely, the moment and the image with which his memoir *Living to Tell the Tale* begins, in medias res: "My mother asked me to go with her to sell the house. [...] She did not have to tell me which one, or where, because for us only one existed in the world: my grandparents' old house in Aracataca."[2]

The year 1936 was indeed a turning point in García Márquez's life, marked by his grandfather's death and the move out of Aracataca. They took his grandmother, Tranquilina, with them and moved to Sincé, a northern town in the Sucre Department, where his father had been born. Without this move, Gabriel García Márquez would not have become the writer he is today. However, the writer he became also responds to the many international borders he has crossed, the books he read, the experiences he survived, and, most importantly, the friends he made along the way.

The same can be said of many writers. What would T. S. Eliot and Ezra Pound have become without the hostility of London? Can we think of Lord Byron without his travels in Italy and Greece? Would Pablo Neruda have written as he did without being able to return to his own home in Chile during the Pinochet dictatorship? García Márquez, however, has been quoted time and again as saying that nothing interesting ever happened to him after the death of his grandfather. It was the end of an era for García Márquez. After that, he says, he felt rather jaded. "Growing up, studying, traveling, none of that particularly attracted me. Nothing interesting has happened to me since."[3] From Sincé, his parents moved to

Sucre. He helped with the moving arrangements as if he were an adult. This was in the year 1939, and García Márquez was 12 years old.

While his parents lived in Sucre, García Márquez was sent to boarding school in Barranquilla. Although the family knew he would be all alone, Barranquilla was more suited for García Márquez's education. Barranquilla has always been the most industrial and most developed of all cities in the Colombian Caribbean region. To most Colombians, this port city is known as Colombia's Golden Gate. It was there, at the Colegio San José, that he would start writing poetry. Little is known about his elementary school days. His own memoir, *Living to Tell the Tale*, seems blurry about this period, as if the solitude he felt as a young child in boarding school was a passage he has kept to himself.

Bell-Villada, whose work on García Márquez is among the most complete we have in English, points out that García Márquez's biography prior to the 1960s is surprisingly dislocated. The dislocations, we agree, come from the lack of factual information available about the number of siblings, his birth date, García Márquez's answers in different interviews regarding his books, his likes, and the almost nonexistent information from 1936 to 1940. By 1936, however, we can imagine a rather slim, introspective, withdrawn 12-year-old whose friends used to call him Old Man because of his temperament and personality. During these years, Gabriel García Márquez was discovering books and authors (an aspect of his biography we discuss in full in a separate chapter). The educational system in Colombia for elementary school is from first grade to fifth. By 1939, the boy who was going to be the world's best-selling author in the Spanish language had finished elementary school at the age of 12. Soon after, without thinking in terms of junior high school, Colombians attend *bachillerato* or *liceo*. Both terms can be transposed to American schooling, if we keep in mind that this level of education goes from the 6th grade to the 12th.

At 1940, the 13-year-old García Márquez made the longest and saddest trip of his young life. Barely an adolescent, he moved away from home again to attend, once more, a boarding school: the Liceo Nacional de Zipaquirá. In May 1982, Plinio Apuleyo Mendoza—a Colombian novelist and journalist, and García Márquez's close friend—published one of the most read and quoted conversations with Gabriel García Márquez. The book was immediately translated and published the year after, in England, as *The Fragrance of Guava*. So, in 1940, the 13-year-old went to high school at a boarding school about 30 miles outside of Bogotá, the capital city of the country.

Getting there by plane now takes about an hour from the coastal Caribbean area where he was living at the time, but in the 1940s, it could take at least a week or longer, depending on the weather conditions and transportation. The trip was one of epic proportions then. It would have started up the Magdalena River (one of the two largest rivers in Colombia; the other is the Cauca in the southwestern part of the country) on a Mark Twain-type steamboat to Port Salgar in the foothills of the eastern Andes mountain range. Thereafter, the trip would have been continued by train—a train ride that goes up the mountain range as the weather changes from hot to cold, the dress code from informal to formal, and the mannerisms from playful and relaxed to reserved and respectful. The ride was a trip from *costeño*-life to *cachaco*-life: from coastal to city life. Cachacos is the name given to the peoples of Bogotá and surrounding areas, a name tinged with both disdain and envy. Cachacos are city dwellers, recipients of the Old Spanish traditions, institutions, wealth, and culture. To young García Márquez, other than the death of his grandfather, this was the saddest change he had ever experienced. The Andean lifestyle of Bogotá was both foreign and contrary to his Caribbean roots. He cried the first time he saw Bogotá.

But as he grew older, the trip became something to look forward to. The coastal students (costeños) would plan ahead and have parties while riding the boat back and forth to school twice a year. As is typical of García Márquez, these memories find echoes in his writing. The most obvious of the references to the Magdalena River steamboat rides to school is the one he calls "the River of Love" in *Love in the Time of Cholera*.

Much of this novel evolves around the Magdalena River. García Márquez evokes his images of it from his teenage years, and his parents' love story. The years at the boarding school at Zipaquirá are his years of coming of age, his own *Bildungsroman*. As is typical of the hero of the *Bildungsroman* novel, the young García Márquez was no longer the same when he returned home from his experience in Zipaquirá.

The lifestyle, social contacts, literary readings, tobacco, alcohol, and geography of the Andean savannah had a profound impact on his growth. The school provided him with a strong education, although his heart, he soon discovered, was not in the hard sciences. Mathematics was rather far from his interest; his passion for the humanities became obvious. His teachers, however, were all fond of him. It was at this school that he became interested in Marxism and developed left-oriented tendencies.

While he was in high school, before his graduation in 1946, García Márquez met a most radical teacher, who introduced him to a new wave of Colombian poetry and the works of the Nicaraguan Rubén Darío, leader

ORIGINS

of the literary movement known as *modernismo* in Latin Ame
Colombian group was known as Piedra y Cielo (Stone and Sky,
suggest a group that aspires to grandiosity while keeping its feet
ground. Teacher Carlos Martín, the youngest of the group of poe
his job and was thrown out of school. Carlos Calderón Hermida, García
Márquez's Spanish teacher, motivated him to write short stories and poetry, as well as directed his literary readings.

Almost 19 years old, in 1946 García Márquez finished high school and went back to his family home in Sucre, not knowing what to do with his life. To this date, his memoir, *Living to Tell the Tale*, helps trace his life, but even in this book, García Márquez was more interested in writing something for posterity than in sharing his life. Somehow, his own novels tell his life story, and this time, when we thought he was going to focus on the facts of his life, his memoir takes the form of a novel. The eight chapters that comprise the book, however, are a tour de force, from his childhood to his first trip to Europe, still single, in 1955.

There is no room for speculation. García Márquez's life as a writer turned out to be what it is today because of his childhood. For the dedicated reader, it soon becomes evident that everything he writes comes from his early childhood. Images, sounds, settings, characters, and frequently even the themes find their origins in Aracataca, in Zipaquirá, in Santa Marta, in Cartagena, someplace in the Colombian landscape, but particularly the Caribbean countryside, for he calls himself a Carib. Most, if not all, of his work can be traced to his own life. His fictionalized characters are representations of real people. He writes about what he knows, with reference to his own experiences. His works are crafted and polished to the minutest detail.

His is a poeticized reality that literary critics in the United States, in the mid-1950s, started calling magical realism. The term, however, was used in Latin American letters as early as 1948, when surrealism seemed to have an impact on literary criticism. German critic Franz Roh used it first in 1925 to refer to the visual arts. Latin American critics and writers, however, were prompt to use it to describe a reality that included the irrational and ancient beliefs of the indigenous and black people of the Americas. García Márquez has captured the attention of readers around the world as a magical realist. Some even see him as synonymous with the term, but there were writers—such as Cuban Alejo Carpentier and Guatemalan Miguel Angel Asturias—who were writing in this style before him. They, too, wrote about a reality where the demarcation between the rational and the irrational was nonexistent. The Venezuelan Arturo Uslar Pietri, who was a friend of both Carpentier and Asturias, is credited with being the first to apply it to Latin American literature as a genre.

To better understand his writings, as we have noted, the reader must learn about Gabriel García Marquez's family, since his fiction includes a coded biographical account of his parents, his grandparents, and, often, of his friends. The combination of myth and reality in his writing gives room to incorporate what he has experienced, read, and observed about the sociopolitical life of Colombia. Although the settings of all his writings are Colombian, with the exception of the book of short stories *Strange Pilgrims*, the plight of his characters is love, the search for love, the lack of love. His fictional world is a human comedy, and most of us find characters with whom we can identify, themes we feel strongly about, or simply stories that are always entertaining. Seemingly local or regionalist, his work is universal. The microcosms he has invented are ageless. The ambitions and frustrations, the anxiety of shame and tenderness, the longing for love and power, and his characters' feelings of immense solitude are all-encompassing. He invented a world that indeed will stand for posterity.

Outside of Colombia, Aracataca is known as the rural town where Gabriel García Márquez was born. Colombia is the fourth largest country in South America after Brazil, Argentina, and Peru. Its population is the third largest in Latin America after Brazil and Mexico. As a country, it is divided into Departments, in the same way that the United States is divided into states. Aracataca is a northern Colombian riverside town, located in the Magdalena Department, built on the side of the Aracataca River. It was founded in 1885. Its climate is tropical with very hot temperatures; humidity can be felt year round, and heavy rainy seasons, from April to June and from August to November, are typical of this Caribbean region.

The image of such constant torrential rains and flooding is captured in the short story "Monologue of Isabel Watching it Rain in Macondo." The title is most appropriate. The pouring rain of this region can often be of biblical proportions. It is not uncommon to see people's homes swept away by the storms. In the story's plot, the railroad tracks are carried away, and people and animals drown, but this terrifying account of a deluge reads as if it were a tropical rain we simply have to come to understand. It is all beyond our imagination, and in the end, the omniscient narrative voice tells us it might have been Isabel's imagination. The story is left open ended. It offers many possibilities for interpretation, and several thematic issues for discussion.

The town of Macondo, the rains, the railroad, the characters, all seem to announce what was yet to come in future writings. We know now that this short story, in fact, was either taken out of or never included in *Leaf Storm*. In any event, one complements the other. The overwhelming storm seen in "Monologue of Isabel Watching it Rain in Macondo" reaches its highest peak in *One Hundred Years of Solitude*, where the rains continued for 4 years, 11 months and 2 days. The universe Gabriel García Márquez was going to call his own with the invention of Macondo, however, would cause him to go through long, trying frustrations and disappointments as a writer.

Today, Aracataca's main economy comprises agriculture, livestock, small family business, and trade. But at the turn of the twentieth century, the banana plantations of the American United Fruit Company were the main economic supplier for the inhabitants of the town, simply called Cataca by the townspeople. The still-visible railway of Gabriel García Márquez's short stories—such as "Tuesday Siesta" and the abovementioned "Monologue of Isabel Watching it Rain in Macondo"—and novels like *One Hundred Years of Solitude* no longer serves as public transportation. A train still comes through town, however, twice a day, carrying coal to Santa Marta, capital city of the Magdalena Department. Today, transport in and out of Aracataca is via State Highway 45.

Present-day Aracataca has a total of 33 neighborhoods, called barrios. It is interesting to note that one of them bears the name "Macondo." Although the barrio has the name mostly recognized and associated with García Márquez, the inhabitants of his childhood town refused to vote in favor of a referendum for a name change. The town's mayor, Pedro Sánchez, was most hopeful and thought the name change would bring tourism to aid the town's economy. Although hard to believe, there were not enough votes in favor of the 2006 referendum to change the town's name to Macondo.

Even though few people find their way to Aracataca, looking for the town where García Márquez was born, there are those who make the long pilgrimage from different corners of the world. Rumor has it that in the late 1960s and early 1970s, there were world travelers who came to Colombia, looking for Macondo as if it were a real place.

At one of the entrances to present-day Aracataca, there is a large billboard showing García Márquez's bust portrait. It is a rather rustic, amateurish, painted mural. In the upper right corner of the mural is an elderly Gabo, wearing glasses, clapping his hands, smiling, sporting his now-gray, ever-present moustache. The mural features yellow butterflies (reminiscent of Mauricio Babilonia in *One Hundred Years of Solitude*), the train station, the town's church, and the old-fashioned coal-engine train: that train whose whistle served to tell time to the townspeople; the same train that the reader finds in much of García Márquez's writing; the train that left with a number of people killed during the banana strike of 1928, both in fiction and in real life. The number of people killed during this event, however, is a difficult myth to decode today. The billboard wall reads "Me siento americano de cualquier país, pero sin renunciar nunca a la nostalgia de mi tierra: Aracataca [Aracataca in capital letters, painted yellow], a la cual regresé un día y descubrí que entre la realidad y la nostalgia estaba la materia prima de mi obra." ("I feel as a Latin American from any Latin American country without ever giving up the nostalgia I feel for my home town: Aracataca, where, once I returned, I realized that between reality and the nostalgia I feel for Aracataca was the essence of my oeuvre.") The billboard may come down sometime, or be changed. It was meant to celebrate his 80th birthday on March 6, 2007. The bottom part of the mural shows a political slogan: "Forging the Future of Macondo," in Spanish, of course, and from side to side, in the style of a banner, the inscription in blue letters, "1927 We Celebrate His 80 Years of Prolific Life 2007,"[4] also in Spanish.

Visitors to Aracataca today find a ghost town, with few people on the streets and hardly any car traffic at all. The road to Aracataca bypasses the town, through its outskirts.

CODA

Gabriel García Márquez lived in Aracataca from his birth in 1927 until 1935. Once his family left Aracataca, it took him 15 years to return, on February 18, 1950. Perhaps this visit opened up the walls in his mind where his memories were stored, because right after this first visit to Aracataca, he broke through those walls and began to write more feverishly than during the two years before. He would not come back to Aracataca again until 1983, the year after he won the Nobel Prize for literature.

Newspapers in Argentina, Mexico, Colombia, Washington, D.C., New York City, and many other places around the globe reported the news of "a magical homecoming" in May of 2007. Now an octogenarian, "Gabo" was once again back in the town where he was born. His triumphant return, on Wednesday, May 30, 2007, was in a vintage train called "the Yellow Train of Macondo" (El Tren Amarillo a Macondo). Having a native son like Gabriel García Márquez is not a small thing for the town of Aracataca. In fact, it is certainly not a small thing for Colombia as a whole. Colombians look upon him as national property. Everyone in Colombia, and the Spanish-speaking world, unquestionably looks up to him. In the United States, we pay more attention to him than to any other

Spanish-speaking writer. Since 1967, with the publication of *One Hundred Years of Solitude*, he has remained the most read Latin American author around the world.

Numerous newspapers, scholars, and journalists worldwide are interested in what he does or does not do. Some come to him to petition his opinion about the ongoing violence in Colombia, as if he could undo the complicated political, social, and economic problems that plague his country. His visit to Aracataca, in May of 2007, was in an effort to help boost the economy of the impoverished town of his childhood. The "Yellow Train of Macondo" on which he arrived is the one that would serve to carry the tourists who come to Aracataca to see the town and the house where he was born.

The Colombian Bureau of Tourism revealed that in 2006, 3,000 "literary visitors" came to see his house and the town. Among them, the improvised museum's guest book shows signatures of Europeans and Americans. The present Colombian Government plans to invest over half a million dollars to restore the house where he was born and officially turn it into a museum by 2008. The museum, two blocks from the main plaza, will carry his name. In today's unofficial museum—his paternal house, the house of the town's telegrapher—world travelers can see his first typewriter, old photos of the writer, his family, and extended family.

NOTES

1. Gabriel García Márquez, *Living to Tell the Tale*, trans. Edith Grossman (New York: Alfred A. Knopf, 2003), 90.

2. Ibid., 4.

3. Luis Harss and Barbara Dohmann, *Into the Mainstream: Conversations with Latin American Writers* (New York: Harper & Row, 1966), 319.

4. I visited Aracataca in July 2007. I wanted to witness the physical places I have read about for nearly 40 years.

Chapter 2
"BOGOTAZO" AND THE BARRANQUILLA GROUP

García Márquez matriculated at the National University (Bogotá, Colombia) on February 25, 1947. In his freshman year, he passed all his courses except Statistics and Demography. The transition from high school to college is sizeable and challenging. Many young adults find the passage difficult, adverse, unsympathetic, and sometimes even undesirable. Some students do not adapt to the newfound freedom and major responsibilities they face, and often drop out. Money issues can be another obstacle, often solvable, although not always. The matter of vocation, however, may pose a most difficult task for independent young adults. Gabriel García Márquez was one of those young adults who was dissatisfied with his decision to go to college. One of the reasons was the fact that he went to college against his will. It was not his decision. As is often the case with middle-class families where no one has a college degree, his parents wanted him to be the first. On the one hand, his father had dropped out of college for economic reasons. On the other, Gabo was the oldest of 11 siblings. With a college degree, he could help take care of the family. He decided to please his parents and enrolled as a student at the National University in Bogotá, the nation's capital. In February of 1947, he matriculated from Law School.

In Colombia, and the rest of Latin America, the degrees of law, medicine, and architecture—to name three fields of specialization—are part of the undergraduate studies curriculum. García Márquez was a 20-year-old Caribbean who did not have the best opinion of Bogotá. To him, the weather was too gloomy and the manners and customs too stiff. In Bogotá, interestingly enough, he felt like a stranger. Coming from a Liberal household, and particularly from the Colombian coastal area, García Márquez would associate Bogotá with centralized power and dictatorship. Colombia, like most Latin American countries, has suffered from centralized power since colonial times. It is in their capital cities that Latin American nations have their highest population, largest economic centers, best universities, and seats of government. Anything of importance—whether political, literary, financial, or otherwise—with few exceptions, converges in the capital cities. The people of Bogotá look at the rest of the country with a certain disdain. The rest of the country, in return, calls them either cachacos or rolos, as if disregarding them, but also acknowledging their elegant dress, good schooling, and manners (see Chapter 1 for more information on cachacos). The younger generations from Bogotá are identified as *rolos*, a newly coined term not usually used for people in their 50s or older; they are exclusively *cachacos*. Divided by regions and political affiliations, or social class, for that matter, Colombians also have identifiable forms of speech—phrasing and intonation—that differ from their lexicon. The people of Medellín, for example, are identified as *paisas*. García Márquez is a *costeño*, from the North Atlantic coastal area. He, however, calls himself a Carib. "I am," he says, "*un caribe puro.*" In 1982, García Márquez published a book of his journalistic work, covering the years of 1954 and 1955, and, appropriately, called it *Among Cachacos*.

Bell-Villada describes García Márquez's days in college: "Floating about in a state of chronic personal depression, he led a life in the main to the lecture halls, the boarding house, and the nearby cafés, where, book in hand, he would show up unshaven and badly dressed."[1] An image we have of him, in contrast, is his tenacious and firm desire to write. He demonstrated that in high school. Most of what he wrote in high school is lost, but in *Living to Tell the Tale*, he states that in those years, he wrote poetry.

In 1947, as a 20-year-old, he was soon going to surprise his friends and those who knew him with his first publications. As it was in high school, however, his passion for letters continued to be poetry, not the short story or the novel. Instead of preparing for his college courses, during the weekends he would ride the trolleys in Bogotá, just to kill time and read poems. "My most salacious form of entertainment (at the time) was to sit, Sunday after Sunday, on those blue-paned trams that took you back and forth from the Plaza Bolívar to the Avenida de Chile for five cents."[2] Around that time, he came into contact with a novel that was going to be instrumental in his shift from poetry to prose. Along those lines, he also met a transcendental and dear friend.

The novel was *The Metamorphosis*, published in 1915 by the Jewish, Czech-born, German writer Franz Kafka (1883–1924). For García

Márquez, reading the opening paragraph of Kafka's *Metamorphosis* (translated into Spanish by none other than the Argentine Jorge Luis Borges) was almost as if he were listening to the stories his grandmother would tell him when he was a child. The friend he met was Camilo Torres Restrepo. Father Camilo Torres, a member of a prominent family in Bogotá, was two years younger than García Márquez. As a Catholic priest, inspired by the Cuban revolution, Camilo Torres joined the guerrilla group Ejército de Liberación Nacional (ELN): the National Liberation Army. "Camilo Torres baptized García Márquez's first son, Rodrigo, and became a popular figure for turning priesthood into a form of rebellion [Liberation Theology]. He was killed by the Colombian armed forces on February 5, 1966."[3] He was only 37. With his death in 1966, he became a martyr of the ELN and an emblem of the 1970s for his maxim, "If Jesus were alive today, He would be a *guerrillero*."

The impact of Camilo Torres on García Márquez comes to the fore in the Nobel laureate's memoir, *Living to Tell the Tale*. The episode dedicated to him is inspirational. Father Camilo Torres seems to jump off the pages more powerfully than the priests who inhabit García Márquez's short stories and novels. Could he, Camilo Torres, have served as a model for the many priests who populate García Márquez's writing? Although most of Gabo's devotees know of their friendship, no one has ever asked García Márquez that question.

The *Metamorphosis* alone secured Franz Kafka a place in world literature. Gabriel García Márquez, on the other hand, through simply reading it, gained enough self-confidence and inspiration to write his first short story. He has been quoted as saying that right after reading the opening paragraph of *The Metamorphosis*, he closed the book, trembling. This is how *The Metamorphosis* starts: "As Gregor Samsa awoke one morning from uneasy dreams, he found himself transformed in his bed into a gigantic insect. [...] His numerous legs, which were pitifully thin compared to the rest of his bulk, waved helplessly before his eyes. [...] 'What has happened to me?' he thought. It was no dream."[4] "'Christ,' [García Márquez] thought, 'so this is what you can do.' [And] the next day he wrote his first story."[5] Apuleyo Mendoza does not provide the name of the short story, but it was "The Third Resignation." It was first published in *El Espectador* (*The Spectator*) of Bogotá.

Bogotá was a cold and distant place for the young Caribbean college student. The city has an altitude of 8,700 feet above sea level. Throughout the year, the days are rather cool and the nights can be unpleasantly cold for people not used to low temperatures. The city's average temperature is 57 degrees Fahrenheit during the day and 48 degrees at night. It rains heavily during April and October, but there are also days of light rain in July and August. García Márquez, at that time, was a chain smoker, so the high altitude made him feel short of breath. While Bogotá was a city where the influence of the supernatural of his childhood was rather removed from society, the advent of Kafka's *Metamorphosis* was a strong connection to his infancy. The tempo and dynamics of the city were those of the most important city in Colombia. The fashions were European, the president of the country did business here, and everything Colombian of great importance seemed to have its epicenter here. Bogotá, García Márquez has said, "is the city which impressed me the most and which marked me the most. The afternoon I arrived in Bogotá, a somber city, it was raining, with the streetcars throwing sparks as each passed a street corner. And everyone was hanging from them. All men were dressed in black, wearing hats, and not a single woman."[6] He made the statement many years after his freshman year in college, when he was 54 years old, a world traveler who had seen most of, if not all, the important cities in the world. He also had homes in several of them.

But during his freshman year in college, he was broke, was not interested in law, and his first publication took him by surprise. It appeared in a weekly literary supplement for *El Espectador* called "Fin de Semana" ("Weekend"). He remembers not having the five cents to buy the newspaper, and no friend was in sight to loan him the money. The chief editor of the supplement was Eduardo Zalamea Borda, a well-regarded journalist, politician, novelist, and critic in Colombia. Zalamea Borda took an interest in García Márquez's first short story and published "The Third Resignation" on Saturday, September 13, 1947. This event and his "learning" about arts and letters in the downtown cafés had not changed his feelings about Bogotá.

He wrote, "I always arranged for the waiters to put me as close as possible to the great master León de Greiff, [...] who would begin his *tertulia* at dusk with some of the most famous writers of the day, and end with his chess students at midnight, awash in cheap liquor."[7] León de Greiff, at the time, was a 52-year-old intellectual poet whose friends were poets, musicians, and painters—Gabo was 20 years old. De Greiff was an influential figure in the poetic and literary Colombian circles. Eduardo Zalamea Borda was one of the intellectuals who would sit at de Greiff's table. De Greiff was a Colombian of Spanish, German, and Scandinavian ancestry, and author of several poetry books. Like many Latin American poets of the second decade of the twentieth century, he was influenced by both French surrealism and by a Chilean poet, Vicente Huidobro (often credited as the founder of the avant-garde Latin American poetry movement known as "Creationism").

García Márquez, although almost penniless, was already getting in touch with leading Colombian intellectuals. Above all, however, Gabo decided to focus on his reading and writing, and ignored his law coursework at the National University. Among other authors, he was reading Fyodor Dostoyevsky and Leo Tolstoy, considered the best novelists of Russian literature, and the French novelists Gustave Flaubert and Stendhal, whose real name was Marie-Henri Beyle. Around that time, he also started reading the literature of the Argentine Jorge Luis Borges, and English authors Aldous Huxley, D. H. Lawrence, and Graham Greene. He must have felt as if he had homework to do and the assignment was literature, not law. He was literally reading almost every author he could, as long as his friends would lend him the books.

During the pivotal year of 1947, Gabriel García Márquez was also first introduced to the literature of the Irish novelist James Joyce, best regarded for his experimental work in *Ulysses* (1922) and *Finnegans Wake* (1939). García Márquez was interested in reading novels, but during the 1940s, poetry was still at the forefront of literature in the Spanish Americas. With poets like the Chileans, Vicente Huidobro and Pablo Neruda, the Peruvian César Vallejo (full name César Abraham Vallejo Mendoza), Cuban Nicolás Guillén, and Mexican Octavio Paz, among many others throughout the Spanish-speaking world, a new form of poetry was being written. Pablo Neruda, born Ricardo Eliécer Neftalí Reyes Basoalto, gained popularity for his poetry, use of language, and political statements. The name "Pablo Neruda" started first as his penname, but sometime later became his legal name. Neruda and García Márquez met years later and became very close friends. With only the authority of his own voice, García Márquez has said that Pablo Neruda was the greatest poet of the twentieth century in any language. An overstatement, perhaps, but Neruda was recognized with the Nobel Prize for literature in 1971.

"The Third Resignation" brought García Márquez the joy of being a published author. His elation, however, was as great as his fear of continuing writing. Upon publishing García Márquez's second short story, "Eva Is inside Her Cat," six weeks after the first one, Zalamea Borda wrote, "[This] is not something that all 20-year-old boys just beginning their relationship with letters can accomplish. [...] With García Márquez, a new and notable writer has been born."[8] "Eva Is inside Her Cat" was published on October 25, 1947, in the same newspaper as the first story—*El Espectador*. At that time, Zalamea Borda and young García Márquez had not yet met. The two publications for *El Espectador* were illustrated. What Zalamea Borda saw in the two short stories published in the *El Espectador* was much different from what the critics wrote about them in the United States, after 1970, when his most famous novel, *One Hundred Years of*

Solitude, was translated. These two stories and those that followed were the spark of the writer who was yet to come. He had a fascination with structure, and at the time, he was merely an apprentice. Emulating Kafka was much too ambitious and his readership rather weak. After all, one must remember, he was enthralled with poetry, not prose.

As it was with his childhood, his first year of college, the only one he completed at the National University in Bogotá, left him with memories as deep as the sea. Only this time, the memories would be both literary and political, and would add to his incredibly dense self-referential writing, which, although it seems fictional, all has a thread tied to reality. Enthralled by his desire to read novels, his absenteeism from university became chronic. He went to parties, dances, and brothels, studied with friends for final exams, did some last-minute cramming, and still managed to pass most of his courses during his freshman year. Interestingly enough, his political interests did not surface at all. That year of 1947, he was also introduced to journalism. It was his friend Camilo Torres, in fact, who introduced him to the journalist Plinio Apuleyo Mendoza. Plinio introduced him to his sister. She, in turn, got him interested in journalism. Plinio Apuleyo Mendoza became his *compadre* when, 12 years later, he served as godfather to Gabriel García Márquez's firstborn son, Rodrigo. The baptism took place at the Palermo Hospital in Bogotá and Father Camilo Torres officiated at the ceremony.

In 1948, at age 21, García Márquez came back to Bogotá from his parents' home in Sucre to start classes as a sophomore. They were so proud of him that they bought him his first typewriter. If leaving Aracataca as an eight-year-old was a turning point, the year of 1948 was going to be a stepping-stone, a crossroads for the young Gabriel García Márquez. This crucial year, in effect, was a crack in time for all of Colombia. For young readers of the twenty-first century, it may seem that the violence we hear about today in Colombia could have started right around this critical year. However, the political feud between the Conservative and Liberal parties can be traced back to the nineteenth century, and the many civil wars Colombia underwent as these two political parties opposed one another. On April 9, 1948, this feud was brought back by the assassination of a Liberal candidate in broad daylight. Jorge Eliécer Gaitán, who two years earlier had lost the presidential election against Mariano Ospina Pérez, was assassinated. He was killed in downtown Bogotá, around lunchtime.

For García Márquez, this caused a rude awakening of his political beliefs, obscured by his limitless interest in literature. But on that day, hundreds of angry people took to the streets, first in Bogotá and then in the rest of the country, to riot in protest of the assassination of their favored candidate to the presidency. If presidential elections had taken place that year, some went on to say, Eliécer Gaitán would have won—but elections would not take place until two years later. What came to be dubbed the "Bogotazo" lasted for three consecutive days and nights. Neither the number of people killed nor the assassin's name has ever been disclosed to please the public. Although the analogy with the assassination of President John F. Kennedy may seem audacious, not many believed that one man alone was the executioner. "Even today, there is no unanimous belief that it was Juan Roa Sierra, the solitary shooter who fired at him from the crowd on Carrera Séptima."[9] The resulting violence lasted three days, but the fighting and deaths continued through the mid-1960s. The death toll, to date, remains unknown. Government offices said a total of two hundred thousand lives were lost; others have stated three hundred thousand. Historians, as well as the public, call this undeclared civil war between Conservatives and Liberals *la violencia* (the violence). The hatred experienced by Colombians during those years is reflected in García Márquez's works *In Evil Hour, No One Writes to the Colonel,* and short stories like "Montiel's Widow." The absurdity of it all is that when Colombians went to the polls, two years later, in 1950, they supported yet one more Conservative Party candidate, whom the rioters had seemed to oppose. They elected President Laureano Gómez, a right-wing extremist of the Conservative Party who ruled the country with an iron fist from 1950 to 1953. In fact, the Liberal Party, due to the wave of violence the country was undergoing, decided not to run after the killing of Liberal leader Eliécer Gaitán. The candidate for the Liberal Party, Darío Echandía, declined his candidacy for the presidency on the basis that there were no guarantees for the well-being of his political party.

With the city of Bogotá literally in flames and in ruins, ringing with shots and explosions, García Márquez moved to Cartagena de Indias, a large walled-city seaport named after the port of Cartagena in Spain's Murcia region. Although he continued to study law at the University of Cartagena, he was definitely more interested in writing. This capital city of the Bolívar Department, today about a five to six hours' drive from the town of his birth, was going to be more benign than Bogotá. His means of living were as precarious as they had been in Bogotá, but here, in Cartagena, on May 21, 1948, he was actually on the payroll of the local newspaper, *El Universal.* His literary readings of the year before were to pay off greatly, as he went on to pursue journalism without having had the proper schooling for it.

He literally had to juggle his law studies at the University of Cartagena during the day and work for the newspaper at night. The newspaper column was called "Punto y Aparte" ("Period, New Paragraph"). He was close to failing as a student at the University of Cartagena. During that time, however, García Márquez enjoyed the sympathy and direction of one of his professors, Mario Alario Di Filippo. He was a lawyer and well-known Colombian intellectual. On August 6, 1975, Di Filippo became a member of the Colombian Academy of Language. García Márquez's work as a journalist eventually became literary journalism, but not without the scrutiny and direction of Clemente Manuel Zabala, who helped the young Gabo in the art of journalistic writing. It would not be until many years later, however, that Zabala's teachings would turn into literary journalism. It was a journalistic approach somewhat similar to that incorporated into literature by the Americans Ernest Hemingway and Truman Capote. In the United States, many consider Truman Capote to be the father of literary journalism, for his non-fiction novel *In Cold Blood* (1965). Although several of García Márquez's important works fit into this genre, the one that gained him worldwide recognition was *Chronicle of a Death Foretold* (1981). Other works in this genre are *The Story of a Shipwrecked Sailor*, *Clandestine in Chile*, and *News of a Kidnapping*.

The offices of the *El Universal* newspaper in Cartagena were located on the street San Juan de Dios. Clemente Manuel Zabala was the director of the newspaper. He had read García Márquez's short stories, published in *El Espectador* of Bogotá, and was rather impressed with his writing. But García Márquez had much to learn about literature and journalism. Zabala, in essence, was García Márquez's editor when necessary. Zabala was the first to read and edit all the originals of *Leaf Storm*.[10] Those were the days when García Márquez used to sleep on the newspaper rolls after the offices of *El Universal* were closed. His parents were living in Sucre, and Gabo did not have an apartment or a room in a boarding house. When he was lucky, he would have enough money to pay for a hotel room, which also functioned as a brothel. His firsthand knowledge of the life of prostitutes has its origin in these days. These were experiences that would later become a recurring theme in his writing. Prostitutes, as symbols of exploitation, would come in and out of his future writing. The most audacious of them all are "The Incredible and Sad Tale of Innocent Eréndira and Her Heartless Grandmother" (1972), and *Memories of My Melancholy Whores* (2004).

The column, "Punto y Aparte," which he wrote in 1948, was more of a chronicle of what was happening in Cartagena. But he also wrote commentaries about George Bernard Shaw, Aldous Huxley's most famous novel, *Brave New World*, and a brief note about American cinema. From May of 1948 to December of the same year, Gabriel García Márquez put his name to 36 newspaper pieces for his column in Cartagena's *El Universal*. While he was learning journalism under Zabala's watchful eye, he was feverishly trying to write his own short stories. *El Espectador* of Bogotá published his third short story, "The Other Side of Death," on July 25, 1948. He was fortunate enough to have come into contact with those who had power in the city, the upper middle class, all members of the Liberal Party, but his passion for writing was all his own.

The most influential figure during his first stay in Cartagena, in 1948, was Clemente Manuel Zabala. During this time, Gabo also met Víctor Nieto Núñez, an important name in Cartagena's public life and a pioneer of radio, radio journalism, and film. Nearly 10 years his senior, today Víctor Nieto Núñez and Gabo are both central figures of the Cartagena International Film and Television Festival, with Nieto Núñez Director of the festival. The international film festival, the oldest of its kind in Latin America, in 2007 honored García Márquez's work in film and the documentaries made about him.

During 1949, Cartagena was going through major changes, and García Márquez, still working as a journalist for *El Universal*, was both a witness and a reporter. The prologue of his novel *Of Love and Other Demons* opens with the date October 26, 1949. At first glance, the facts we read in the prologue have historical value and the reader, thereafter, may assume that as the story of Sierva María de Todos Los Angeles unfolds, it is based on reality. However, García Márquez himself publicly denied that the facts mentioned in the prologue ever happened.[11] According to Gustavo Arango, October 1949 was a month of important religious and political events in Cartagena, which may have both influenced and affected the creation, many years later, of the novel *Of Love and Other Demons*. Journalist, novelist, and critic Gustavo Arango records that in October 1949, the only *El Universal* article García Márquez signed, on October 7, with his full name was the one about the death of Edgar Allan Poe. It was a note on the one hundredth anniversary of the death of the American poet and short story writer, who died on October 7, 1848, at the age of 39. The title of the article was "Poe's Life and Novels" ("La vida y novela de Poe"). The newspaper article provides an incredible opportunity to look into the life of a 22-year-old who has a strong opinion on the subject he's writing about. Poe's life, he writes, "was the fulfillment of a tragic itinerary. Like those of his American contemporaries—Nathaniel Hawthorne and Herman Melville—Poe left in each one of his words the testimony of a neurosis that took over all aspects of his psychological universe."[12] He goes on to state that he is a reader of the detective novel, as genre. He adds that without Poe's narratives of mystery and the macabre, and short stories like "The Murders in the Rue Morgue," we would not have such writers as Thomas de Quincy, whom many see as the father of the detective novel, nor would Conan Doyle, S. S. Van Dine, and Ellery Queen enjoy the prestige they do today. He closes the article with a wish in the first personal singular pronoun: "I hope this, the one hundredth anniversary of his death, marks a just and definitive date to value the work by Edgar Allan Poe."[13]

By the end of 1949, then 22 years old, having dropped out of college at the University of Cartagena, García Márquez moved to Barranquilla. His professor at the University of Cartagena, Mario Alario di Filippo, who thought Gabo was a genius, gave him the money for the move.[14] When Gabo left for Barranquilla, according to Carlos Alemán, a friend from Gabo's youth, "Mercedes was already in Barranquilla. Her father had a drugstore in the Boston *barrio*. Gabito always kept an eye on her; he would visit her constantly. He left Cartagena for Mercedes and because they [*El Heraldo*] paid him better."[15] Today the city of Barranquilla is a two-hour drive from Cartagena, on a relatively good, paved two-lane road. Barranquilla is a more industrial, more economically sound city than Cartagena. Esthetically, however, there is no comparison with anywhere else in Colombia: the walled city of Cartagena is peerless.

Typical of all the moves Gabo made throughout his life, moving to Barranquilla was also a good stepping-stone for the development of the aspiring young writer. Although now living in Barranquilla, García Márquez continued to publish in *El Espectador* of Bogatá. In 1949, he published two short stories there: "Diálogo del espejo" ("Dialogue with the Mirror") and "Amargura para tres sonámbulos" ("Bitterness for Three Sleepwalkers"). These two short stories were his fourth and fifth publications. According to Jacques Gilard, the former is still reminiscent in style of Kafka's influence. The latter, however, has traits of the inspiration that García Márquez took from Faulkner's *The Sound and the Fury*.[16]

In Barranquilla, Gabo wrote for the newspaper *El Heraldo*. The central figures and major influences of his stay in the city of Barranquilla were the journalist, novelist, and intellectual José Félix Fuenmayor, alongside Ramón Vinyes, a playwright, journalist, and businessman. Vinyes, Bell-Villada says, was more of a literary father to García Márquez. Gilard, on the other hand, observes that this Catalan, who was going to be a significant figure for Gabo, had in fact read Faulkner in 1939, in France, and Virginia Woolf by 1940. Vinyes wrote a literary column for *El Heraldo* called "Reloj de torre" ("Clock Tower"). Although García Márquez only knew Ramón Vinyes for rather a short time (Vinyes died in 1952), he has great, long-lasting memories of him. In the back of the house where he was born in Aracataca, the House-Museum undergoing restoration, there is a plan for a small auditorium that will bear his name: Ramón Vinyes, "El sabio Catalán" ("The Wise Catalan"). The group of young journalists, Álvaro Zepeda Zamudio, Germán Vargas, and Alfonso Fuenmayor, and the elders, Félix Fuenmayor and Ramón Vinyes, would become yet another group of contributors to the rapid literary growth García Márquez was undergoing while away from the university classrooms. Gabo, in essence, became a self-taught *literati* through his friends. In the coastal city of Barranquilla, Gabo got together with these friends for both work and seminal discussions—*tertulias*—at a bohemian café called Happy. Their conversations were invariably about politics, combined with literature—or perhaps the other way around.

The president of Colombia was the engineer Mariano Ospina Pérez, member of the Conservative Party. He had won the presidential election of 1946 and survived the infamous Bogotazo of 1948, when Jorge Eliécer Gaitán was killed. Of the group of friends currently called the Barranquilla Group by some literary critics, García Márquez is fond of mentioning primarily three names: Álvaro Cepeda Zamudio, Germán Vargas, and Alfonso Fuenmayor; the latter is the son of José Félix Fuenmayor. The three of them—Alvaro, Germán, Alfonso—plus Ramón Vinyes appear at the end of *One Hundred Years of Solitude* as characters, with their own names, as does García Márquez's wife, Mercedes.

It was around this time, through the influence of the Barranquilla friends, that García Márquez came into contact, or rather became more involved, with the literature of Defoe, Dumas, Woolf, Melville, and Hawthorne. Of the group of friends, he was the only one who had not read *A Journal of the Plague Year* by English writer Daniel Defoe, and *The Count of Monte Cristo* by the Frenchman, Alexandre Dumas. Alvaro Zepeda gave him *Mrs. Dalloway* by Virginia Woolf as a present—the only book written by a female that he has been quoted as reading during those times. He also read Herman Melville's *Moby Dick*, and Nathaniel Hawthorne's *The House of the Seven Gables*. In his memoir *Living to Tell the Tale*, he said the latter book marked him for life; indeed a strong statement, but he does not say how or why. To this list, Gilard adds the Americans John Dos Passos, Ernest Hemingway, John Steinbeck (winner of the Nobel Prize for Literature in 1962), Erskine Caldwell, and the English author Aldous Huxley. While García Márquez was sick, without anything to read at his parents' home in Sucre, his friends from the Barranquilla Group sent him a box of books to read.[17]

When he started to write for *El Heraldo*, on January 5, 1950, he had an editorial column called "La Jirafa" ("The Giraffe"). This time, as a

23-year-old, he did not put his name to his writing, but wrote under the pseudonym Septimus. His signing as Septimus was most likely inspired by his new discovery of Virginia Woolf's novel *Mrs. Dalloway* (1925). It is interesting, however, that Gabo would select Septimus for his *nom de plume*. Septimus is an anxious, manic-depressed character who ultimately commits suicide in Woolf's novel, *Mrs. Dalloway*.

His work for the Barranquilla newspaper *El Heraldo* kept him very busy. For the month of January, he wrote 14 columns under the name Septimus; 14 in February; and 27 in March. March and May were the two months when he wrote the most articles in 1950, both months with 27 entries each. His notes, signed "Septimus," dealt with a large variety of issues: Eva Perón's appendectomy, Ingrid Bergman, Nostradamus, President Truman, Rimbaud, and Verlaine. Among the many pieces he wrote that year, one, written in April, was about the Nobel Prize for Literature. The title he used was "Once Again the Nobel." He was defending the rumor that the Venezuelan-born writer and politician Rómulo Gallegos might be the winner of the Nobel Prize for 1950. The Venezuelan author, who became president of Venezuela in February of 1948, did not win then, or ever. In his column, Gabriel García Márquez argues that the Chilean poet Gabriela Mistral was not worthy of receiving the Nobel Prize in 1945, as Pablo Neruda was already around, and to his evident consternation, he adds that William Faulkner may never get it. With emotion, he writes, "In the United States, there is someone named William Faulkner, someone who is the most extraordinary that there is among the world's modern novelists, no more, no less."[18] Gabo shows in this article that he had no time to research the news he wrote about. William Faulkner, in fact, had received the Nobel Prize the year before! He corrects himself later the same year, in November, with an article titled "Faulkner, Nobel Prize." This time, however, he quotes Faulkner's home as Oxford, Missouri, as opposed to Oxford, Mississippi.

García Márquez had strong feelings about many issues. The same month he published the piece about Faulkner and why he would never get the Nobel Prize, he wrote about the status of the Colombian novel; the headline was "The Problem with the Novel?" In sum, the crisis he saw was the lack of influence on the Colombian novel by writers like Joyce, Faulkner, and Woolf. It was too soon for him to be undertaking literary analysis in an area of expertise that was not his, but he did. The fascination he felt for literature, and the company he kept with older friends, mainly the Barranquilla Group, seemed to have led him to write as he did in regard to Truman's Capote short story "Miriam," and Ernest Hemingway's novel,

Across the River and into the Trees. The short story was too long to be good; the novel was a good example that Hemmingway was on his way out. "Hemingway's life of the last few years seems to be a strategic farewell, a voluntary death like that of suicide, but more realist, more rational, of course."[19] Young Gabo was wrong when it came to Hemingway's farewell from letters, but right when he made the analogy with suicide. Two years later, Hemingway published *The Old Man and the Sea* and received the Pulitzer Prize in Fiction for it in 1953. In 1954, Ernest Hemingway was awarded the Nobel Prize for Literature. However, at the age of 61, anxiety-ridden and depressed, he took his own life, on July 2, 1961.

The Barranquilla Group, perhaps driven by their intellectual ambition, started *La Crónica*, a tabloid magazine that combined literature with sports news. This was a weekly publication, first published on April 29, 1950. Alfonso Fuenmayor was the director, and García Márquez was the editor in chief. The two of them would bear most of the responsibility for putting out the weekly publication, but the rest of the Barranquilla Group were members of the Board and contributed with their writing. While the magazine's Board of Directors published its own literary interests, what they were reading, it was also a form of self-promotion for their own writing. José Félix Fuenmayor published seven short stories, García Márquez published six, and Álvaro Cepeda Zamudio published four. However, the magazine, wrote Jacques Gilard, became one of the best of its kind in Colombia. Not a small triumph, considering that *Crítica* (*Criticism*), edited by Jorge Zalamea, was publishing in Bogotá at the same time.[20] Jorge Zalamea was considered then, and now, to be an influential author, essayist, critic, and poet. *La Crónica*, on the other hand, allowed García Márquez to show off his drawing abilities. Many of the stories featured in the magazine were illustrated with his own artwork (Chapter 1 describes how sketching was one of his artistic abilities as a young child). "The Night of the Curlews" was one of the short stories he published in *La Crónica*. The magazine ceased publication in June of 1951.

By February of 1951, García Márquez had moved back to Cartagena, but continued to work in partnership for the *El Heraldo* newspaper. The move was perhaps prompted by the fact that his parents had moved from Sucre to Cartagena. We say "perhaps" only because García Márquez, for any number of reasons, lived with his parents for only very short periods at a time. Their moving to Cartagena would not have been a strong enough reason to just let *Crónica* die. He might also have intended to continue with his studies at the University of Cartagena. But that was not the case, as all he ever wanted to do was write.

During 1951, now living in Cartagena, he worked for *El Universal* again, to make ends meet. His name, however, did not appear on any of the pieces published. Why? A good answer is the fact that he continued to write for Barranquilla's *El Heraldo* to pay off a loan he had taken from them to help his family buy furniture for their move to Cartagena.

By February of 1952, Gabo had returned to Barranquilla. It was as if he had never left. From Cartagena, he kept sending his newspaper articles for publication in Barranquilla's *El Heraldo,* to repay the loan. Now he was back to work at the newspaper again, writing his column, "The Giraffe." For each of these pieces, the Barranquilla newspaper would pay him three pesos. During 1952, Gabriel García Márquez had two major character-forming experiences. On one hand, he endured the death of his mentor and intellectual "father figure," Ramón Vinyes, who died in Barcelona. On the other, he experienced the rejection by Argentine publishing house, Losada, of his manuscript for the novel *Leaf Storm.* Losada had planned to publish a Colombian novel to help its sales in Colombia, and García Márquez submitted the manuscript for *Leaf Storm.* Losada, whose director was Guillermo de Torre, selected *El Cristo de espaldas* (*Christ Turns His Back*) by the Colombian writer Eduardo Caballero Calderón. This realist novel deals with the Colombian violence that reached unimaginable proportions after the 1948 Bogotazo.

Before 1952 was over, García Márquez had left *El Heraldo*. For the special Christmas edition, the newspaper published his short story "El invierno" ("Winter Time"). This story would later be published with the familiar title, "Monologue of Isabel Watching it Rain in Macondo."

In June of 1953, General Gustavo Rojas Pinilla seized power through a coup d'état and became president of Colombia from that date on, until May 10, 1957. He ruled as a dictator, brutally opposing any form of opposition or rebellion.

In 1953, García Márquez was employed selling books, as hard as it may be to imagine. The experience, however, provided him with a closer look at the towns of the Atlantic Colombian region, where he would try to sell encyclopedias.

CODA

For a few months after the publication of his first short story, García Márquez worked as a journalist in the coastal cities of Cartagena and Barranquilla. His journalism during these years, as critics point out, would not be remembered today if it had not been for his short stories and novels. His work as a journalist, nevertheless, has continued to the present.

His journalism provided him not only with the opportunity to publish his short stories, but endowed him with the necessary tools to polish his writing. A good number of his newspaper articles and reportages were serious drafts of his literary ambition. His own style, his sense of humor, his use of language, his tendency to exaggerate and fictionalize reality—typical of his literary style—are found in the journalism he began writing as early as 1948, when he was 21 years old. His work in Cartagena and Barranquilla, the friends he made, the Barranquilla Group, and his opportunity to travel throughout the Atlantic coastal area gave him a strong sense of independence and an iconoclastic way of writing that he would not have developed in Bogotá. His journalism from 1948 to 1953, and the short stories he published along the way, are testimonials to this apprenticeship period as a writer.

NOTES

1. Gene H. Bell-Villada, *García Márquez: The Man and His Work* (Chapel Hill: University of North Carolina Press, 1990), 46.

2. Plinio Apuleyo Mendoza, *In Conversation with Gabriel García Márquez: The Fragrance of Guava*, trans. Ann Wright (London: Verso, 1983), 41. Note: Throughout Colombia, in every city or town where there is a main plaza (a main square in the center of town), it is called Plaza Bolívar.

3. Rubén Pelayo, *Gabriel García Márquez: A Critical Companion* (Westport, CT: Greenwood Press, 2001), 1.

4. Apuleyo Mendoza. *In Conversation*, 41–42.

5. Franz Kafka, *The Complete Stories*, ed. Nahum N. Glatzer and trans. Willa and Edwin Muir (New York: Schocken Books, 1971), 89.

6. *Gabriel García Márquez: Magic and Reality*, videocassette, directed by Dr. Ana Cristina Navarro and produced by Harold Mantell (Princeton, NJ: Films for the Humanities, Inc., 1981).

7. García Márquez, *Living to Tell the Tale*, 246 (see chap. 1, n. 1).

8. García Márquez, *Living to Tell the Tale*, 251 (see chap. 1, n. 1).

9. García Márquez, *Living to Tell the Tale*, 290 (see chap. 1, n. 1).

10. Gustavo Arango, *Un ramo de no me olvides: Gabriel García Márquez en El Universal* (Cartagena, Colombia: El Universal, 1995), 107–8.

11. Gustavo Arango quotes from conversations with Carlos Alemán, a friend of García Márquez during these years. Taken from Arango, *Un ramo*, 273.

12. Gabriel García Márquez, *Obra periodística 1, Textos Costeños*, compiled by Jacques Gilard (Bogotá, Colombia: Editorial Norma, 1997), 96–98. (The translation is mine.)

13. Ibid., 98. (The translation is mine.)

14. Arango, *Un ramo de no me olvides*, 273. (The translation is mine.)

15. García Márquez, *Obra periodística 1*, 275. (The translation is mine.)
16. Ibid., 13. (All the translations used to refer to this book from Jacques Gilard are mine.)
17. Ibid., 20.
18. Ibid., 173.
19. Ibid., 257–58.
20. Ibid., 24.

Chapter 3

CINEMA, EUROPE, AND MARRIAGE

> When the history of the Colombian cinema is written, García Márquez's work about it will deserve a special chapter. Not for the films he never had a chance to make [during the 1950s], but for his contributions as a film critic.
>
> —Jacques Gilard

In 1954, nine hundred pesos a month was enough money to convince García Márquez to relocate to Bogotá and work for the daily newspaper, *El Espectador*. Plenty of money, indeed, if one takes into account that each entry for *El Heraldo* in Barranquilla, where he had worked before coming to Bogotá, was worth a mere three pesos each. Even when he produced as many as 27 entries a month, 27 "Giraffes" (derived from "La Jirafa," his column for *El Heraldo*, which he wrote under the pseudonym "Septimus"), the grand total would not even approach his new salary at *El Espectador*: more than a nine-fold increase!

This was fully an economic windfall for the young Gabriel García Márquez, and he was once again in the capital of the country. Seven years earlier, in February of 1947, he had lived in Bogotá when he matriculated from law school at the National University. He was back in the same gloomy city of the *cachacos*, whose manners, he had thought, were too stiff, and among whom he had felt like a stranger. This time, however, he would be there on his own terms, not just to please his parents. They had sent him to Bogotá expecting him to earn a college degree. But he never finished his college education.[1] This time, it was all about himself. He was 26 years old, still single, and although literature was his only love, what he wrote would primarily be journalistic articles. In this new phase of his life, journalism would continue to provide him with the means to support himself, travel within the country, and eventually go to Europe. Yet this young man, who spent time at clubs, bars, social gatherings, and had earned a name for himself, still did not have a steady girlfriend. And when he did, it was a phantom one, who seldom, if ever, would be seen with him: Mercedes Barcha Pardo.

His job at *El Espectador* was to write a weekly film column, the first of its kind in Colombia. This new task began on Monday, February 22, 1954, just a week before his 27th birthday. The fact that the Board of Directors of the newspaper had trusted him with a newly created column was, without a doubt, recognition of the journalistic work he had done in the past. He had worked for six years as a journalist after dropping out of college in 1948. Writing about films was not altogether new to Gabo, but having his own weekly column with a nationally distributed newspaper must have seemed intimidating for this young *costeño,* a coastal man who always seemed at odds with the *cachaco* ideology: the dominant, centralist idea that everything Colombian is best if it originates in Bogotá. Was García Márquez ready to have his own movie column? What, after all, did he know about moviemaking, directing, scriptwriting, and the art of cinema in general? Did offering a newly created movie column to a young journalist and short-story writer represent a certain naïveté within the Colombian press?

We know his passion for cinema was somehow inherent to his persona, almost built-in. When he was a small boy, his maternal grandfather, Colonel Nicolás Ricardo Márquez Mejía, used to take him to the only movie house in the town of Aracataca, where he was born. García Márquez was always a raconteur, always a movie enthusiast, but it was not a discipline he had worked on the way he had with literary-oriented material. We know that in his early 20s, he was reading as many novels as he possibly could, particularly the Greek classics, and the leading European and American writers of both the nineteenth and twentieth centuries. Little is known about his training in the cinema during the first part of the 1950s. His formal studies on the cinema did not take place until 1955, in Rome.

In Gabriel García Márquez's compilation of journalistic work from May 1948 to December 1952, there are indications of his great interest in film. As early as September 1948, he had written commentaries on cinema. At that time, while writing for the Cartagena newspaper *El Universal,* he was supporting what Sir Charles Spencer Chaplin Jr., known the world over as Charlie Chaplin, had said about the American film industry. Chaplin, the famous mime, was unhappy with what film critics had said about his film *Monsieur Verdoux.* Chaplin co-wrote it with Orson Welles, directed it, and played the main character, who gives the film its title. García Márquez's judgment, like Chaplin's, was that Hollywood was more interested in how a movie does at the box office than what the movie does for the audience. Both Chaplin and García Márquez were critical of the Hollywood moneymaking philosophy we still see today. García Márquez's journalistic feature, "El cine norteamericano" ("The North American Film Industry"), his first about film, was written in September 1948, exactly five months after his career as a columnist began.

During 1949, his work as a press officer was almost nonexistent; he wrote a few pieces about literature, and commentaries about Colombian personalities, but nothing on the subject of film. In January of 1950, however, he wrote a satirical article about Eva Perón, then First Lady of Argentina (until her death in 1952). García Márquez viewed the Argentine political affairs of the times as analogous to an ostentatious film in which Evita (Little Eva), as the Argentine people called her, is nothing more than "a blurry image from a mediocre film."[2]

His film writing around this time seems to have echoed the news from the cables *El Espectador* got from the United Press (UP), the Associated Press (AP), or other sources. Of a total of five films he reviewed in 1950, one film particularly caught García Márquez's attention. He mentioned two reasons: (1) because it was the first English-speaking movie filmed in Argentina; (2) because Richard Wright, the protagonist of the film, was also the author of the novel. The novel, which shares the same name as the film, was mistakenly reported by the young Gabo as *Black Blood*. However, the title of Richard Wright's novel was *Native Son*, but the film indeed had premiered in Buenos Aires as *Sangre Negra* (*Black Blood*). It is possible that the only mistake Gabo made was accepting the misinformation from the cable as he wrote his piece for *El Universal*. This, we could say, was still part of the apprenticeship of the journalist he was becoming. He had no formal schooling in journalism, whether investigative, movie review or any other form. He learned dexterity as he went along. But the self-made journalist was now, in 1954, a film columnist in Bogotá. Once again, as is the case with the scattered literary foundation of his youth, the members of the Barranquilla Group can be credited with the knowledge Gabo needed to exercise his new role as a film critic; two in particular, Alfonso Fuenmayor and Germán Vargas. The two names are always associated with García Márquez in the 1950s. Their friendship, however, lasted a lifetime. Fuenmayor died in 1994 in his native town of Barranquilla. Germán Vargas had died over two decades earlier.

When Gabriel García Márquez started his tenure as a columnist for *El Espectador*, the political unrest Colombia was undergoing in 1954 under the dictatorship of Gustavo Rojas Pinilla was everywhere. The military dictator had seized power in a coup d'état on June 13, 1953. The civil turbulence and clash with the government forces resulted in many casualties. The oppression, abuses, and corruption affected all sectors of public life. In literature, it was dubbed *la violencia* (the violence). García Márquez's writing, however, focused on literature, not on *la violencia*. He would write about it years later, when he was in Paris. His writings related to film and investigative journalism. It was through these two forms of journalistic work that his larger literary works would eventually be published. In 1954, nevertheless, *El Espectador* published his short story, "Un día después del sábado" ("One Day after Saturday"), reflecting not the violence the country was experiencing at large, but rather a literary violence camouflaged in the short story. While some of his investigative chronicles of 1954 are worthy of mention for their literary sharpness, other than "One Day after Saturday," he published only one more short story, "Un hombre viene bajo la lluvia" ("A Man Comes under the Rain"). Both short stories were published in the Sunday edition of *El Espectador*, alongside his movie column.

The same year, his friend and member of the Barranquilla Group, Alvaro Cepeda Samudio, published a book of short stories titled *Todos estábamos a la espera* (*We Were All Waiting*). Cepeda Samudio was also interested in the cinema. In that year, 1954, he made an experimental black and white film, *La langosta azul* (*The Blue Lobster*), which has been erroneously associated with García Márquez. Gabo had nothing to do with the film. The credits, however—for those who may have the opportunity to see it (the film is nearly impossible to get)—do list both Alvaro Cepeda Samudio and Gabriel García Márquez as directors and screenwriters of the film. "The paternity of *The Blue Lobster*, in actual fact, belongs totally to Alvaro Cepeda, who was the screenwriter and director, plus the protagonist. When the film was made, García Márquez was in Bogotá."[3] Incidentally, Alvaro Cepeda's book of short stories was considered then, as it is today, an important work in Colombian literature. A year younger than García Márquez, he died in 1972, at the age of 46, in New York City. He was fluent in English, studied journalism at Columbia University, and played a great role in García Márquez's developmental years as one of the *literati* and also as a film devotee.

By the end of 1954, García Márquez's reputation as a journalist was well recognized throughout Colombia, due to *El Espectador*'s national reach. His opinions, although valuable in terms of improving the thinking of the readership of his column, will be better served, as Gilard points out, when movie historians look at the evolution of Colombian cinema.

CINEMA, EUROPE, AND MARRIAGE

García Márquez's contributions in 1954, however, were somewhat lacking in depth. His limited knowledge of film theory was not always offset by his intense enthusiasm. He knew his reading public had only some knowledge about cinema. Most likely, he was interested in guiding the public as to which films they should see and which to ignore. He wrote with that intent, but he often wrote beyond that need. Like most writers, he ended up writing for himself and for his friends.

Jacques Gilard, as he examined García Márquez's first year as a movie columnist for *El Espectador*, wrote that the enormous mistakes García Márquez made in 1954 were due predominantly to his esthetic opinions and lack of film knowledge. Gabo could only look at cinema on the surface. Gilard was talking about García Márquez's body of work at the time,[4] but focused on Gabo's end-of-the-year newspaper article. García Márquez had written a long piece titled "A Critical Review of Bogotá's Year in Film." García Márquez selected *Dieu a besoin des hommes* by Jean Delannoy as, in his own opinion, the best picture of the year. The quality films of that year, he wrote, were the French ones. It all started, Gabo stated, with Julien Duvivier's *El santo de Enriqueta*. But Gilard saw the French cinema of that year, which García Márquez saw in Bogotá, as being of mediocre level. Gilard thought *Dieu a besoin des hommes* by Jean Delannoy was rubbish. The divergence of their statements makes the reader wonder which of the two critics is reacting more emotionally. García Márquez, however, was judging Delannoy's film as better than those by the Italians Michelangelo Antonioni, Vittorio De Sica, and Alberto Lattuada; the Spaniards Luis García Berlanga, and Luis Buñuel; Americans Joseph L. Mankiewicz and John Ford; the Englishman Alfred Hitchcock; the Austrian-born, naturalized American Fritz Lang, and several others.

Was Gabo giving the director the importance he really deserved? The French expert on García Márquez added that his opinions were nevertheless somehow didactic for both the Colombian reading public who were reading his column and for Gabo as a writer. He was learning how to follow the camera's eye, how to understand the movie script, how to relate to the characters' dialogue. Writing this movie column was a formative experience. While his movie reviews provided him with the ability to write short stories as if through a camera's eye, his investigative reporting put him in direct contact with the reality Colombia was experiencing under the dictatorship of Rojas Pinilla. Some, if not all, of these traits were to be displayed in his first novel, *Leaf Storm*, the following year.

His work as an investigative journalist began in August of 1954, with a three-part reportage he titled "Reconstruction and Balance of Antioquia's Catastrophe" ("Balance y reconstrucción de la catástrofe de Antioquia").

García Márquez was reporting to the country what it (and he, at the same time) did not know about the rest of the country. Colombia is a pluralistic and diversified country with people of all races. Among his "discoveries," during the year of 1954, he found himself reporting about Chocó state, the African heart of Colombia. Colombia has the second largest population of blacks in South America, after Brazil. His reportage on El Chocó was a four-piece newspaper article accurately titled "The Chocó Colombia Does Not Know." He wrote in support of the people to denounce the abandonment and indifference, and the abuses, suffered by the people of Chocó state at that time, during the 1950s. He also addressed the subjects of university education as well as public transportation. The newspaper's Board of Directors sent him wherever they thought there was news for the paper. Of all of his types of investigative journalism, the most talked-about piece was the one he wrote in March of 1955, the story of Luis Alejandro Velasco, a shipwrecked Colombian sailor.

The first newspaper piece had a long and sensationalist entry titled "The Shipwreck Survivor Spent 11 Days on a Fragile Raft." This was followed by a subtitle: "How Sailor Velasco's Girlfriend and Parents Received the News." The story boosted newspaper sales and Gabo's reputation at several levels. His popularity as a reporter made his name highly recognizable. *El Espectador* was a Liberal paper with national distribution. The story about the shipwrecked sailor was serialized into 14 episodes, plus one more special Sunday supplement to close the story. The story did not bring Colombia to a standstill, but certainly captivated the reading audience for over a month! His political ideology, on the other hand, saw the shipwrecked sailor's odyssey as an opportunity to openly and strongly criticize Rojas Pinilla's corrupt dictatorship. Of eight castaways, Luis Alejandro Velasco, the shipwrecked sailor, was the only one to survive the wreckage of *The Caldas*, a Colombian navy destroyer. The vessel had left Mobile, Alabama, for Cartagena, Colombia, never to reach shore. "The ship's journey had been characterized by shady dealings—overweight contraband and life rafts unequipped with food or water."[5] Velasco told his story to García Márquez. The hostilities between the news media and the government were exacerbated by the pictures included in the last installment. Most of Gabo's investigative journalism comprised solid pieces of well-crafted reporting with a twist of denunciation. Gabo was then linked to the Communist Party, but was writing for a bourgeois Liberal newspaper. Whether it was to protect him from the Rojas Pinilla regime of abuses or to protect the interests of the owners of *El Espectador*, Gabriel García Márquez was sent to Europe, to cover the July 1955 "Big Four" Geneva Summit. He was there among a thousand journalists from around the world. The summit was to discuss finding an end to the Cold War, which had begun after the end of World War II. The Big Four were the United States, Great Britain, France, and the Soviet Union. It was the first time in 10 years that East and West were coming together to try to negotiate peace.

His first trip to Europe in 1955 provided García Márquez with yet one more window of opportunity to assess his own worldviews. No matter how well cemented his ideologies were, looking back from afar was going to influence his way of thinking. The newspaper he worked for, *El Espectador* of Bogotá, announced his trip to Geneva with a photograph of the 28-year-old. After covering the Big Four Geneva Summit in July in Switzerland, García Márquez moved to Italy. He spent time working for *El Espectador* in Rome, as well as in Venice, where he attended the Film Festival. His writing was well received in Colombia, but his access to the news in Europe was secondhand. He was, in a way, reporting from what the leading newspaper reporters were saying, and from what he would see, and interpret on his own. His reports in Colombia were firsthand interviews, fresh news. His name alone, and the name of his newspaper, gave him access to prime news. In Europe, however, he was a complete unknown, as was *El Espectador*. These two facts may have considerably contributed to both his way of thinking and writing. If he was at the center of things, the Geneva Summit or the Venice Film Festival, his role was more of a "spectator," and his reporting for *El Espectador* (how interesting that the name of his newspaper carries precisely the same meaning) was a combination of the news with much of his own interpretation and commentary on the reports. While in Rome, for example, he wrote about the Pope's summer vacation at his Castelgandolfo residence. The papal castle is located in a small village with the same name, Castel Gandolfo, about 15 miles from Rome. Typical of García Márquez's writing, the papal episodes would be echoed in his short story "Big Mama's Funeral." In it, the Pope comes to Colombia for the burial of the matriarch, Big Mama. John Paul II—the Traveling Pope, as some historians have called him—made García Márquez's fiction reality when he visited Colombia in 1986.

The year 1955 must have felt tumultuous for García Márquez, traveling from one country to another and not being able to speak the language. In October of 1955, he visited Poland and the then-Czechoslovakia as a prelude to a longer trip he would make the following year. By December of 1955, García Márquez had left Rome and moved to Paris, but not without first taking classes at the Centro Sperimentale di Cinematografia in Rome. The Italian school of moviemaking in vogue at the time was neorealist. The sense of "new realism" was sought by having ordinary people take the roles of seasoned actors in an effort to recreate real life, in an attempt to portray the human condition in any form, as long as it was raw, natural, and even crude, if necessary. The front-runners were the influential Vittoria de Sica, Roberto Rossellini, and Federico Fellini.

García Márquez wanted to learn directing, but there were no classes offered in that field at the time. He settled for learning about *la Moviola*, the movie camera. It was there, while studying cinema at the Centro Sperimentale, that he met the Argentine Fernando Birri. Years later, in Cuba, Birri would direct García Márquez's film *A Very Old Man with Enormous Wings* (*Un señor muy viejo con unas alas enormes*, 1988). While García Márquez studied at the Centro Sperimentale for a short time, Birri graduated from the school. Today Fernando Birri is credited with founding the first film school in Latin America, specializing in documentaries.

To close the year, his first in Europe, Gabo spent Christmas of 1955 and New Year's Eve in the company of Plinio Apuleyo Mendoza.

In Paris, reading the newspaper *Le Monde* soon after the New Year, García Márquez learned the newspaper he worked for had closed down. Not a good start for 1956. All of a sudden, he was unemployed, albeit for a very short while. In less than a month and a half, the owners of *El Espectador* had begun circulating another paper, in somewhat the same vein, *El Independiente* (*The Independent*). *The Espectador* was not shut down by the oppressive dictatorship of President Rojas Pinilla, but rather as a protest against the dictatorship. So, García Márquez was employed by *El Independiente*, but the new newspaper ran for less than two months and then ceased publication on April 15, 1956. Readers of volume three of Garcia Marquez's journalism collection, *Obra periodística 3: de Europa y América*, may notice that there are no entries for the months of January, February, and March. The period of poverty and sacrifice often referred to in his life and adventures started here. However, his good fortune, his great friends, and his pen would make ends meet. All of a sudden, he had plenty of time to write. Unexpectedly, he experienced the immense solitude his characters experience in his fiction. The year of 1956 would prove productive for his writing. From time to time, he would receive small amounts of money from his friends in Barranquilla. His friend Plinio Apuleyo Mendoza offered him the opportunity to write for the weekly *Elite*. This rather prestigious paper was published in Caracas, the capital of Venezuela, and Plinio was editor in chief. Although the fee was small, García Márquez could make some money through this venue, while he continued to live in Paris. Once again, Gabo wrote for the Venezuelan weekly *Elite*—as he had done for the Colombian newspapers—chronicles of what was taking place in Europe, accounts of what he saw, and stories on his assessment of the temperament of European lifestyle. He had no opportunities for interviews or access to galas, receptions, or political affairs. All this time, meanwhile, he was writing *No One Writes to the Colonel*, the short stories for the book *Big Mama's Funeral* and *In Evil Hour*.

By January of 1957, he had finished writing *No One Writes to the Colonel*. How and with whom he celebrated his birthday that year is not known. That year he turned 30. In May, however, during the first part of the month, his friend Plinio Apuleyo Mendoza was in Paris once again. This time, Plinio was in Paris in the company of his sister, Soledad. Plinio had resigned from his post of editor in chief for the Venezuelan weekly, *Elite*. Plinio and García Márquez were together on May 11 when they heard the news that the dictator of Colombia, General Gustavo Rojas Pinilla, had fled the country. One can only imagine the joy they and millions of Colombians felt. The news was being reported in Europe the day after the fact. Rojas Pinilla's entry into the annals of Colombian history reads: President of Colombia, military dictator, from June 13, 1953 to May 10, 1957. He died on January 17, 1975. García Márquez and Plinio, along with hundreds of Colombians, were living in self-imposed exile. As if in a mammoth celebration, the three of them decided, while on a stop in Frankfurt, Germany, to make the trip García Márquez recorded and published as *90 Days behind the Iron Curtain* (*De viaje por los países socialistas, 90 días en la "Cortina de hierro."*). The book describes their visit to the Socialist countries from June to September of 1957. However, it encodes the truth by disguising them as seemingly fictional characters. On the first page, one reads:

> There were three of us out there. Jacqueline was French, of Indo-Chinese origin, a magazine designer for a Parisian magazine. The other one was Franco, a freelance journalist for magazines in Milan, and the third one was me. My passport is stamped to prove it. The adventure began at a café in Frankfurt, on the morning of June the 18th. Franco had bought a French car for the summer and had no idea what to do with it. So he said, "Let's go find out what's behind the Iron Curtain."[6]

The book's chronicles were originally published in two magazines: the Colombian *Cromos* (*Colored Prints*) and the Venezuelan *Momento* (*Moment*). The opening of the book form, however, quoted above, was the only one the trio made together: García Márquez, Plinio, and his sister, Soledad Mendoza. Plinio is the freelance journalist from Milan; his sister,

Soledad, is Jacqueline, the French designer of Indo-Chinese descent; and García Márquez is "me," the narrative voice speaking in first person singular.

After visiting Eastern Germany, the three of them drove back to Paris in the Renault 4CV (the car Franco had bought and did not know what to do with). The French car manufacturer Renault ceased production of the Renault 4CV in 1961. Once in Paris, Soledad Mendoza flew back to Caracas. Her brother and García Márquez went to Moscow together, to the Communist Youth World Festival, after which García Márquez went on to Hungary, and Plinio returned to Paris. The book form, *90 Days behind the Iron Curtain*, does not follow the same order that the trips were taken. The visit to Poland and Czechoslovakia was made in 1955. Of this visit, no pictures were published, although there are most likely some pictures floating around somewhere. The Spanish publication *El olor de la guayaba* (*The Fragrance of Guava*) displays a total of 14 pictures: 12 within the book, one on the front cover, and one on the back jacket. Of all the pictures, only one is of the "90 days behind the iron curtain." It shows García Márquez with a group of young Russians, Colombians, and peasant women. However, the book *90 Days behind the Iron Curtain* was published without any pictures. Reading the book is, nonetheless, still attractive today, with its twists of fiction. The Iron Curtain countries, in Gabo's descriptions, even then, somehow read as a myth. "The Wall" had to come down with the passage of time. It was simply a matter of time, but in the 1950s, it was impossible to imagine.

The book *90 Days behind the Iron Curtain* seems to close the gap between journalism and literary fiction. In a book titled *Cuando era feliz e indocumentado* (*When I Was Happy and Undocumented*), published years after the articles were written and published in newspaper form, Garcia Marquez called 1957 "The World's Most Famous Year" ("El año más famoso del mundo"). The attention-grabbing title narrates "the news" of a year in review: Gabo's review. It starts with January's farewell to British Prime Minister Sir Anthony Eden, whose post was taken by Harold McMillan. He quickly moves on to report Humphrey Bogart's death from cancer on January 6. Two other important deaths that month were those of the Chilean poet, Gabriela Mistral, and the Italian music director, Arturo Toscanini. There are entries for each month. For May, he reports the downfall of Colombian dictator Rojas Pinilla. His reporting is in chronicle style. He refers to James Dean's death the year before, comments on Mao Tse-tung, talks about Nikita Khrushchev on American television, mentions the marriage of Sophia Loren to Carlo Ponti in Mexico, and the death of Christian Dior. The newspaper article closes with a commentary on President Eisenhower's poor health.[7]

CINEMA, EUROPE, AND MARRIAGE

By the end of 1957, Plinio Apuleyo Mendoza was editor in chief of the Venezuelan weekly *Momento*. He managed to convince the director of the publication, Carlos Ramírez MacGregor, to hire García Márquez to work for *Momento*. Gabo flew to Caracas the day before Christmas Eve. His first European round trip was completed in two and a half years. January of 1957 saw the end of yet another Latin American dictatorship: on January 23, 1958, the Venezuelan dictator, President Marcos Pérez Jiménez, fled the country.

Months later, in June, the Colombian newspaper *El Espectador* began publishing again. While García Márquez's journalistic career continued to be the focus of his daily life, in 1958 he finished three short stories: "La viuda de Montiel" ("Montiel's Widow"); "La prodigiosa tarde de Baltazar" ("Balthazar's Marvelous Afternoon"); and "Un día de éstos" ("One of These Days").

But of all the events of 1958, perhaps none was bigger than his marriage. On Friday, March 21, 1958, at 11:00 A.M., the 31-year-old Gabriel José García Márquez married Mercedes Raquel Barcha Pardo. The religious ceremony took place in the coastal city of Barranquilla, at El Perpetuo Socorro Church. She wore an electric blue dress; Gabo was dressed in black.[8] The wedding took place in near secrecy. Little, if anything, has been published about the marriage ceremony or the courtship. Their wedding vows, however, have been kept for all these years—except for, some may say, the fidelity vow. This suspicion was rekindled during the 2007 celebration of Gabo's 80th birthday. The Mexican newspaper *La Jornada* (*The Working Day*) inexplicably chose to publish a photo taken by photographer Rodrigo Moya back in 1976, in which García Márquez is sporting a black eye, ostensibly received at the hands of Peruvian writer Mario Vargas Llosa. While never fully explained, the bad blood between the two men was rumored to be due to Gabo's betrayal and adultery. Nevertheless, in 2007, gossip or not, newspapers around the Western world talked about it. *The New York Times* published the same photograph mentioned above. But García Márquez's marriage to Mercedes Barcha has remained intact. His private life, although often encoded in his writing, has been kept away from the public; intentionally, no doubt.

Tracing García Márquez's life, one might think Plinio Apuleyo Mendoza is one of his best friends. But he did not attend his wedding. Will Gabo himself talk about it in the next volume of *Living to Tell the Tale*? When they returned to Caracas after the wedding, Plinio received them at the Maiquetia airport in Caracas, better known as Simón Bolívar International Airport. Plinio described García Márquez's wife, Mercedes Barcha, as a woman who did not speak a word in three days. Physically, he described her as "dark skinned and svelte, with a deer's dark, unsociable eyes." She was "thin as a rail with great big slanted eyes." She was, Plinio says, "the phantom girl, the sacred crocodile," and he found it difficult to describe her.[9]

Gabo and Mercedes Barcha first met in the town of Sucre, at a student party, when she was only 13. She had finished elementary school and he was a junior in high school. According to Dasso Saldívar, García Márquez asked Mercedes to marry him without having to think about it twice. The young girl, however, paid no attention to such a loquacious proposition.[10] The fact would later be turned into a fictional account in *One Hundred Years of Solitude*. In real life, the two families were friends; in the novel, they are not. Both in real life and in the novel, the groom is the oldest of the family, the firstborn. Both in the novel and in real life, in the bride's family, there are seven siblings. In both real life and in the novel, such a marriage does not seem to make sense. In real life, the couple has to wait 13 years before they marry; in the novel, they marry, even though the young girl still wets her bed. Both in the novel and in real life, however, the couples marry in the same month. In the novel, the legendary Colonel Aureliano Buendía marries Remedios Moscote, "one Sunday in March before the altar Father Nicanor Reyna had set up in the parlor [when] little Remedios had reached puberty before getting over the habits of childhood."[11] At the time of the wedding in the novel, Colonel Aureliano Buendía is not yet a legend. In real life, the wedding is on a Friday in March, and García Márquez is yet not a legend, either. In the wondrous tale of *One Hundred Years of Solitude*, the couple had no children of their own, but the promiscuous Colonel Aureliano Buendía procreates 17 bastard children with 17 different women. All children are named Aureliano, plus one more, named Aureliano José. García Márquez and Mercedes Barcha had only two sons and neither was named Aureliano.

Mercedes Barcha, the "sacred crocodile" who has kept a rather low profile throughout their marriage, was born in Magangué, Colombia, on November 6, 1932. Her paternal grandfather, Elías Barcha, was an Egyptian emigrant. "He lived to be nearly a hundred. His true vocation, other than being a merchant, was to read people's fortunes in the sediment of a cup of coffee."[12] Mercedes' father, like her grandfather, was also a merchant. By the time García Márquez met them, in the town of Sucre, they owned a pharmacy. Mercedes was the eldest of eight siblings. Although her desire was to go to college to study bacteriology, her schooling stopped after she graduated from high school.[13]

García Márquez has masterminded his life and his career from the very beginning. His work for *Momento* in Caracas continued after he came back

CINEMA, EUROPE, AND MARRIAGE 43

from his wedding in Colombia, and he carried on writing political articles as if he were a citizen of Venezuela. The winds of change, of political adjustment, were, on the whole, visible in Latin America. Both Colombia and Venezuela were undergoing political change, with the stepping down of their dictators, as mentioned above. Cuba, on the other hand, has been international news since 1956, with its revolutionary army under the command of Fidel Castro and top lieutenants, Raul Castro (Fidel's brother), and the Argentine physician Ernesto (Che) Guevara.

The visit of Richard Nixon, then vice-president of the United States, to Caracas created tremendous turmoil, mayhem, and opposition. On April 27, Nixon started a vice-presidential trip that would include eight Latin American countries. On May 13, he made a stop in Caracas. The press dubbed the riot caused by his visit "12 minutes of terror." Nixon himself described the experience as one of the worst in his life. The Venezuelan working class, university students, and sectors of the middle class rioting in the streets saw Nixon as a supporter of the government represented by the brutality of Marcos Pérez Jiménez, who had fled the country in January of the same year, only to find refuge in the United States. Nixon's motorcade was stoned. President Dwight Eisenhower sent United States marines to the Caribbean bases as a form of precaution. The stoning of Nixon's motorcade was similar to what he had faced days earlier in Lima, Peru. The sentiment against the Pentagon's policies toward Latin America, judging from the riots, was strong, to say the least, but the polls conducted by *Life en Español* and some of the leading Latin American newspapers reported the opposite. *Momento,* in Caracas, was no exception. As neither Plinio Apuleyo Mendoza nor Gabriel García Márquez supported the editorial published by the director of *Momento,* both resigned immediately. "Plinio Apuleyo Mendoza remembers that neither García Márquez nor Paul de Garrat had yet arrived at the newspaper's offices that morning. The only witness to the heated discussion was Herrera Campins. Upset by the authoritarianism *of Momento*'s director and his political blindness, Plinio Apuleyo Mendoza ended up telling him 'Eat shit!', and walked out, slamming the door. As he was leaving, he bumped into García Márquez. He [García Márquez] decided to leave the magazine on the spot, and together they walked out."[14]

A little over a month after the incident with the director of *Momento,* on June 27, 1958, according to Plinio Apuleyo Mendoza, all the members who had left *Momento* were employed by *Venezuela Gráfica* (*Graphic Venezuelan*). Plinio playfully wrote that in Caracas, everyone knew it as *Venezuela pornográfica* (*Pornographic Venezuelan*). Evidently, having a job was more important than the quality of the employment. García Márquez had a family to feed and look after, so he took the post, but decided not to put his name on any of the articles he wrote.[15] The United States, meanwhile, ended military aid to Cuba. On New Year's Day, Fulgencio Batista fled into exile and Fidel Castro and his troops took over the government of Cuba. It was as if every dictator in Latin America was bound to leave office one way or another. Juan Domingo Perón had stepped down in Argentina in 1955; dictator Manuel A. Odría allowed national elections in Peru in 1956; Colombia ousted Gustavo Rojas Pinilla in 1957; and Marcos Pérez Jiménez fled Venezuela in 1958. The triumph of the Cuban revolution in 1959 was a breath of fresh air. The feeling that democracy had triumphed was everywhere. By the time the military tribunals organized by the Castro regime against the opponents began to take place, García Márquez and Plinio Apuleyo had been invited to come to Cuba. They were present, but did not write about the nationally televised tribunal trial of Jesús Sosa Blanco. Sosa Blanco was tried and executed by firing squad on February 23, 1959.

On February 7, changes were made to the Cuban Constitution of 1940. The death penalty was instituted and the right to expropriate private property was approved. On February 16, Fidel Castro named himself Prime Minister of the country and elections were never to be held again. Modern history was to record, year by year, what was happening in Cuba. By 1961, many countries and intellectuals around the world broke relations with Cuba. Mexico was the only Latin American country that did not do so. García Márquez, at this time, was not the close friend of Fidel Castro he is today. Castro did not befriend García Márquez until the 1970s.

Among the changes the Castro government brought about was the formation of its own press. Created by the imagination and skill of Argentine journalist Jorge Ricardo Masetti, Prensa Latina (Latin Press) was created. One of the main goals of Latin Press was to counterbalance the domination of the international press, mainly that originating in the United States. The Cuban government envisioned a form of press that would publish the news from their own viewpoint; they would call it Operación Verdad (Operation Truth). Plinio Apuleyo Mendoza opened the first Latin Press agency in Bogotá at the end of February. García Márquez, however, flew back to Caracas and continued his work for *Venezuela Gráfica*. Two months later, nevertheless, in May, García Márquez flew to Bogotá to work with Apuleyo Mendoza and began work for Latin Press. Gabo's wife, Mercedes Barcha, was pregnant. For García Márquez, 1959 held a string of events that were almost like fiction. The same month his first son was born, the Colombian Book Festival produced the first re-edition of *Leaf Storm*, his first novel. His son Rodrigo, today a movie director, was born in Bogotá on Monday, August 24, 1959. His baptism took place at the same hospital where the baby was born. Plinio Apuleyo Mendoza served as his godfather, making him Gabriel García Márquez's *compadre*. The improvised religious ceremony, which traditionally takes place at a church, was officiated over by none other than Father Camilo Torres. The month before, Ricardo Masetti had made a stop in Bogotá to see how Plinio and Gabo were doing with working together. In the end, Masetti decided that Latin Press could not afford to have them working together. They needed to open yet another office elsewhere. García Márquez flew back to Cuba with Masetti. He was delighted to receive three months of training, an opportunity that allowed him to come into close contact with Rodolfo Walsh, an Argentine short-story writer Gabo had read and admired. Walsh was in charge of Servicios Especiales (Special Services) for Latin Press. Gabo's three-month training in Havana was in preparation for opening an office in Montreal. With the training over, he flew to Bogotá to pick up his wife, Mercedes, and his baby son, Rodrigo. On the way to New York City, the family made a stop in Mexico City. He wanted to visit his friend, Alvaro Mutis, whom he had not seen in five years. Once in New York City, the García Barcha family waited for their visas. The Canadian visas never arrived!

CODA

For García Márquez, the second half of the 1950s saw the confirmation of his ideology and his writing style. His European stay of over two years substantiated what he thought of Colombia, but gave him a broader sense and allowed him to see not just Colombia, but Latin America as a whole. What he thought of Europe, on the other hand, was authenticated by his own experience, firsthand. The polarities of West versus East, Capitalism versus Communism, were two loud expressions he heard and saw firsthand. He was disheartened by the living conditions he saw, and the seeming totalitarianism of the Communist regimes. His sympathy and support for Communist ideals found a "true example" as he traveled through Communist countries. His experience is best discovered in two books of journalism: *90 Days behind the Iron Curtain* and *When I Was Happy and Undocumented*. The latter recounts his stay in Venezuela. Both texts were published years after the articles were written and published in newspapers. The publication of *Leaf Storm* in 1955 did not establish him as a novelist. At best, it allowed him to start signing his literary works with the re-edition of *Leaf Storm* in 1959, when he was photographed alongside Eduardo Zalamea Borda, the critic who had first taken an interest in García Márquez's writing. He had published Gabo's first short story, "The Third Resignation," on Saturday, September 13, 1947. Although this was a great moment in García Márquez's life, even though he had gone to Europe and back, he continued to be considered a journalist first, then a short-story writer. His fame was limited to Colombia and certain circles.

The turn of events in his life, his isolation in Paris, and his insistence in elaborating, over and over, on the same themes and the same characters brought his first great work to paper: *No One Writes to the Colonel*, first published in the Bogotá magazine *Mito*. But no one wanted to publish it as a book. When it was published in book form, the following year, only 800 copies were sold. The print run was two thousand copies.[16] The fall of the Colombian and Venezuelan dictatorships, along with the triumph of the Cuban revolution, would fuel his imagination to continue writing under the scope of two opposing forces, love and the lack of love, immense solitude, the search for power, and death. He was still growing as a man, as a person, as a husband, as a father. His marriage to Mercedes Barcha Pardo no doubt influenced his writing, but not his style. Although seemingly poor, often exaggerated to romanticize the experience, the European years showed a man whose lifestyle allowed him to travel extensively. Moreover, the political impact of the 1950s was as profound as the adventures he underwent.

NOTES

1. Refer to Chapter 2 for more information on this subject.

2. García Márquez, *Obra periodística 1*, 102–3 (see chap. 2, n. 12).

3. Gabriel García Márquez, *Obra periodística 2, Entre Cachacos*, compiled by Jacques Gilard (Bogotá, Colombia: Editorial Norma, 1982), 22.

4. Ibid., 7–68.

5. Bell-Villada, *García Márquez*, 51 (see chap. 2, n. 1).

6. Gabriel García Márquez, *De viaje por los países socialistas: 90 días en la "Cortina de Hierro"* (Colombia: Ediciones Macondo, 1978), 9. (The translation is mine.)

7. Gabriel García Márquez, *Cuando era feliz e indocumentado* (Barcelona: Plaza & Janés, 1975), 7–29.

8. Dasso Saldívar, *El viaje a la semilla: la biografía* (Madrid: Santillana, 1977), 370–72.

9. Plinio Apuleyo Mendoza, *Aquellos tiempos con Gabo* (Barcelona: Plaza & Janés, 2000), 62–64.

10. Saldívar, *El viaje*, 370.

11. Gabriel García Márquez, trans. Gregory Rabassa, *One Hundred Years of Solitude* (New York: Perennial Classics, 1998), 89.

12. Saldívar, *El viaje*, 371.

13. Ibid., 371.

14. Gabriel García Márquez, *Obra periodística 3, De Europa y América*, compiled by Jacques Gilard (Bogotá, Colombia: Editorial Norma, 1983), 49.

15. Apuleyo Mendoza, *In Conversation*, 65 (see chap. 2, n. 2).

16. Saldívar, *El viaje*, 390.

Chapter 4

NEW YORK, MEXICO CITY, AND MAKING FILMS

Fate has terrible power.
You cannot escape it by wealth or war.
No fort will keep it out, no ships outrun it.

—*Sophocles*, Antigone

In the 1960s, the life of Gabriel García Márquez took the literary twists and turns that, combined with his childhood memories, shaped the writer who would eventually create his masterpiece, *One Hundred Years of Solitude*. It was as if his good fortune, his fate, would take a turn he had never expected. In 1961, after a stay in New York City, he decided to move to Mexico City. The stay in New York was short, barely five months in length. However, those months, from January to May, were rather tumultuous. He worked as assistant to the editor in chief, Jorge Ricardo Masetti, for the Latin American News Agency Prensa Latina (Latin Press). Prensa Latina was, and still is today, an independent news agency with headquarters in Havana, Cuba. Jorge Ricardo Masetti, an Argentine journalist, was its director and founder. A close friend of Ernesto "Che" Guevara, Masetti wanted Prensa Latina to broadcast what was happening in Cuba under Castro's newly formed government.

The Argentine Rodolfo Walsh, and the Colombians Plinio Apuleyo Mendoza and Gabriel García Márquez, were among the journalists who worked on launching Prensa Latina. The nascent Cuba Libre (Free Cuba) government, under the leadership of Fidel Castro, wanted the world to read about what was happening in Cuba from its own perspective. To that effect, Prensa Latina was part of Operación Verdad (Operation Truth).

The newspaper today, in its online version, can be read in several languages, including English.

Gabriel García Márquez had moved to New York at the start of 1961 to work for Prensa Latina. By May of the same year, however, he had resigned. Prior to his resignation, he had made a visit to Havana in March. This trip, he wrote, turned him into an erratic or meandering correspondent for Prensa Latina.[1] His apparently abrupt leaving was due to at least two reasons. On the one hand, he was receiving constant death threats from the upper-class, anti-Castro Cubans in exile. On the other hand, he wanted to support director and founder Jorge Ricardo Masetti, who had also decided to leave the news agency. In addition, García Márquez had an obligation to his young family. Rodrigo, his firstborn, was not yet two years old. Masetti's determination to leave Prensa Latina was influenced by a desire to work in Cuba alongside his friends, Che Guevara and Rodolfo Walsh. Masetti later went to the country of his birth, Argentina, to help organize a guerrilla movement. He would be killed in Argentina in 1964.

For Gabriel García Márquez, returning to his native Colombia must have been out of the question. The Colombian violence that erupted in 1948, first in Bogotá and then throughout the country, due to the killing of the Liberal leader Jorge Eliécer Gaitán on April 9, 1948, was still ongoing. By the 1960s, the Colombian Communist Party had several guerrilla groups, known as Fuerzas Armadas Revolucionarias de Colombia (FARC)—Armed Revolutionary Forces of Colombia. FARC was originally started to defend the farm workers from the abuses of the landowners, but its tactics soon changed. To finance themselves, the members began kidnapping landlords first, and then political and prominent figures of Colombian society, for the purpose of extortion. As a counter-reaction to FARC, to defend themselves the landowners organized their own armed faction. They armed and trained people who were already working for them as laborers. Before they knew it, this step backfired on the landowners. Once these farm workers realized their power, they started acting on their own and attacked the very landowners who had armed them. Debatably, they were the ones who began growing large areas of coca leaves where they used to grow coffee. The drug lords, on the other hand, were gaining strength, and they too had their own organized armed forces. The resulting violence became part of everyday Colombian life. The violence we read about nowadays can be traced back to the societal problems of those years.

In light of Colombia's chaos, Mexico was a more hospitable destination, where García Márquez could pursue his ambitions. Mexico was safer, more progressive, and a much better place to work and live (Mexico's guerrilla war did not break out until 1967). The Mexican economy and social stability were often referred to as the "Mexican Miracle" at the time. Mexico's movie industry was a leading market in the Spanish-speaking world. Culturally, newly founded publishing houses, ERA in 1960 and Joaquín Mortiz in 1962, joined the ranks of the most established names in the book industry, namely Porrúa and Fondo de Cultura Económica, in addition to several publications controlled by leading Mexican universities.

García Márquez decided that the trip from New York to Mexico City needed to be made by bus. He craved seeing the fictionalized Yoknapatawpha County in northern Mississippi, the background of William Faulkner's short stories and novels. So the 34-year-old Gabo, his wife Mercedes Barcha, and their young son rolled through the Carolinas into Georgia, Alabama, Mississippi, Louisiana, Texas, and into Mexican territory, finally reaching Mexico's capital, Mexico City. The American Deep South was no longer merely a literary reference for him. He was exposed, no doubt, to the harsh indignities of segregation. Bus stations, in particular, had separate waiting rooms, with separate restrooms, drinking fountains, and separate concession stands, if there were any, for people other than white. We wonder where they, as a Hispanic family, might have sat on the bus and in the bus stations. Did all this remind him of Paris in the 1950s, when he was often mistaken for a Moroccan? Only he could tell.

The Freedom Riders, organized by student activists, were brutally attacked by angry white mobs in May of 1961. These incidents were reported both nationally and internationally. The racial segregation, violence, and prejudice in the Deep South formed a sad chapter in American history. Alabama and Mississippi must have had a significant and negative impact on the García-Barcha family.[2]

Gabriel García Márquez and his family made the trip in 20 days. Mario Vargas Llosa, writing about the journey, quotes García Márquez as saying: "We spent 20 days on the road, eating hamburgers and milkshakes. We saw the rough side of the United States in Atlanta (many hotels we stopped at did not want to give us a room because they thought we were Mexicans). In another town in the South, we came across a sign that read 'dogs and Mexicans not allowed.'"[3] It is interesting that his remarks failed to mention the larger picture of the racial problems the Deep South was undergoing, although the quote clearly indicates that they had faced a form of the venomous racial discrimination of 1961 America.

One can only wonder what he may or may not write about when the second volume of his memoirs is published. The first volume ends with two notes. On the personal side, he receives the first letter from his then-girlfriend, Mercedes Barcha. The other refers to his work. He is in Geneva, as journalist for *El Espectador,* to cover the Geneva Conference of Heads of Government, known as the "Big Four" of 1955: Dwight D. Eisenhower, 34th President of the United States; Nikolai Bulganin, Prime Minister of the USSR; Edgar Faure, Prime Minister of France; and Anthony Eden, Prime Minister of Great Britain.

The García-Barcha family arrived in Mexico City on a hot summer day. Their arrival coincided with the date of Ernest Hemingway's gruesome suicide, killing himself with a shotgun in Ketchum, Idaho, on July 2, 1961. Soon after the family arrived, García Márquez started work as a journalist. Journalism was one of several jobs he held to earn a living. His first article was published in the magazine *Siempre!* (Yes, with one exclamation mark only. The Spanish language uses two; one at the beginning of a word, phrase, or sentence, and one at the end, but not in the magazine's title.) *Siempre!* was a rather prestigious magazine, with wide distribution throughout Mexico. The magazine was founded in June 1953 by lifelong journalist José Pagés Llergo, who served as director until he died in December 1989. The magazine is still published today, in hard copy, as well as on the Internet.

It is interesting to note that the title García Márquez selected for his first journalistic piece in Mexico was "A Man Has Died of Natural Death." He wrote it the same day he arrived, and it appeared a week later, on July 9. The commentary was on Hemingway's suicide. The irony of the title, the dark sarcasm, is open ended. What did he mean? Was it what he expected, from a man like Hemingway? It is hard to say, since García Márquez never met Hemingway in person.

García Márquez worked as a newspaper journalist, but the Colombian author really wanted to write movie scripts, not daily or weekly articles. His role as a journalist had been established during his years in Colombia, Venezuela, Rome, and Paris as a correspondent, and his stay in New York as assistant to the editor in chief for Prensa Latina. His motivation to become a successful novelist, on the other hand, had not yet been accomplished; at best, it was still in the making. But Mexico City was going to be the right place for both ambitions: making films and writing, in that order.

In Mexico City, Gabo soon encountered some of the leading Mexican intellectuals and artists, particularly those who sympathized with the Mexican political left. Some of them were and still are literally the movers and shakers of culture in Mexico: Carlos Fuentes, Juan Rulfo, Manuel Barbachano, Carlos Monsiváis, José Emilio Pacheco, Elena Poniatowska, and Homero Aridjis, among many others. Of this group, Carlos Fuentes is perhaps the one who helped García Márquez the most, and who has remained one of his closest friends. Fuentes, Rulfo, and Barbachano were instrumental in García Márquez's ambition to make films. Of these friends, Carlos Monsiváis is a well-known chronicler, journalist, and literary and film critic. His opinions, often ironic, are time and again considered canonical. Pacheco and Aridjis are well-regarded poets. Pacheco, a poet and novelist, became a member of the Mexican Academy of Language in 2006. Aridjis plays an important role in Mexican environmental causes. As a political figure, like Fuentes, Aridjis also served as Mexican ambassador to the Netherlands and Switzerland. Poniatowska's career started as a newspaper reporter and evolved into one of the leading names in Latin American literature. With such a group of friends, and the inner drive to make films and write, García Márquez was well situated. He was probably broke, but far from being poor, as he is often romanticized by many who have written about him during the years prior to the summer of 1967. At home, as is typical of a Mexican middle-class household, the family had a maid who came in to help with the household duties. His lifestyle actually mirrored that of the Mexican upper-middle class, with whom he kept in close contact.

García Márquez's determination to make films was nothing new. During his early days as journalist for *El Espectador* (*The Spectator*), in Bogotá, he wrote a movie review column, the first of its kind for that newspaper. While still working for this paper, he studied cinema in Italy in the mid-1950s. For him, making films was as important as writing the perfect novel. He had the opportunity to study film, albeit briefly, at the Centro Sperimentale di Cinematografia in Rome. His role as journalist also gave him the opportunity to work in the film industry indirectly, as a film critic. In September 1955, while working as a foreign correspondent for *El Espectador,* he attended the XVI Exposition of Cinematography in Venice, Italy. He covered the entire 16-day event. It was after this event, later in December, that he studied cinema in Rome. Those were the days when Gregory Peck and Kirk Douglas, Sophia Loren and Gina Lollobrigida were the big stars, before the term "superstar" was coined.

The friends he made in Mexico's metropolis were primarily involved with the world of letters, but they were also interested in cinema. García Márquez's talent and charisma, in addition to the power of his friends, accelerated his career in both literature and the film industry. During 1961 and 1962, however, he worked largely as a journalist. In that capacity, he reached the decision to become editor in chief of two magazines with rather small distribution, *Sucesos* (*Incidents*) and *La Familia*. Nevertheless, these two Mexican publications had nothing to do with literary issues. He agreed to edit them as long as he did not have to write a single article for them. Vargas Llosa documented the fact that during these two years, García Márquez did not even have a typewriter in his office.[4] Was García Márquez ashamed to work there? *Sucesos* was not comparable to *Siempre!*, the magazine where he had published the article about Hemingway's suicide, but neither was he on the payroll of *Siempre! Sucesos* magazine was interested in current issues in all types of genres. It was a weekly publication of news and analysis. Cuba, for example, was among its main interests. Furthermore, it was interested in what was happening in Mexico's film industry. Their front-page news was on a par with the heartbeat of the country and the continent. *La Familia*, on the other hand, was more or less a doctor's waiting-room magazine, dealing with home care, fashion, and trivia.

Neither of the two magazines could compare to *Siempre!* This publication enjoyed the contributions of the best Mexican journalists, and, often, economic support from the Mexican government. The orientation, however, was alternative and left wing, with a twist of popular culture. García Márquez was careful about the public image he wanted to create. His decision not to write for either *Sucesos* or *La Familia* was motivated by this concern.

The only new literary material he wrote in 1961 was the short story "El mar del tiempo perdido" ("The Sea of Lost Time"). It was published in *Revista Mexicana de Literatura* (*Magazine of Mexican Literature*). Once again, he published only one short story, but unlike his previous publications, this one was in a prestigious literary magazine. *Revista Mexicana de Literatura* was cofounded in 1954 by Octavio Paz and Carlos Fuentes, both members of the Mexican cultural elite. Octavio Paz would become the recipient of the Nobel Prize for Literature in 1990.

"The Sea of Lost Time" deals with the theme of a stranger in town, Mr. Herbert, as one of the opposing forces that shapes the story. The other force is the townspeople. The setting is an impoverished coastal town in the Guajira Peninsula. An omniscient narrator gives voice to the characters, who seem to sketch a larger story and are more developed than those in his previous short stories. The design is "threefold: the fragrance of roses that wafts in from the ocean and pervades everything, the arrival of tall, ruddy-faced Mr. Herbert, with his philanthropic schemes, and the long swim to the ocean's bottom and discovery of a live sunken city, as well as a 'sea of the dead' with its corpses perfectly intact."[5]

This short story, in effect, as critics pointed out, is a prelude to *One Hundred Years of Solitude*. "In this short story, García Márquez described, for example, a man who takes his wife to see ice for the first time, a prelate who levitates, and a whole town that seems like a dream world. This town looks much like the Macondo of José Arcadio Buendía, its founder, and the end of *One Hundred Years of Solitude*."[6] The similarities with *Solitude* stretch from the characters to the images drawn, it is true, but the insistence on the reference to getting to see something for the first time is not to see ice, as the quote above insists. In "The Sea of Lost Time," it is the image of money. Tobias, whose make-up is at the center of the narrative, "took Clotilde to see what money was. They made believe they were betting enormous sums at roulette, and then they figured things up and felt extremely rich with all the money they could have won."[7]

The image is, no doubt, from the memory bank of his childhood, from those stories he had heard at home, at his grandparents' house, when men in Aracataca made bundles of money from the banana-bonanza. But the representation of the mammoth ship that seems to besiege the impoverished coastal town, the presence of Mr. Herbert, and the scent of flowers are strongly reminiscent of a journalistic account he wrote after his second visit to Cuba in March 1961. In it, it becomes obvious that the ship that inspired the short story is none other than the *USS Oxford*. This was a spy ship that served the United States Navy from 1960 to 1969. García Márquez's second visit to Cuba was evidently months before he moved to Mexico City, and two years after the United States embargo against Cuba.[8] This same story, years later, was published again as "The Incredible and Sad Tale of Innocent Eréndira and Her Heartless Grandmother." This is how Garcia Marquez described the real ship that gives way to the one in the short story: "A CIA ship, *The Oxford* was equipped with all sorts of spying devices. The ship patrolled the Cuban territorial waters for several years, to make sure that no capitalistic country, except those few who dared, would go against the embargo on Cuba."[9]

In 1961, *La mala hora* (*In Evil Hour*) won the Esso Literary Prize for best Colombian novel. The Esso Prize, worth three thousand dollars, was supported by the Colombian Academy of Language. Nevertheless, *In Evil Hour* was not the title García Márquez used for the manuscript, but the title the judges of the Esso Prize gave to the novel, substituting it for the original, *Este pueblo de mierda* (*This Crappy Town*). The organizers of the contest, furthermore, sent the text to Spain to be published. The editors in Madrid, Graphic Arts Luis Pérez, as is the often the case with colonialist thinking, decided to make changes without consulting the author. They changed what they considered Latin Americanisms or obscure wording. Not only that, they also "poisoned the novel with errata. When he received the first copy of *In Evil Hour*, in 1962, he realized that the printed book was a parody of the original. He rejected the print. In the second publication of the novel, published in Mexico in 1966, García Márquez added, 'On this occasion, the author has permitted himself to put back *the idiomatic mistakes* and *the stylistics atrocities* in the name of his own sovereignty and arbitrary will. This is, therefore, the first edition of *In Evil Hour*.'"[10]

These two publications of the same book became an episodic event best understood when one recognizes that García Márquez has always been extremely careful with the use of language. Hence, he never approved the earlier publication. *In Evil Hour* was a realist novel. While he was in Paris, in 1956, the novel started to take shape, first as a short story. As the story developed into a novel, he began to lose interest in it. *In Evil Hour* was put aside and the writing of *No One Writes to the Colonel* took precedence. Based on the violence that was happening in Colombia, *In Evil Hour* depicts the fear endured by its inhabitants. The town of the novel, seemingly fictional, is supposed to be Sucre, a town and municipality located within the Department that bears the same name. One of the values of the novel is the strength and refusal of the community to surrender to an unveiled violence besieging the townspeople. Individual characters give way to the whole community; the tension is between the two political factions in town, as represented by the characters.

No One Writes to the Colonel not only took writing precedence, but it also took primacy in publication. It was first published by Editorial Aguirre in Medellín, capital of the Department of Antioquia and the second most populous city after Bogotá. Of all his works published before *One Hundred Years of Solitude*, this short novel, a novella, is the one considered the most structured and polished. The main character, the old colonel, displays an inner strength superior to all the misfortunes placed upon him by the bureaucracy, which fails to pay him his pension, after decades of waiting, as a veteran of the civil war. The town is very similar to that in *In Evil Hour*. The two novels complement one another. The old colonel suffers the force and power of an antagonizing political faction that killed his only son for distributing clandestine, subversive leaflets. The old colonel is an idealist, almost a dreamer. His wife, on the other hand, seems to be the voice of reason.

The two novels can be seen as a denunciation of the violence unleashed after the killing of Jorge Eliécer Gaitán in 1948. Of the two, *No One Writes to the Colonel* is more biographical. A rooster plays an important role within the novel. As absurd as it may seem, it is through the rooster that the whole town comes together. The schoolchildren and the townspeople see the rooster as a symbol of strength and pride. Pride is

NEW YORK, MEXICO CITY, AND MAKING FILMS 57

the only thing left for these people, who otherwise live under the most precarious of circumstances. The plot, the viewpoint, and the economy of language made the critics take note of García Márquez as a skilled writer. Sales, however, were slim. At the time of the book's publication, he did not envision it as a film, but in 1999, Arturo Ripstein turned it into one and showed it at the Cannes Film Festival. García Márquez has strong opinions about adapting books for film. He once said, "I can't think of any one film that improved on a good novel, but I can think of many good films that came from very bad novels."[11]

He seems to speak his mind rather freely, but one can also hypothesize that *No One Writes to the Colonel* was published before *In Evil Hour* because the culprits, the novel suggests, were still in power in the mid-1950s. The president of Colombia during those years, General Gustavo Rojas Pinilla, was responsible for the closure of *El Espectador*, the newspaper that García Márquez to Europe as a correspondent. The dictatorship of Rojas Pinilla, from 1953 to 1957, was insinuated in the novel. "The mayor of the fictionalized account is supposed to be modeled after a relative of his wife, Mercedes. He was a real criminal who wanted to kill Mercedes' father. So he, Mercedes' father [García Márquez's father-in-law] was always armed."[12] Fiction and fact were once again intertwined, woven together. Another fact, however, is that neither the Spanish nor the Mexican publication of *In Evil Hour* found commercial success, but some literary critics received it favorably.

The events and the skirmishes surrounding the two novels are worthy of note, but García Márquez did not write any fiction in 1961 other than the short story "The Sea of Lost Time." It is hard to understand why a writer such as García Márquez would not have published anything other than that short story. The four volumes of his journalism somehow skip the 1960s. Volume three, *De Europa y América* (*Of Europe and America*), covers up to May of 1960, and volume four, *Por la libre*, includes selected newspaper articles from 1974 to 1995. So the Mexico City years, the early 1960s, indeed constitute a period of writer's block. He tortured himself with the idea that he could not write anything worthy of his own approval. The short story "The Sea of Lost Time," however, was certainly a story closer to the *magnum opus* he was intending to write, which he thought would be titled *The House*. His intentions were right; the title, as we discuss in Chapter 5, was not.

The year 1962 was marked by two significant events in his personal life. At the age of 35, García Márquez became a father for the second time. On the 16th of April, Gonzalo was born in Mexico City. And in that same year, according to his youngest brother, Gabriel Eligio[13] (known in the family as Yiyo), García Márquez was introduced to Carlos Fuentes. This was the year that Carlos Fuentes published his internationally acclaimed novel, *The Death of Artemio Cruz*. García Márquez was suffering from writer's block, while Carlos Fuentes was publishing constantly. To date, Carlos Fuentes is the most prolific of Mexican writers. While *The Death of Artemio Cruz*, also linked to Faulkner's 1930 *As I Lay Dying*, was published by Joaquín Mortis with great fanfare, García Márquez published a book of short stories he had written in years past: *Los funerals de la Mamá Grande* (*Big Mama's Funeral*). The publication took years to sell, although the University of Veracruz Press printed only 2,000 copies. From this book collection, the short story "There Are No Thieves in This Town" was made into a film.

Whether an oversight or not, it is worth mentioning that while Gabo was quick to write about Hemingway's suicide in 1961, a year later, he seemed to have ignored the death of the author he considered his master: the Mississippian William Faulkner. On a Friday morning, July 6, 1962, William Faulkner died of a heart attack at Wright's Sanitarium in Byhalia, Mississippi. He was 65 years old. The novelist William Styron wrote a four-page, illustrated essay in the July 20 issue of *Life* magazine, covering the funeral, which took place the day after Faulkner's death. *The New York Times, Time, Newsweek, The Saturday Evening Post*, and leading newspapers and magazines in the United States and around the world acknowledged his death.

After two years of working as editor in chief for *Sucesos* and *La Familia*, García Márquez resigned. It was obvious that this was not what he wanted to do. In 1963, now 36 years old, while working at his publicist's office for the Walter Thompson agency—thus far just another way to make a living—the opportunity to produce a film script was offered to him. The film producer, movie director, and screenwriter Manuel Barbachano was responsible for producing the film *El Gallo de Oro* (*The Golden Cock*), based on a short story by Juan Rulfo. Fuentes and García Márquez were invited to work on writing the adaptation. The film was released in 1964. The film had been worked on by others before, but to no avail. Like déjà vu, this new adaptation was not successful either. What was wrong with his pictures? The adaptation of "There Are No Thieves in This Town" was also a failure, but García Márquez would not know that until 1965. Perhaps the problem was the transfer from one medium to another. He thought he should write for the movies as genre, write for literature alone, and keep both separate. He did. His misfortunes, however, may or may not have been connected with transferring from one genre to the other. That year, Henry Fielding's novel, *Tom Jones*, was adapted for the big screen by screenwriter John Osborn. The film won four Oscars. Another film adaptation of 1963 is the acclaimed version of *Cleopatra*, with Elizabeth Taylor as Cleopatra and Richard Burton as Marc Antony. García Márquez undoubtedly went to see these two films. I am not making comparisons, but mere references. Budgets, actors, and actresses do contribute greatly in filmmaking.

In the United States, 1963 was marked by the two films mentioned, but above all by the shocking news, the world over, of President John F. Kennedy's assassination on November 22, while visiting Dallas, Texas. The year before, President Kennedy had been greeted by an unprecedented Mexican tickertape parade, and a seven-mile-long crowd of a million and a half spectators cheering him and First Lady Jacqueline Bouvier Kennedy.

In 1964, García Márquez wrote the movie script *Tiempo de morir* (*A Time to Die*). Unlike his previous efforts in writing for the cinema, the results were more favorable. The film was directed and produced in Mexico, a year later, by the Ripstein brothers, Arturo and Alfredo, Jr. The script, on the other hand, although it was not intended as a literary piece, was published in *Revista de Bellas Artes* (*Magazine of Fine Arts*). It was as if his intention to get things done was being forced. *A Time to Die* was a Western, intended to attract both the Mexican and the international public. Years later, García Márquez said he was not happy with the results. He had not wanted the film to be a Western, but had had no control over that. The violent plot, with a rural setting, deals with the themes of revenge and honor. These same themes frame the novels *No One Writes to the Colonel* and *In Evil Hour*. The film was favorably received by movie critics, but somehow there was something missing and the work did not attract a larger audience. Some of his friends thought he did not know how to get to the people. His treatment of both literature and film needed perfecting; he was not grabbing the reader's, nor the viewer's, heart and attention. He, however, continued to write about the same themes with the same recurring background.

The main character in *A Time to Die* is released from jail after 18 years, for killing a man in a duel (based on a biographical account). The two sons of the deceased man want to avenge the death of their father. Fate and repetition play a significant role: cyclical time. One of the two sons provokes the ex-convict until he agrees to fight him in a duel. Like his father before him, he is killed. The younger brother then kills the supposed villain by shooting him in the back. The film is one more attempt to deal with the thematic issues that will eventually all come together in *One Hundred Years of Solitude*. These issues have a real-life foundation in what seems to be fiction. García Márquez's own grandfather had killed a man in a duel.

In 1965, the film adaptation of "There Are No Thieves in This Town" was ready to meet its fate. The film found its way to the Locarno Film Festival in Italy. He worked on several other movie scripts, but none was commercially successful. Not even his collaboration with Carlos Fuentes on the adaptation of *Pedro Páramo*, a novel by the celebrated Mexican author Juan Rulfo, succeeded. Rulfo also wrote the short story "The Golden Cock," García Márquez's first movie venture. From 1961 to 1965, he was frustrated with the film industry, and also upset that he could not find the precise tone for the novel he had been trying to write since 1948: *La casa* (*The House*). The first half of the 1960s must have seemed like a steep mountain, not at all magical, which he had to climb. The movie *There Are No Thieves in This Town*, from the short story of the same name, was packed with names who were shining stars in their own right, but they were not actors. That was a big mistake. Any movie buff interested in Spanish American letters would feast his eyes looking at names like Luis Buñuel, Carlos Monsiváis, Juan Rulfo, and Juan José Gurrola on the big screen. García Márquez himself played a ticket seller in the film. In his own words, anybody who was somebody in art and literature appeared in that film.[14] The comment is an exaggeration on his part, typical García Márquez hyperbole. However, the Spaniard Luis Buñuel, considered one of the most important movie directors within and outside the Spanish-speaking world, played the role of the priest in the film.

NOTES

1. Gabriel García Márquez, "Los cubanos frente al bloqueo" ("Cubans in the Face of the Embargo"), *Por la libre, Obra periodística 4 (1974–1995)* (*No Toll, Journalist Work, Volume 4 (1974–1995)*) (Colombia: Editorial Norma, 1999), 221–33.

2. I am using both family names to refer to them as a family. Barcha is his wife's maiden name. Their son, therefore—the only son at that time (they only had two boys)—is Rodrigo García Barcha. The Spanish naming tradition is explained in Chapter 1: Origins. As a family, they are not the Garcías, as we would call them in English, but the García-Barcha family.

3. Mario Vargas Llosa, *García Márquez: historia de un deicidio* (*The Story of a Deicide*) (Barcelona, Spain: Barral, 1971), 66. (The translation is mine.)

4. Ibid., 67.

5. Bell-Villada, *García Márquez*, 1990 (see chap. 2, n. 1).

6. Gabriel Eligio García Márquez, *Tras las claves de Melquiades: historia de* Cien años de soledad (Colombia: Editorial Norma, 2001), 578–79.

7. Gabriel García Márquez, *Collected Stories*, trans. Gregory Rabassa and J. S. Bernstein (New York: Harper Perennial, 1999), 235.

8. García Márquez, "Los cubanos frente al bloqueo," *Por la libre, Obra periodística 4*, 221–33. (The translation is mine.)

9. Ibid., 221–33.

10. Vargas Llosa, *García Márquez*, 75. The Spanish publication, by Talleres Gráficos Luis Pérez, 1962, printed in Madrid, had 224 pages. The Mexican publication, by Era, 1966, had 198 pages. (The translation and emphasis (italics) are mine.)

11. Peter H. Stone, "Gabriel García Márquez," in *Latin American Writers at Work, The Paris Review*, ed. George Plimpton (2003), 153.

12. Gabriel Eligio García Márquez, *Tras las claves*, 403.

13. Gabriel Eligio, nicknamed Yiyo by the family, is the youngest of the 11 siblings of the García Márquez family, the children of Gabriel Eligio García and Luisa Santiaga Márquez Iguarán.

14. *Gabriel García Márquez: Tales beyond Solitude*, videocassette, directed by Holly Aylett and produced by Sylvia Stevens (London: Luna Films Limited, 1989).

Chapter 5

THE MYTH OF *ONE HUNDRED YEARS OF SOLITUDE*

> It always amuses me that the biggest praise for my work comes for the imagination, while the truth is that there's not a single line in all my work that does not have a basis in reality. The problem is that Caribbean reality resembles the wildest imagination.
>
> —*Gabriel García Márquez*

One Hundred Years of Solitude was published in 1967 in Buenos Aires, Argentina. Four decades after its publication, readers around the world continue to see it as a literary phenomenon with countless interpretations. The myriad of ways of approaching the text go from a textual reading as fiction alone—the story of six generations of the Buendía family—to numerous studies taking political, social, psychological, historical, and mythical approaches, using various meticulous literary theories. "*One Hundred Years of Solitude* offers a richness and a density that allows succeeding generations of readers to add further comments to its already abundant critical legacy."[1] As a work of fiction, any reader detached from Latin American reality will enjoy (not without a strong will to read it throughout) a most amazing tale, written in a seemingly linear, old-fashioned style of storytelling. In effect, that is what the author intended. He wanted to be able to tell the most fantastic tales without a moment's hesitation, as if it were all matter-of-fact. The result was *One Hundred Year of Solitude*, as we know it today.

The actual writing of the novel began in 1965. In spite of this, García Márquez is fond of saying that he really began writing the novel many years earlier. It may seem a poetic exaggeration, but many scholars estimate that it was 17 years in the making. What came to be *One Hundred Years of Solitude* (hereafter either *Solitude* or the full title) was supposed to be called *The House*. "I wanted the whole development of the novel to take place inside the house. I later abandoned the title *The House*, but once the book goes into the town of Macondo, it never goes any further."[2] In this chapter, we will trace his life from the genesis of the novel, universally considered his *magnum opus*, to the year after it was published in the United States.

In 1965, 38-year-old García Márquez was still living in Mexico City. He had very little time alone to enjoy the solitude that permeates his oeuvre. His job as editor in chief for the two Mexican magazines, *Sucesos* and *La Familia*, was not something he enjoyed. He had accepted that job on the condition that he did not have to write a single line for them. The worst of it all was his inability to write. He had faced writer's block for several years, since his arrival in Mexico. He arrived in Mexico City in 1961, and, four years later, had no intention of leaving. Mexico City has always been one of the poles of culture in Latin America, the other being Buenos Aires in Argentina. The place was right; his circumstances were not.

Before *Solitude*, Gabo had published four books: *La hojarasca* (*Leaf Storm*), *Los funerales de la Mamá Grande* (*Big Mama's Funeral*), *La mala hora* (*In Evil Hour*), and *El coronel no tiene quien le escriba* (*No One Writes to the Colonel*). These first four books can be seen as attempts to write *The House*. The plot of *Leaf Storm* (1955) describes a family at odds with the community for the right to give an outcast a Christian burial. All the action is imaginary. The time frame of the story elapses 25 years before the death of the doctor, through the stream of consciousness of an old colonel, his daughter, and his grandson. Today, García Márquez aficionados can see *Leaf Storm* as part of *One Hundred Years of Solitude*. The same can be said of the short stories found in *Big Mama's Funeral* and the novels *No One Writes to the Colonel* and *In Evil Hour*.

The setting itself is named in full in the title "Isabel Watching it Rain in Macondo." This short story, in turn, can be seen either as a draft of *Leaf Storm*, or as a piece taken out of the novel. The setting of *Leaf Storm* is also Macondo. When the town is not expressly called Macondo, it is simply described as "the town." In *Big Mama's Funeral*, three of the short stories take place in Macondo and four happen in "the town." Because of these recurrences, some readers find him repetitious, if not boring. But these four early works are more than short drafts and revelations. They are not just supplementary, sudden flashes that announce stages of *Solitude*. Each work fashions real life in the tropics; each unveils the foibles of the universe the characters share with peoples in other latitudes, whether in the Spanish-speaking world or elsewhere. The writer is not simply repeating himself in order to master technique. The characters appear and reappear in different stories as archetypes in a fictional world that feeds from the real world. The reader identifies the priest, the strong mother, the child, and the proud old colonel, and tracks them as the booklover enters the fictional world, as if in a continuum. Gabo's will to develop a fleshed-out, well-rounded old colonel comes to fruition in *No One Writes to the Colonel*, but the first attempt is in *Leaf Storm*.

It was in July of 1965, while driving to Acapulco, Mexico, that García Márquez's intention to write the novel he had always wanted to write suddenly took shape in his mind. In the mid-1960s, the drive to Acapulco from Mexico City would take as long as 10 to 12 hours. This stretch of road is part of the Pan-American Highway, a celebrated route in film, literature, and real life. It extends from Fairbanks, Alaska, to the tip of Argentina. That 12-hour drive, even with two children in the car, was sufficient time for García Márquez to put together the pieces of the puzzle, and envision the novel in its entirety. His son, Rodrigo, born in Colombia, was then six years old, and Gonzalo, born in Mexico, was barely three. The infamous writer's block, five years in length, was over. If anyone had mentioned *No One Writes to the Colonel* to him, it would have been like pins and needles, for this work was considered masterful and he could not produce anything similar or close to it. But in 1965, his literary future was about to change.

Commercially, up until 1965, his novels and short stories had been poorly received, and he had never received any author's royalties. During the first half of the 1960s, in Mexico, he was better known as a screenwriter and as a publicist. His literary work in Mexico, as well as in Colombia, was well respected among friends and certain literary critics, but limited to a small reading public. In fact, if it had not been for his close friendship with Carlos Fuentes, he would not have been included in Luis Harss' celebrated book, *Into the Mainstream* (1967).

In 1964, Harss was set to write *Into the Mainstream* for Harper and Row, to include authors who were making an impact, albeit small, in the United States and Europe. There was not much criticism available about the writers he had in mind, so personal interviews were the best way to prepare the manuscript for the book. His long journey started in Paris, France. The most avant-garde of all Latin American writers at that time was Julio Cortázar, and his residence was in Paris. His 1963 *Rayuela* was an experimental novel, considered a masterpiece, and one of the best written in the Spanish language in the last century. By 1966, it had been translated into English as *Hopscotch*.

In 1965, Harss was in Mexico to interview both Carlos Fuentes and Juan Rulfo for inclusion in his book. Fuentes and Rulfo were authors with a large readership; their books were "best sellers" with sales of over five thousand copies. Today that number seems almost laughable, but García Márquez himself was not a best-selling author at that time, and his books were printed by small publishers. Harss' book, however, was expected to be published first in Spanish by Sudamericana in Buenos Aires. Carlos Fuentes wanted Harss to include García Márquez in the book, but Fuentes was not just lionizing a friend for the sake of it. Fuentes was convinced that with every book, Gabo was becoming a better writer, and the difference between *Leaf Storm* and *No One Writes to the Colonel* was obvious. Fuentes not only convinced Luis Harss of Gabo's uniqueness with respect to writing, but also provided Harss with copies of García Márquez's four books to date. Harss was convinced that Fuentes was not simply glorifying a friend. However, García Márquez was not in the city, and Harss did not want to leave Mexico without talking with him.

He managed to have an interview with him, but had to drive two hundred miles west of Mexico City to Pátzcuaro, a colonial gem town in the state of Michoacán, famous for its lake, its ancient traditions, and its folk art. This is how Harss described García Márquez in *Into the Mainstream*: "He is stocky but light on his feet, with a bristling mustache, a cauliflower nose, and many fillings in his teeth. He wears an open sport shirt, faded blue jeans, and a bulky jacket flung over his shoulders."[3] He was on location, filming. By the time Luis Harss left Mexico to fly to Argentina, he was convinced of García Márquez's great skill in *No One Writes to the Colonel*. Two years later, when *Into the Mainstream* was published by Harper and Row, Harss' book soon became "a reference source" in the United States for those who wanted to learn about the writers who were changing the shape of Latin American literature. The chapter about García Márquez was a close reading of the four books he had written, and a succinct biographical account of the Colombian novelist.

In 1965, in the United States, those who were reading Latin American authors were looking at the Argentines Jorge Luis Borges and Julio Cortázar, the Cuban Alejo Carpentier, the Mexicans Juan Rulfo and Carlos Fuentes, the Guatemalan Miguel Angel Asturias, the Uruguayan Juan Carlos Onetti, the Peruvian Mario Vargas Llosa, and the Brazilian João Guimarães Rosa. Most of these would be known, the following year, as members of the Latin American "boom." García Márquez, however, was the only one whose works had not yet been translated into English. He was virtually unknown. His name was unfamiliar not only in the

United States, but even in Latin America. The translation of *One Hundred Years of Solitude* had to wait until 1970.

The myth surrounding *One Hundred Years of Solitude*, now over 40 years old, started with the way it was published in September 1967. On one hand, the book was somehow supposed to be published by a different publishing house, most likely the newly created ERA in Mexico City, and not by Editorial Sudamericana in Buenos Aires. However, in 1965, the literary director of Sudamericana, Francisco Porrúa, was ready to go to any lengths to secure the publication of a novel that was yet to be written. But Porrúa knew little or nothing about García Márquez. He came to know of him through Luis Harss' intention to include the unknown Colombian as one of the authors in the book he was writing. Porrúa was the editor in chief of *Los nuestros* (*Our Own*), the English free translation of which—or interpretation, really—is *Into the Mainstream*.

As Carlos Fuentes had done in Mexico City with Harss, talking up the literary uniqueness and skill of García Márquez, Harss was doing in Buenos Aires. Harss lent Porrúa García Márquez's four books to date. Porrúa was immediately convinced. Like many before him, Harss wrote that the four books prior to *Solitude* were somehow interconnected. He noted, "A single source has fed all his books, which grew side by side in him like different aspects of a single basic image. In fact, [...] all were more or less written together, each an echo of the others, a hint containing its sequel or, inversely, deriving from it."[4] So through Harss, who in turn had listened to Fuentes, the contract that Sudamericana secured to publish *One Hundred Years of Solitude* was signed on September 10, 1966. A month later, *Los nuestros* (*Into the Mainstream*) was published in Spanish.

García Márquez, on the other hand, was sharing bits and pieces of it with his friends and journalists, as well as two chapters with Francisco Porrúa of Sudamericana. It is interesting to note that the translation of Harss' book into English has no correlation with its original in Spanish; nevertheless, obviously, Harss did not oppose Harper and Row in this regard. When he quotes within his own text, however, he uses his own translations. For the rather poetic *No One Writes to the Colonel*, he uses *No Letter for the Colonel*.

According to Gabriel García Márquez's youngest brother, Gabriel Eligio (notice the repetition of the name; the youngest was named after their father: Gabriel Eligio), *One Hundred Years of Solitude* must have been written between July of 1965 and no later than August of 1966. It took 12 months to write the novel, not 17 as often quoted by so many, García Márquez included. It is a fact, however, that he was driving to Acapulco, Mexico, with his wife and two children when the epiphany of the novel came to his mind. A romanticized, erroneous belief is that they immediately turned around and returned to their home in Mexico City. They did not! With García Márquez at the wheel, they all drove to the Mexican port. By the time the family got to the world-famous Mexican beach town of Acapulco, the novel was nearly fully framed in his head.[5]

As Gabo said to many interviewers, he could have dictated it in full to a typist. They got to Acapulco and he sat down at his hotel room table and wrote the opening sentence: "Many years later, as he faced the firing squad, Colonel Aureliano Buendía was to remember that distant afternoon when his father took him to discover ice."[6] This is undoubtedly the most popular opening of any novel ever written in Spanish, other than *Don Quixote*.

The full length of the novel was written in his house at 19 Loma Street, in the upper-middle class neighborhood of San Angel Inn, in Mexico City. The writer William Kennedy substitutes the number 19 for number 6, although in the same street, and in the same neighborhood. According to Kennedy, as García Márquez drove to Acapulco from Mexico City, he envisioned the first chapter. Gabo, according to Kennedy, could have dictated the entire chapter on the spot if he had had a tape recorder with him.[7] There are small variations in dates and events from journalist to journalist and from scholar to scholar, as García Márquez is known for contradicting himself. He told Luis Harss in *Into the Mainstream* that after reading Faulkner, he wanted to be a writer, but to Plinio Apuleyo Mendoza in *The Scent of Guava*, he said it was after reading Kafka that he wanted to be a writer. And in his memoir, *Living to Tell the Tale*, he says he always knew he wanted to be a writer.

"Mr. García Márquez [said the interviewer, Claudia Dreifus], there's so much that's been written about you and so little of it is true."[8] The insinuation had to do with his political beliefs and the commentaries on the civil wars of the 1980s in Central America, mainly in El Salvador, Guatemala, and Nicaragua; the Argentine dispute over the Falkland Islands with Great Britain; and his friendship with the Cuban Fidel Castro. While the undeclared Guatemalan civil war was not as prominent in the consciousness of the American press, a great deal of attention was put on the Nicaraguan Contras (Spanish for "against"; the Contras were counter-revolutionaries), and the brutal Salvadoran civil war. In each country, the fight for a better form of government and stopping to abuses of human rights was at the forefront. The fighting did not stop during the 1980s and continued through the 1990s.

The number of casualties may seem hyperbolic, but as is often the case in Latin America, reality surpasses most forms of imagination. The

THE MYTH OF ONE HUNDRED YEARS OF SOLITUDE 69

number of victims was in the hundreds of thousands, enough to scare anyone and make people solve both the national and international problems experienced in the Central American Region. A bit of imagination and a small amount of social consciousness from the parties involved might have helped to end the conflict, but that was not the case. Killings, kidnappings, torture, executions, rape, and the seizing of civilians' properties were commonplace in the Kafkaesque reality of each of the three countries.

The Falklands War, or Malvinas War, was also an undeclared war. The twentieth century can be remembered by our inability to recognize the meaning of war. This time, in 1982, the countries involved were Argentina and Great Britain. The dispute was brief and the number of dead combined did not exceed a thousand, according to the press. In the end, Great Britain regained control of the islands the Argentines had invaded on April 2, 1982. Somehow, this was an ill wind that blew some good. Argentina's defeat discredited the military government, and helped to restore civilian rule from 1983 to the present.

Gabo's friendship with Fidel Castro has endured the test of time and the vast criticism of people the world over. Even his closest friends have had something to say about it. Plinio Apuleyo Mendoza, who compares Fidel Castro to Soviet leader Joseph Stalin, told a reporter for *The New Yorker*, "We will hear about all the atrocities that happened during his rule [Castro's]. And I don't think it will help Gabo to have been such a friend of his."[9]

The account published by Gabriel Eligio García Márquez, known as Yiyo to family and friends, in 2001 contradicts some of the mythical entries that have been documented regarding *One Hundred Years of Solitude*. His is undeniably one of the most thorough studies ever written about the birth of *Solitude*. His report includes letters, an extensive bibliography, and direct contact with many players in the production of the novel. Like the author of *One Hundred Years of Solitude*, Gabriel Eligio also heard the stories Gabo writes about. He did not hear them from his grandparents; he heard them from his parents. Sometimes indirectly, when not directly, he heard and saw what his oldest brother, Gabriel García Márquez, was experiencing and writing. No other biographer of García Márquez has ever collected more information to document one book alone. Through him, we learned there were 40 writing pads, all of which García Márquez and his wife, Mercedes, burned in their house on La Loma Street (the Hilly Street) in Mexico City, on which the structure of the novel was recorded to help the author keep track of it. Yet, in 630 pages, Gabriel Eligio states there are no documents to pinpoint when exactly the novel began or when it was finished. We favor many of his entries, without ignoring what others wrote before him.

The title of the novel came to Gabriel García Márquez at some point after the writing began. We know he thought the novel's title would be *The House*, but in a letter to the literary director of Sudamericana, dated October 30, 1965, he quotes the title we have known all these years. At that time, he had written about 400 pages.[10] The English version is 448 pages in total. Here, bear in mind, we are referring to typewritten pages, one side only. The novel was nearly half finished; the Spanish version has more or less the same number of pages, depending on the edition. The novel was, in effect, coming out as he had told his interviewers.

Another myth that encircled *One Hundred Years of Solitude* relates to the time of writing. Many wrote that he did not leave his house in Mexico City during the time he was writing the novel. However, in March of 1966, at age 39, he traveled to Cartagena de Indias, Colombia, where his parents were living, to participate in Cartagena's VII Film Festival. He was there as part of a Mexican delegation that was presenting the film *Tiempo de morir* (*Time to Die*), for which he had written the script. The judges of the Cartagena Film Festival selected *Time to Die* as the winner of the movie festival. The director of the picture was the Mexican Arturo Ripstein, then 21 years old. This film, in fact, was Ripstein's *opera prima* as a movie director. Years later, in 1999, he directed the acclaimed adaptation of Gabo's novel, *No One Writes to the Colonel*. The 1966 trip to Colombia would allow García Márquez the opportunity to come into close contact with the scenario of the novel he was writing, *One Hundred Years of Solitude*. There he was, in his beloved Aracataca, his place of birth, and the physical setting for the imaginary Macondo.

As stated earlier, the seeds of *One Hundred Years of Solitude* were visible in all previous writings. Most of us clearly see today that before *Solitude* was published, it was as if García Márquez had been writing the same book over and over, until *Solitude* came along that fateful day when driving to Acapulco. The four preceding books all foreshadowed the setting, the characters, the themes, the style, the language. "*One Hundred Years of Solitude* encompasses the beginning and the end, the *alpha* and the *omega*, the genesis and the apocalypse, of Macondo and its people."[11] Anything and everything with which García Márquez had experimented before in each book was taken to its highest form. The mythical invention of Macondo is indeed a genesis: "Macondo was a village of twenty adobe houses, built on the bank of a river of clear water that ran along a bed of polished stones, which were white and enormous, like prehistoric eggs. The world was so recent that many things lacked names, and in order to indicate them, it was necessary to point."[12] The tone, however, was new.

THE MYTH OF ONE HUNDRED YEARS OF SOLITUDE 71

The success of the novel was heralded by García Márquez's friends, whose comments served as ambrosia for a writer who, on the one hand, seemed to have faced writer's block after publishing *No One Writes to the Colonel*, and, on the other, wanted to succeed in the film industry. No one anticipated the triumph of the novel as much as the Mexican novelist Carlos Fuentes. Soon after Fuentes published the article, "García Márquez: *Cien años de soledad*. La Cultura en México" in *Siempre!*, segments of *One Hundred Years of Solitude* began to appear elsewhere. The Peruvian novelist Mario Vargas Llosa mentions *Eco* from Bogota, Colombia; *Mundo Nuevo* from Paris, France; *Diálogos* from Mexico; and *Amaru* from Lima, Peru.

As Vargas Llosa points out, this created a lot of enthusiasm and great expectations about the novel.[13] "Not since *Madame Bovary* [by the French author Gustave Flaubert] has a book been received with the simultaneous popular success and critical acclaim that greeted *One Hundred Years of Solitude*."[14] Carlos Fuentes' piece of writing has been quoted many times over. The English translation:

> I have just finished reading the first 75 pages of *One Hundred Years of Solitude*. They are absolutely magisterial...All "fictional" history coexists with "real" history, what is dreamed with what is documented, and thanks to the legends, the lies, the exaggerations, the myths...Macondo is made into a universal territory, in a story almost biblical in its foundations, its generations and degenerations, in a story of the origin and destiny of human time and of the dreams and desires by which men are served to destroyed.[15]

The novel was subsequently published in Buenos Aires in June 1967. The cover of the first edition, which was never repeated, depicted the silhouette of a galleon floating amid trees against a blue background, which contrasts with three geometric yellow flowers on the lower part of the cover in the foreground.[16]

According to Jorge Luis Borges, the Argentine poet, essayist, and short-story writer, *One Hundred Years of Solitude* is a book "as profound as the cosmos and capable of many endless interpretations."[17] Harold Bloom, on the other hand, said, "My primary impression, in the act of reading *One Hundred Years of Solitude*, is a kind of aesthetic battle fatigue, since every page is rammed full of life beyond the capacity of any single reader to absorb."[18] Bloom's reception is both ambiguous and less favorable than that of Borges. No book is infallibly good and readable for everyone. *Solitude* is no exception. Like *Hopscotch* by Julio Cortázar, *The Death of Artemio Cruz* by Carlos Fuentes, *Ulysses* by James Joyce, and *Absalom! Absolom!* by William Faulkner, *One Hundred Years of Solitude* calls for a tenacious reader. All these novels require a determined reader who is not easily bothered by the complexity of modernist literary technique.

In 1967, Gabriel García Márquez was a happy and pleased 40-year-old. The commercial success of his fifth novel was extraordinary. The first edition sold out in two weeks. Soon after, the Argentine press presented him with the Premio Primera Plana (Front Page Prize). On June 20, 1967, a few weeks after *Solitude* was published, Gabo and his wife were in Buenos Aires. That night they attended the premiere of a play at the theater, Institute di Tella. He was surprised, in a city where he had been a total unknown weeks before, that "the entire audience rose as the couple entered. At that very moment, García Márquez thought to himself, 'It seemed as if fame were falling down on me from heaven, wrapped in a blinding array of wing-flapped sheets, much like Remedios the Beauty' [in *One Hundred Years of Solitude*]."[19]

Before 1967 was over, García Márquez had decided to move to Barcelona, Spain, because it was suddenly difficult to find privacy in any Latin American country. While both enjoying and suffering from the attention celebrity brought, García Márquez attended, before moving to Barcelona, the XIII International Congress of Iberian and Latin American Literature, held in Caracas, Venezuela. Venezuela awards the prestigious Rómulo Gallegos Prize for best novel, and that year the prize was presented to Mario Vargas Llosa for *La casa verde* (*The Green House*). The two authors, who had not yet met, shared the limelight: Vargas Llosa for being novelist of the year, and García Márquez for the fact that *One Hundred Years of Solitude* was considered a masterpiece. The two became close friends thereafter. Their friendship, however, had its up and downs, and a sensationalist break-up worthy of news worldwide. The soap-opera denouement is dealt with in Chapter 10.

But Barcelona was no exception: privacy was difficult to find there, too. The Spaniards also wanted autographs, television, radio, and newspaper interviews. Time alone was something that eluded Gabo. The American novelist William Kennedy described García Márquez's place in Barcelona. "The apartment is modern in its furnishings, with wall-to-wall carpeting, floor-to-ceiling drapes, the color scheme beige, brown, and orange. The hi-fi, which García, and no one else, operates, is a significant object in the room, and in García's life. He treats his records as if they were fine crystal."[20] Kennedy also mentions the living-room shelves and García Márquez's books. The authors' names are those we hear often: the Polish-born, English novelist Joseph Conrad; Greek biographer Plutarch; Franz

Kafka; Virginia Woolf; Austrian poet, essayist, and short-story writer, Stefan Zweig; Scottish novelist A. J. Cronin (in full, Archibald Joseph Cronin); Jorge Luis Borges; François Rabelais; and British author Frederick Forsyth.

The interview with Kennedy is of particular importance for the documentation of Gabriel García Márquez's readings and opinions about authors he considers influential in his writings. Graham Greene is at the top of the list, along with Faulkner. Although Kennedy's interview insinuates the parochialism we suffer in the United States regarding Latin American issues and its writers, he learned that the translation for *One Hundred Years of Solitude* had to wait a whole year because Gregory Rabassa, the translator García Márquez wanted, was booked for a year. "I'll wait," García Márquez told his publisher. Kennedy is certainly right when he adds, "A decision for which anyone attuned to the English translation must be grateful."[21] One can imagine García Márquez was carefully crafting his grand entrance into the American book market: Gregory Rabassa had won the 1967 National Book Award for his 1966 English translation of Julio Cortázar's novel *Hopscotch*.

His literary agent, on the other hand, the Catalan Carmen Balcells, had secured the English translation for García Márquez's first four books: *Leaf Storm*, *Big Mama's Funeral*, *In Evil Hour*, and *No One Writes to the Colonel*. All efforts paid off when Rabassa's translation was finished. Gabriel García Márquez was a world-famous writer whose entry to the United States, interestingly enough, had been banned since 1961, due to his political beliefs. His books were read throughout the United States, *One Hundred Years of Solitude* had a cult following in certain colleges, but the author himself was not allowed to set foot on American soil. The reason was his alleged membership in the Communist Party. While no membership records are available, he was briefly involved as a journalist for the Latin American news agency Prensa Latina, the news agency of the Castro regime.

The impetus demanded by putting together such a work of genius in 1967's *One Hundred Years of Solitude* was still dominating Gabo's writing. The obsession with writing about his childhood, the images of the people he knew, and the Caribbean places he had seen would not leave him. The year 1968 was a crack in time for Western world cultures, but in his writing, at first glance, it almost seems as if it simply came and went, although we know that was not the case. How could anyone not be aware of the social unrest throughout the world?

In the United States, we witnessed the Vietnam War escalating even further as North Vietnam was bombed. There were protests against the war around the world, and student revolts broke out in Spain, Mexico, Prague, Paris, and the United States, just to mention some of the countries that were reacting to the world order and their own internal social and political problems. In March of that year, President Lyndon B. Johnson announced that he would not seek nor accept the Democratic Party nomination for another term as president. The month after, in Memphis, Tennessee, Martin Luther King, Jr. was shot and killed on the balcony of the Lorraine Motel on April 4. Born in 1929, civil-rights activist Luther King, Jr. was only two years older than García Márquez. Later that same year, the unthinkable happened again: Senator Robert Kennedy was assassinated in the ballroom of the Ambassador Hotel in Los Angeles, California, on June 15.

A journalist at heart, Gabo could have written columns about these world events, perhaps even written about the romance and wedding of Jacqueline Kennedy to Aristotle Onassis. From interview questions regarding the music he listens to, we can imagine Gabo fully aware of the Beatles' release of "Hey Jude," and the hippie movement. This counterculture movement was influencing fashion and the American way of life as much as that of the rest of the Western world. San Francisco was the epicenter of the movement, and that summer of 1968, to those who followed the change, was the summer of love. Whatever is common to popular culture, we know, is not foreign to Gabo. He feeds on it, whether as a journalist or as a fiction-writer.

García Márquez's everyday life in Barcelona was lived under the dictatorship of General Francisco Franco. Franco's long, dictatorial rule was particularly harsh on Spain's press, and definitely on anything Catalan, the language and region of Barcelona. Protests against the regime were docile, except for the university students, who repeatedly clashed with police. But Gabo would not write about this, either. The Franco dictatorship, according to García Márquez, was different from the one he wanted for his book *The Autumn of the Patriarch*, a volume about a literary tradition in Latin America regarded as the "Dictatorship Novel." García Márquez considers this book completely historical. "I realized at one point," he said, "that I myself had not lived for any period of time under a dictatorship, so I thought if I wrote the book in Spain, I could see what the atmosphere was like, living in an established dictatorship. But I found that the atmosphere was very different in Spain under Franco from that of a Caribbean dictatorship."[22] Was he being tactful and selective with his words? Does the reader find similarities with the Spaniard Francisco Franco, the Argentine Juan Domingo Perón, the Dominican Rafael Trujillo, or the Chilean Augusto Pinochet? The answer rests with the person who reads the novel. This is one novel critics find difficult to read, due to its technical complexity. We know he was writing *The Autumn of the Patriarch* while in Spain, but again, this novel took many years to complete. It is one he feels very strongly about, but literary critics in the United States found the book to be inferior to *Solitude*.

What he wrote in 1968 can be seen as echoes left by *One Hundred Years of Solitude*. It seems as if he was determined to write exclusively about the geographical area where he grew up, and the characters he knew. In 1968, according to Vargas Llosa, García Márquez wrote five short stories, but the fifth was meant to be a film. His interest in film was stimulated by the previous success of the motion picture *Time to Die*. The stories were "A Very Old Man with Enormous Wings," "The Handsomest Drowned Man in the World," "Blackman the Good, Vendor of Miracles," "The Last Voyage of the Ghost Ship," and "The Incredible and Sad Tale of Innocent Eréndira and Her Heartless Grandmother." The dates of publication varied in both Spanish and English. He would have to wait 16 years for "The Incredible and Sad Tale of Innocent Eréndira and Her Heartless Grandmother" to be made into a film (as *Eréndira*), and four more for "A Very Old Man with Enormous Wings," although the latter was not originally expected to become a picture.

The spell of Macondo as setting is substituted by a town near the sea in "A Very Old Man with Enormous Wings," "The Handsomest Drowned Man in the World," and "The Last Voyage of the Ghost Ship," but the images of magical realism permeate the five stories. The influence of *Solitude*, we have stated, is obvious in all five. Another unifying aspect is the use of political, social, and religious satire. Satire is one of the fundamentals that frame the portrait of daily life in the narratives. After reading any of his novels and short stories, we come to realize that satire and irony are the basis of criticism for testing and contesting moral and ethical values. This is true within these five stories. However, it is not so much from the writer's viewpoint, but rather from the reader's perspective.

Of all five stories, the one that strikes the reader for its innovative technique is "The Last Voyage of the Ghost Ship." On one hand, the whole story is told in one sentence, from beginning to end. On the other, the shift of the narrative voice from the omniscient narrator to the character and then back again to the omniscient within the story makes the reader question the reading itself. This story, unlike "The Incredible and Sad Tale of Innocent Eréndira and Her Heartless Grandmother," "A Very Old Man with Enormous Wings," and "The Handsomest Drowned Man in the World," loses itself into nothingness. The high level of experimentation makes the plot a story without a design. The plan, of course, is precisely that; make believe there is no design. The ploy is similar to waking up from a dream we think we remember, but we really do not and cannot. The lack of punctuation leads to confusion. The one-breath sentence vanishes into a voiceless fade-out. Who is the character who announces we will find out who he is, as the story opens? The opening of the story, this idea of seeing something for the first time, is reminiscent of the first sentence in *Solitude*. In that book, we see a child; here we see a man.

Two of the five stories were meant for children: "A Very Old Man with Enormous Wings," and "The Handsomest Drowned Man in the World." Nevertheless, when the former was taken to the screen, that quality was lost in the intention to make it successful at the box office. The sexual overtones not present in the short story make the film risqué and unwatchable for children. All five stories were published in the United States 10 years later, under the title *Innocent Eréndira and Other Stories*. While the plot of "A Very Old Man with Enormous Wings" as a short story is not difficult to read from a moral viewpoint, the storyline of "Innocent Eréndira" is the opposite. This happens when the reader is fundamentally not willing to or cannot interpret the narrative beyond the surface level. While the plot of "Innocent Eréndira" (who is not innocent at all) can be seen from several different angles of exploitation, the reader first sees child prostitution, child exploitation, and grows disgusted by it. The allegory of substituting a grandmother who sells her 14-year-old granddaughter's virginity to a widower known to pay well becomes offensive to many readers. This theme, however, is one García Márquez exploits as a literary tool, for his views on women are altogether different.

By 1969, now 42 years old, with plenty of money from his royalties, he spends his days as a full-time writer. There is no need to ever make a living doing something other than writing, traveling, and attending ceremonies in his honor, either to receive a prize for *One Hundred Years of Solitude* or simply as a guest of honor. The success of *Solitude* in Buenos Aires, when the novel first appeared, is continued that year in Italy and France. Critics in Italy awarded *Solitude* the 1969 Chianchiano Award, and in France, the critics bestowed on him the prize for best foreign book (Prix du Meilleur Livre Etranger). In the United States, *Solitude* was translated in 1970, to more popular success. The American critics selected it as one of the best 12 books of the year. So the story of a Latin American family, the Buendía family, appeals to Americans, Italians, French, and many other nationalities alike.

By 1971, nearly half a million copies had been sold in Spanish-speaking countries alone, and his four earlier books were reprinted again for a public who wanted to read more about the creator of Macondo. Latin

Americans read him voraciously. Many booklovers find the characters resemble some of their parents in their mannerisms, in their pessimism, in their sadness. Others read it as an allegory of the types of Latin American governments. The plot of the novel is mostly sad, but closer to the end, two members of the Buendías find love: Aureliano and Amaranta Ursula. They are the ones who complete one of the many cycles and myths enclosing the novel: the fear of giving birth to a baby with a pig's tail due to incest. She, his aunt, is unaware of their kinship. The two of them share pure love, a feeling denied to any other of the previous generations of Buendías. With biblical insinuations, she dies after giving birth. The newborn is eaten by ants and the father, the very last of the Buendías, yet one more Aureliano, comes to realize that the manuscripts he has been translating from Sanskrit are the story of his whole family, all generations, and written one hundred years before. "And he began to decipher the instant that he was living, deciphering as he lived it, prophesying himself in the act of deciphering the last page of the parchments, as if he were looking into a speaking mirror."[23] The climax of the novel for the reader outside the text, we who have the book in our hands, is the same that the character within the novel experiences. We are simultaneously reading what he is deciphering. He knows and we know that he, Aureliano Babilonia, the last of a dynasty of sorts, is bound to be wiped out from the surface of the earth. Because "everything written on them [the parchments] was unrepeatable since time immemorial and forever more, because races condemned to one hundred years of solitude did not have a second opportunity on earth."[24] That is how the novel ends, a lapidary ending announcing that regardless of what happened after the ultra success of the novel, there would be no second parts, no films, nothing other than the novel as we have known it in English since 1970, when it was first published in the United States.

Publishing houses around the world got wind of it, and 18 translation contracts were signed, before or after 1970. They were in the United States, France, Italy, Finland, Brazil, Sweden, Germany, Russia, Norway, Poland, Romania, Czechoslovakia, Yugoslavia (with two translations, one in Serbo-Croatian and one in Slovenian), England, Denmark, Japan, and Hungary.[25] The worldwide fame Gabriel García Márquez enjoys is well deserved, although it is rather premature to talk about it as a classic. *Solitude* was published over 40 years ago. It has passed many tests. Its reading is still fresh, and the passage of time proves that. Some critics have called it "an instant classic."

In 1971, García Márquez was questioning whether he would accept an honorary doctoral degree from Columbia University. Around that time, there was much talk among world-renowned intellectuals about the handling of Cuban poet Heberto Padilla versus Fidel Castro. García Márquez was not necessarily in the eye of the storm, but he had refused to sign a second letter petitioning on behalf of the poet, who was in prison. Would he be misjudged for accepting the degree? Would it hurt his credibility? After all, he had been banned from stepping on American soil since 1961. A special visa was granted, and García Márquez accepted the honorary degree from the university. It was the university, he would say, that awards the degree, not the politicians.

CODA

Today, the number of readers of *One Hundred Years of Solitude* is in the millions. There are versions of it in more than 40 languages. There is a special edition to celebrate the 40th anniversary of its publication, this time done under the careful scrutiny of the Royal Academy of the Spanish Language, in association with the different Language Academies of the Spanish Americas. The author himself participated in the proofreading before it went to press. The printed edition was published in Colombia on March 6, 2007, the day of his 80th birthday.

After the presentation section of the edition, the introductory pages are written by Alvaro Mutis, a Colombian poet, novelist, and essayist who befriended García Márquez when Gabo was 20 years old. Their friendship has lasted over 60 years. Mutis was a friend and a Maecenas for the aspiring young writer, and has accompanied Gabo throughout his life. They were together in Stockholm when García Márquez was awarded the Nobel Prize. Their celebrations together are legendary. They have shared friends, books, and music. They have traveled together on three continents. Mutis' words are followed by those of Carlos Fuentes. He writes a tribute with the title "To Give America a Name." America, for most Latin Americans, starts in Alaska and ends at the tip of Argentina, at the South Pole. The Mexican novelist also talks about his friendship with Gabo. They met in Mexico City in 1962. As noted in this chapter and Chapter 3, their friendship was instrumental for García Márquez's international reception, particularly in the English-speaking world.

After Mutis and Fuentes, in tribute to the novel is an abstract from Mario Vargas Llosa's voluminous work, *Historia de un deicidio* (*The Story of a Deicide*). García Márquez and his wife, Mercedes Barcha, collaborated with Vargas Llosa while he was writing the book. Vargas Llosa's commentaries on the novel, first published in 1971, are followed by some from Victor García de la Concha and Claudio Guillén. De la Concha is a Spanish philologist who has served as Director for the Royal Academy of the Spanish Language since 1998. Guillén, a Catalan poet of international renown, was Professor Emeritus at Harvard University. He died in 2002.

This special edition of *One Hundred Years of Solitude* is a must-have for book lovers around the world. It was presented to Gabriel García Márquez at the IV International Congress of the Spanish Language, celebrated in Cartagena, Colombia, in March 2007. Many scholars, friends, politicians, and members of the press gathered that day for the presentation of the book. Carlos Fuentes was one of them, along with the King and Queen of Spain, and former U.S. President, Bill Clinton.

Why do people love *One Hundred Years of Solitude* as much as they do? I think the lasting impression has to do with the fact that this novel is possibly the most realistically human of all modernist novels written in Spanish, other than *Don Quixote*.

NOTES

1. Aníbal González, "Translation and the Novel: *One Hundred Years of Solitude*," in *Gabriel García Márquez: Modern Critical Views*, ed. Harold Bloom (New York: Chelsea House Publishers, 1989), 271.

2. Stone, "Gabriel García Márquez," in *Latin American Writers at Work*, 152 (see chap. 4, n. 11).

3. Harss and Dohmann, *Into the Mainstream*, 310 (see chap. 1, n. 3).

4. Ibid., 318.

5. Gabriel Eligio García Márquez, *Tras las claves*, 70 (see chap. 4, n. 6).

6. García Márquez, *One Hundred Years of Solitude*, 1 (see chap. 3, n. 12).

7. William Kennedy, "The Yellow Trolley Car in Barcelona: An Interview," in *Conversations with Gabriel García Márquez*, ed. Gene H. Bell-Villada (Jackson, Mississippi: University Press of Mississippi, 2006), 59–78. The Argentine writer Kennedy mentions is Luis Harss, who was not Argentine, however, but Chilean born. Harss is a novelist in his own right and the one, if only indirectly, responsible for García Márquez's reception in the United States, through his book *Into the Mainstream* (1967).

8. Claudia Dreifus, "*Playboy* Interview: Gabriel García Márquez," in *Conversations*, ed. Bell-Villada, 95.

9. John Lee Anderson, "The Power of García Márquez," *The New Yorker*, September 27, 1999, 56–71.

10. Gabriel Eligio García Márquez, *Tras las claves*, 78 (see chap. 4, n. 6).

11. Pelayo, *Gabriel García Márquez*, 91 (see chap. 2, n. 3).

12. García Márquez, *One Hundred Years of Solitude*, 1 (see chap. 3, n. 12).

13. Vargas Llosa, *García Márquez*, 78 (see chap. 4, n. 3).

14. Regina Janes, *One Hundred Years of Solitude: Modes of Reading* (Boston, Twayne Publishers, 1991), 13.

15. As quoted in William Kennedy, "The Yellow Trolley Car in Barcelona: An Interview," in *Conversations*, ed. Bell-Villada, 73.

16. Juan Gustavo Cobo Borda, *Para llegar a García Márquez* (Bogotá, Colombia: Ediciones Temas de Hoy, 1997), 101. (The translation is mine.)

17. Ibid., 106. Cobo Borda quotes Borges; the translation is mine.

18. Harold Bloom, ed. *Gabriel García Márquez: Modern Critical Views* (New York: Chelsea House Publishers, 1989), 1.

19. Mariana Solanet and Hector L. Bergandi, *García Márquez para principiantes* (Argentina: Era Naciente RSL, 1999), 118. (The translation is mine.)

20. Kennedy, "The Yellow Trolley Car in Barcelona: An Interview," in *Conversations*, ed. Bell-Villada, 71–72.

21. Ibid., 73.

22. Stone, "Gabriel García Márquez" in *Latin American Writers at Work*, 142 (see chap. 4, n. 11).

23. García Márquez, *One Hundred Years of Solitude*, 447 (see chap. 3, n. 12).

24. Ibid., 448.

25. Vargas Llosa, *García Márquez*, 78 (see chap. 4, n. 3).

García Márquez attended sports ceremonies in Revolution Square, Havana, in November 2002 with longtime friend, Cuban president Fidel Castro. AP Photo/José Goitia.

By 1982, the year in which he won the Nobel Prize for literature, García Márquez had long since achieved international fame, and the "Boom" movement—of which he was one of several leading figures—had been succeeded by a far more diffuse South and Central American literary culture. AP Photo.

With his wife, Mercedes Barcha, García Márquez made a triumphal return in May 2007 to his childhood home in Aracataca, Colombia, the prototype of his famous Macondo of One Hundred Years of Solitude. *AP Photo/William Fernando Martínez.*

In January 1999 García Márquez attended peace talks between Colombia's president, Andres Pastrana, and FARC, Colombia's largest guerilla group, held in San Vicente del Caguan, Colombia. AP Photo/ Ricardo Mazalan.

Gabriel García Márquez, wearing a traditional liqui-liqui *rather than formal attire, receives his Nobel Prize medal at the presentation ceremony in Stockholm, Sweden, on December 8, 1982. Associated Press.*

Erected to celebrate García Márquez's return to Aracataca in 2007 after a 25-year absence, a billboard highlighting his tribute to the town depicts the author with the magical yellow butterflies of One Hundred Years of Solitude. *Courtesy of Rubén Pelayo.*

For the characters and places depicted in One Hundred Years of Solitude, *García Márquez drew heavily on his vividly remembered childhood in Aracataca. At the opening of the novel, Col. Aureliano Buendía (García Márquez) recalls this house on "that distant afternoon when his father took him to discover ice." Courtesy of Rubén Pelayo.*

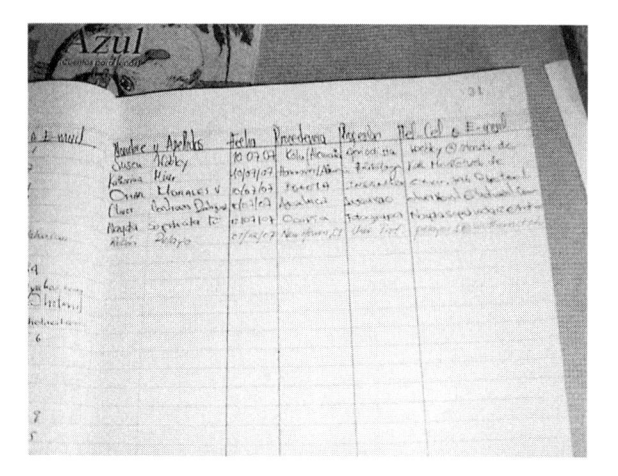

The names and far-flung places recorded in the guestbook at the García Márquez museum in Aracataca—temporarily housed at the Administraciòn Postal Nacional's Casa del Telegrafista, where García Márquez's father worked—bear testimony to the author's international appeal. At the upper left is a copy of Rubén Darío's Azul *(Blue), a volume of children's stories. Courtesy of Rubén Pelayo.*

Chapter 6

WORLD FAMOUS, SEPTEMBER 11, 1973

> Capote and Mailer developed their interests in the nonfiction novel, or New Journalism, from their careers as fiction writers. García Márquez, on the other hand, followed an opposite course, going from journalism to literature.
>
> —*Gloria Jeanne Bodtorf Clark*, A Synergy of Styles, *22*

In 1970, the 43-year-old Gabriel García Márquez published in book form a piece of investigative journalism he first wrote for *El Espectador*, the national Colombian newspaper headquartered in Bogotá. Although today García Márquez's work is often translated soon after the book is published, *Relato de un naúfrago* was not. When it was first published as a journalism piece in 1955, the story boosted Gabo's popularity and reputation (see Chapter 3). But when the reporter's feature was published as a book in 1970, its reception was lukewarm, both in Spain and the Spanish-speaking world. Sixteen years later, the English translation, *The Story of a Shipwrecked Sailor*, also came and went without much fanfare.

During the first half of the 1970s, García Márquez had become a celebrity, living off the fame, reputation, and economic success derived from *One Hundred Years of Solitude*. As early as 1971, Ernesto González Bermejo[1] observed he was already being considered "one of the greatest writers, or the greatest writer in Spanish, the Amadís of Latin America, the Cervantes of Colombia, author of *One Hundred Years of Solitude*, one of the most important or *the* most important of contemporary novels."[2] Hyperbolically or not, the appeal of *Solitude* was global. Everybody was still talking about *One Hundred Years of Solitude*. In fact, it often seems that most people have not stopped talking about it now, more than 40 years after its publication in 1967. The English translation, however, was not available until 1970. In spite of this, some academics, several critics, and large numbers of college students in the United States had read the novel in the original Spanish soon after its publication in 1967. An American college-educated multitude had already been reading in Spanish the works of the Argentines Jorge Luis Borges and Julio Cortázar; the Chileans María Luisa Bombal and Pablo Neruda; and the Mexicans Carlos Fuentes and Juan Rulfo, among others.

In 1971, Uruguayan journalist Ernesto González Bermejo interviewed the Colombian magician of words for the Cuban press, Prensa Latina (Latin Press). The dialogue between González Bermejo and García Márquez focused on *Solitude*. When González Bermejo asked, "Where has the best criticism of *One Hundred Years of Solitude* appeared?" Gabo answered, "It's unfortunate to have to say so, but the best criticism has been done in the United States. They're professional, conscious readers, well trained, some of them progressive, others as reactionary as they're supposed to be, but as readers, they're fantastic."[3] Why would it be *unfortunate* that the best readers of *Solitude* are Americans? Were the ideas, messages, or metaphors of *Solitude* intended for a particular or different public? What did the Russians make of it? How about the Japanese, and the Greeks, and the peoples of Africa? Was it *unfortunate* because a large number of the readers who were publishing, and continue to put out literary criticism on the subject of *One Hundred Years of Solitude* in the United States, were either Cuban or Cuban-Americans or other Hispanics living in the United States? Some were professors of literature at leading American universities, and some still are. They, in fact, might be the ones García Márquez was crediting as "the fantastic readers" of *One Hundred Years of Solitude*. Then, of course, there has been a group of American journalists who every so often have been granted interviews throughout the last 40 years, some of whom are writers in their own right.

During the 1970s, García Márquez's opinions were valued for what he said or chose not to say. When the subject is Cuba, his remarks are carefully crafted, perhaps skillfully and cautiously uncompromising, as the above quote proves. The interview he was giving was intended for the Cuban public. But not all Latin American writers felt like García Márquez. Some of the members of the intellectual literary circle of authors who had once been taken with the Cuban revolution were in an uproar by 1971 because of the turn of events in Cuba. García Márquez, however, seemed to have ignored or pretended to ignore what was going on. Nevertheless, he had always opposed the death penalty ever since it was instituted by Castro's regime.

By 1971, his name alone was news. The impact of his words, politically speaking, had much impact by the 1970s. As we would soon discover, his silence would carry a great deal of importance as well. Such was the advent of the "Caso Padilla," the "Padilla Affair." Heberto Padilla was a Cuban intellectual, an advocate of the Cuban revolution, a poet who, after living in the United States prior to the triumph of the Cuban revolution, returned to Cuba once the revolution was victorious. While the Cuban Diaspora we hear so much about in the United States left the island, Padilla flew back instead. "In 1959, Mr. Padilla, then 27, had enthusiastically embraced the revolution, which brought him back home from the United States, where he had been working as a radio commentator and translator. He became one of the founding editors of Lunes de Revolución [Revolutionary Mondays], a literary journal, and worked for Prensa Latina [Latin Press], the Cuban news agency, and Granma, the Cuban Communist Party newspaper, as a foreign correspondent based in Moscow and London."[4]

Outside of Cuba, however, Heberto Padilla was an obscure poet. In 1971, accused of being a counterrevolutionary, his name gained international attention when he was imprisoned for criticizing Castro's administration. Interestingly enough, the charges against him originated from a poetry book, Fuera del juego (Out of the Game), which the Cuban Union of Writers and Artists had seen worthy of the Julián del Casal Poetry Prize in 1968. In 1971, he and his wife, Belkis Cuza Malé, were arrested. His wife, like her husband and many others, was critical of the Castro government. Among others, internationally known writers like Mario Vargas Llosa, the Spaniard Juan Goytisolo, Carlos Fuentes and Octavio Paz, Plinio Apuleyo Mendoza, Julio Cortázar, and Jean-Paul Sartre protested the arrest and broke ties with the revolution they had once supported. A letter was written, titled "The First Letter to Fidel," asking for explanations and to reconsider the arrest. A total of 54 intellectuals signed the letter. The Italian novelist Alberto Moravia and New York-born writer Susan Sontag also defended Padilla. For some international left-leaning authors, the event completely changed their viewpoint on the Cuban revolution. The rumor was that the one signature missing was that of Gabriel García Márquez. Did he or did he not sign the letter? Was it important, one way or the other? In certain circles, whether he had signed the letter to Fidel Castro or not was indeed of great consequence. This will be a task for historians, if a copy or the original of the letter exists. What we have today are contradictions. Some say he signed, others say he did not, and others say that Plinio Apuleyo Mendoza signed on his behalf.

By April 29, 1971, the "Padilla Affair" took a turn for the worse. On that date, the poet made a public, humiliating self-criticism, accusing himself of being a counterrevolutionary. His 4,000-word "confession," a 15-page communiqué—if we think of it as a typewritten, double-spaced document—incriminated many other Cuban intellectuals. His "declaration of guilt" included his wife, Belkis Cuza Malé, and novelist Lezama Lima, one of the most influential names in contemporary Latin American literature. The script Padilla read was an ill-wrought parody that resulted in a second letter to Fidel Castro. This time, the letter was written by Mario Vargas Llosa. Some say Gabo did not sign the second letter, either. Others say he did. Perhaps García Márquez will clear up the mystery of the signature affair when he publishes his forthcoming volume of memoirs. What we know today is that when Heberto Padilla finally left Cuba in the early 1980s, to come to the United States, it was with the help of García Márquez.[5]

But in 1971, aside from the fact that the Padilla Affair can be pinpointed as one of the reasons for the beginning of the breakup of the group of novelists who are often identified with "the boom" of Latin American writers, García Márquez was involved in many other affairs. Some were political, several social, a few involved cinema, and some he always kept for himself, his family, and his closest friends. The latter, of course, we may never come to know about. His friends, on the other hand, were themselves world news. With friends like Pablo Neruda, Gabo continued to make connections with world figures who would become his own comrades. One of them was French President François Mitterrand, who Gabo met at Neruda's house in Paris in 1971, while Neruda was Chile's ambassador to France. At that time, Mitterrand was the leader of the French Socialist Party, not president. Neruda had invited Gabo and his wife, Mercedes, on the occasion of Neruda's nomination for the Nobel Prize of Literature. But Mitterrand was only one of the influential names Gabo would meet that evening: "Neruda wasn't just the initial link with Mitterrand; he also introduced his Colombian friend to French celebrities and a Swedish official."[6] The French celebrities were Régis Debray and Henri Cartier-Bresson. The Swedish official was the poet, novelist, and literary critic Artur Lundkvist.

When Lundkvist died in 1991, his obituary in the *New York Times* talked about the influence he had had in the Swedish Academy, which awards the Nobel Prize for Literature. "He was instrumental in bringing the works of many Spanish and Latin American writers to his colleagues' attention, often translating the works himself."[7] The article adds the names of Pablo Neruda and the Mexican poet Octavio Paz, the 1990 Nobel

Laureate; the South African Nadine Gordimer; and the French writer, Claude Simon, but does not mention García Márquez. All the guests at Neruda's table were influential people affiliated with Socialist causes. Debray had been released from a Bolivian prison the year before (1970) because of his connection with Ernesto Che Guevara.

With regard to the high-profile French guests, when Mitterrand became president of France, he appointed Debray as his advisor on Third World Affairs. Cartier-Bresson, who died in 2004, is considered one of the greatest photographers of the twentieth century, but he was also fond of drawing and painting. Today his photographs sell for thousands of dollars. Being introduced to famous, influential people is important in anybody's career, but developing a friendship is up to the parties involved. Mitterrand would become president of France a decade later. Gabo's friendship with the politician would pass the test of time. In the next chapter, the 1980s, we will talk about Mitterrand's inauguration and the friends who accompanied him—García Márquez included, of course.

The 1970s follow the telegrapher's son from Aracataca, a Colombian writer in his 40s whose life, all of a sudden, was everybody's business, globally. In May of 1971, García Márquez was getting ready to come to the United States, and this move alone put him in the eye of the storm. The Padilla Affair had been highly publicized as an anti-Castro response on behalf of the intellectual left, which had supported the Cuban revolution, now over a decade old. Therefore, coming to the United States was something Gabo would have to think about carefully. He did not want the international press to assume he had broken with Fidel Castro's regime. "For anyone who didn't know that this decision [coming to Columbia University] had been made earlier, it might lead them to believe that I was going to United States because I had broken with Castro. I therefore made a statement to the press, completely clarifying my position on Castro, my doctorate, and my return to the United States after 12 years, during which time I had been refused a visa."[8] He was in disbelief that Columbia University had chosen him. "The last thing I ever expected in this world was a doctorate of letters. My path has always been anti-academic. […] And I asked myself, 'what should I be doing in a literary academy in cap and grown?' At my friends' insistence, I accepted the title of *doctor honoris causa*."[9] While his global reception in connection to Castro was important, it was about more than just Castro, per se. García Márquez was also friends with Salvador Allende, Omar Torrijos, Carlos Fuentes, and Graham Greene, among many other well-known public figures. His friendship with Castro, however, seems to have led to an obsessive interest on the part of the media, some academics, and many people in general. But in the 1970s, García Márquez was also a supporter of the Chilean Popular Front, the Sandinistas in Nicaragua, and the Montoneros in Argentina. In the same interview mentioned above, García Márquez added, "My ambition is for all Latin America to become Socialist, but nowadays people are seduced by the idea of peaceful and constitutional socialism. This seems to be all very well for electoral purposes, but I believe it to be completely Utopian. Chile is headed toward violent and dramatic events."[10]

He was right in foretelling violent and dramatic events in Chile. Soon after Salvador Allende became president of Chile, a civil war of sorts erupted in the country. Not all Chileans supported their president and the changes he was making. One significant change was the nationalization of the country's mining industry. While the change would help the mining workers and the country's economy, the private international sector would take a measurable blow. Copper mining in Chile was controlled by three American firms: Anaconda, Kennecott, and Cerro. The social unrest throughout the country immediately became world news. College students, intellectuals, and people from the middle classes were out on the streets, demonstrating in favor of the government action, but they were not alone. There were those who favored the old-fashioned ruling class and foreign interests. According to *Time* magazine, in January of 1971, "None of the more than 150 U.S. firms in Chile have given up and left. Though expropriation of most, if not all of them, seems only a matter of time, none are willing to antagonize Allende unnecessarily before knowing just when or where he will strike next."[11] The time came in 1971, on Monday, July 26, when Chile was proclaimed by Salvador Allende "Owner of the Future" after the amendment for nationalizing the copper mines passed. "Newspapers, billboards and walls blossomed with the slogan: 'Chile has put on its long pants! Finally the copper is ours.'"[12] Chile was experiencing national pride and unrest, but with Pablo Neruda winning the Nobel Prize for Literature, Chileans and their friends thought their place in history was right. Neruda's Nobel Lecture, on December 13, 1971, was rightly titled "Towards the Splendid City." But the poet's Banquet Speech—like García Márquez's ominous foretelling, "Chile is headed toward violent and dramatic events"—also spoke of ominous things to come. Alluding to his work as poet, he said, "I render my thanks and return to my work, to the blank page which every day awaits us poets so that we shall fill it with our blood and our darkness, for with blood and darkness poetry is written, poetry should be written."[13] But neither Neruda nor García Márquez could ever have imagined what was to take place in Chile in 1973.

García Márquez's literary career, on the other hand, was on hold. No new literary material, whether short stories or a novel, was published in 1972 except for translations of previous works. In the United States that year, we had *Leaf Storm and Other Stories*. The ripple caused by *One Hundred Years of Solitude* in 1972 resulted in García Márquez receiving the international Rómulo Gallegos Literature Prize. This award, given every two years for the best novel, is named after the Venezuelan novelist Rómulo Gallegos, former president of Venezuela. Relatively new, the Prize was created in 1964, but the first time it was awarded was in 1967. The first winner of the prize was Mario Vargas Llosa, for his novel *La casa verde* (*The Green House*). Among other winners, the prize has been given to Carlos Fuentes, Argentine Mempo Giardinelli, and Chilean Roberto Bolaño. When it was first instituted, the prestigious prize was worth a hundred thousand bolívares, along with a gold medal and a diploma.

In 1972, *One Hundred Years of Solitude* was selected out of 139 novels from 18 different countries. The prize is given in the month of August, to coincide with the birth of Rómulo Gallegos. That same year, in the United States, García Márquez was awarded the Neustadt International Prize for Literature. The biennial prize is sponsored by the University of Oklahoma and *World Literature Today*. First established in 1969, the award consists of fifty thousand dollars, a replica of an eagle's feather cast in silver, and a certificate. Among the 11 candidates for the 1972 Neustadt Prize were Octavio Paz (Nobel Laureate in 1990), and Polish writer Czesław Miłosz (Nobel Laureate in 1980). Two years before winning the Nobel Prize, Miłosz had won the Neustadt Prize. Octavio Paz was victorious in 1982. To date, the only American to have won the prize is the Massachusetts-born poet Elizabeth Bishop, in 1976.

On March 8, 1973, from Barcelona, García Márquez wrote a note to Dr. López Escauriaza on the occasion of the 25th anniversary of *El Universal* newspaper, in Cartagena, Colombia, where he had begun his career as a journalist. "My dear Dr. López," he wrote. "I believe that on few occasions, such as today, I realize the passage of time, as when I remember that today is the 25th anniversary of the newspaper you founded, the one where maestro Zabala did his work as he pleased and where I began to learn the only useful thing I've done in this world: the job of journalist. Receive my heartfelt embrace. Gabriel García Márquez."[14] Among his many qualities is his genuine sense of appreciation for those who have helped him through his formative years. Not long after the 1970s, García Márquez stopped writing letters and signing them. He became totally disheartened by the fact that some of his letters were being sold.

As in the year before, no new literary material was published. In 1973, we had the English translation of *Innocent Eréndira and Other Stories*, 11 short stories and a novella that gives the book its title. That tale is one of abuse and exploitation, as the original title suggests: "The Incredible and Sad Tale of Innocent Eréndira and Her Heartless Grandmother." Although the story can be read on many different levels, the reader cannot escape the oppression Eréndira endures while being prostituted by her own grandmother. Though Eréndira, 14 years old, is not really innocent (she planned to kill her grandmother), she is indeed taken advantage of by the older woman. The images of exploitation the narrative portrays are brutal. *Innocent Eréndira* was first published in 1972. By then, Gabriel García Márquez's mass appeal allowed him to publish almost anything, although he would only publish as much as he wanted. Around the world, the reading public wanted more from the "magic realist" Colombian author. He was already some sort of world sensation. His short stories and previous books, which had had a poor reception until then, were now sought after. Readers and moviegoers, furthermore, were given the chance to experience Eréndira's misfortune on film. The movie version was released in 1983. The storyline shows a 14-year-old forced to practice prostitution. She sells sexual services, but unlike the "queen," the prostitute in "The Woman Who Came at Six O'Clock," who does it because of a powerful system of patriarchy, Eréndira is exploited by her grandmother, hence subverting the system from patriarchy to matriarchy. The reader may or may not look at the narrative as sexist, chauvinistic, bigoted, and unfair, and all other possible words labeling men who abuse women. The storyline is as monstrous as the grandmother (she has green blood). To end the suffering, Eréndira kills her grandmother. The symbolism of the story may or may not reach all readers. At the surface level, the plot describes an elderly woman who has no moral or ethical consideration for her granddaughter, an unscrupulous pedophilic matriarch. Gabo is caught on film saying, "I knew the girl, Eréndira, and the grandmother. But I don't think she was her grandmother. She was the owner of a sort of traveling brothel that would go from town to town."[15] So as wickedly as the story unfolds, we are reading both fiction and some form of reality. The tyrannical older woman, whether related by blood or not, was a real person, as was the young girl.

The story, nonetheless, can certainly be looked at from different viewpoints. Once the reader goes beneath the surface, the writing calls for an active, investigative, inquisitive booklover who can look at the story as poetic prose in which references and the characters hold hidden meanings (symbolism). Despite the fact that the meaning is veiled, the elements needed to put the pieces together are there in the story. The reader, however, has to decode them from where he or she stands. The 300 years of Latin American colonization immediately come to mind. The colonial period can easily be juxtaposed: *Innocent Eréndira* then represents the young colonies that were exploited under Spanish and Portuguese rule, followed by the French. If one chooses to see it that way, the exploitation of Eréndira is rather similar to that of the so-called New World. Ruy Guerra, the Portuguese movie director, screenwriter, and actor who directed the film, went on camera to say, "The whole of Latin America is made up of exploitations. People are exploited at a political and economic level, at a human level, between men and women, and at an ethnic level." Guerra, however, is quick to add, "But you will never get me to say it [*Innocent Eréndira*] deals in metaphors, even if they exist. It's not for me to say, but for you to find out."[16] Guerra is not evading responsibility. It is the reader, indeed, who decides what he or she reads, and from which perspective.

We mentioned the economic and political changes Chile was undergoing under Salvador Allende and the nationalization of industries owned by foreign companies, a form of exploitation. Allende, the first democratically elected Marxist president of any nation, was killed on—a date predestined to be awful—September 11, 1973, by the Chilean army under the rule of General Augusto Pinochet. The events of that September 11th and its aftermath became part of the world consciousness, but particularly for Chileans, Latin Americans, and peoples with leftist ideals. Pinochet's coup was a bloodbath in which the four branches of Chile's armed forces attacked their fellow countrymen to overthrow Allende, his government, and anybody who sympathized with his ideals. While some Latin American countries had freed themselves in the 1960s from their own dictatorships, Chile ended a democracy and began a 17-year-long totalitarian dictatorship under General Augusto Pinochet Ugarte.

García Márquez responded to such events in the way he knew best, with his pen. "He has very close links with social-democratic tendencies and progressive liberals. In a continent faced with the vicious alternatives of a reactionary, militarist, pro-American right and a hard-line, pro-Soviet left, he prefers other kinds of popular democratic options. Since the Latin American right almost always supports military dictatorships, it is naturally hostile to him."[17] The fourth volume of his journalism work starts with an entry that reads "Chile, the Coup, and Gringos." There is no wonder he considers himself a journalist first. Or, as he puts it in the quote above, "The only useful thing I've done in this world [is] the job of journalist." His journalism is as spellbinding as his fiction is mesmerizing. In his account, the coup begins at the end of 1969, with a dinner party at the Pentagon in Washington, D.C. The investigative newspaper report brings a chill to the spine as he unveils a type of information to which the *very few* would have had access. Names, places, times, and even what they had for dinner are mentioned. When Gabo refers to Henry Kissinger, one can almost hear the German-born, naturalized American former Secretary of State of the United States speaking. Then the write-up moves on to document the historical aspects that made Chile what it was before the coup—its economy, its historical democratic form of government, its literary past—to come forward to September 4, 1970, when the socialist doctor Salvador Allende—a mason, he adds—was elected president.

His account brings to attention the role of the CIA, the economic blockade, and the sabotage by the Chilean upper class, which was against Allende. When he comes to describe the Chilean army, he uses the subheading "The Most Bloodthirsty Army in the World." He quotes Salvador Allende: "Anyone who believes that a military coup in Chile will be like any other in Latin American countries, with a simple change of guard at The Moneda [The neoclassical presidential palace, Chile's White House], is fully wrong. Here, if the army acts out of legality, there will be a bloodbath. It will be another Indonesia."[18]

Once again, Gabo traces the history of the Chilean armed forces from the seventeenth century to the twentieth, providing chilling facts. He ends the entry with numbers that are far beyond the imaginable, if one considers that this is real life, not fiction. These are Chileans killing Chilean civilians. He writes, "Four months after the coup, the balance was atrocious: almost 20,000 people killed, 30,000 political prisoners subjected to savage tortures, 25,000 students expelled from schools, and more than 200,000 workers without jobs. The worst part, however, was yet to come."[19] The investigative article ends with the subheading, "The True Death of a President." The account is as sad as it is realistic. Every sentence is crafted with the intent to communicate the last minutes of President Salvador Allende as he gets cornered, inch by inch, ever so slowly in the presidential residence, as if through the lens of a camera. But no device is as good as the imagination when the writer is as detailed and as meticulous as García Márquez. Allende died while exchanging gunfire with the army patrol that broke into his office. Once he was dead, "all the officials, as in a rite of caste, took one more shot at his body. To finish him, a sub-official demolished his face with the butt of his rifle. The picture exists: the photographer Juan Enrique Lira of the newspaper *El Mercurio* took it. He was the only one allowed to photograph the cadaver."[20] The President's wife was allowed to see his body, in the coffin, but she was not permitted to see his face. García Márquez closes his journalistic account with a historical statement that resonates throughout the ages, "The drama took place in Chile, to the Chileans' misfortune, but it will go down in history as something that happened, without remedy, to all mankind of our times, and it will remain in our lives forever."[21]

In 1974, the 47-year-old Gabriel García Márquez founded *Alternativa* (*Alternative*) with the help of other Colombian intellectuals, mainly Orlando Fals Borda and Enrique Santos Calderón. It was a left-wing magazine that ran through 1980. The periodical was conceived as a counter force to the established forms of communication controlled by the State. It was written in accessible language, so that anyone could read and understand politically oriented issues, often dealing with the working class and government affairs. *Alternativa*, as the title suggests, was the other voice, the single attempt to be most pluralistic. In that fashion, *Alternativa* was interested in propagating the voice of the different factions of the Colombian guerrilla and guerrillas elsewhere where there was intent to institute alternative forms of free thought. Although the magazine has now disappeared, the García Márquez reader can find some of the best journalism he once published in *Alternativa* magazine in his book, *Por la libre, Obra periodística 4 (1974–1995)*. No translation is available for *No Toll, Journalism Work, Volume 4 (1974–1995)*.

While *Alternativa* was a Colombian publication aimed at the general reading public, García Márquez published no new fiction in 1974, while he continued to live in Barcelona. But that year, multifaceted Gabo attended the San Sebastián International Film Festival, in San Sebastián, Spain. Over half a century old, the festival has attracted an endless list of film industry personalities. Among the film directors, the list includes names from Federico Fellini to Francis Ford Coppola, and from Luis Buñuel to Pedro Almodóvar. The list of actors and actresses who have participated in and been honored at the event is as long as the names of the films the best movie fans can possibly remember since 1953, when the festival began, to the present. San Sebastián is located in the Basque region of Spain.

García Márquez's attendance, however, was not as a mere spectator. In that year, 1974, he participated in the film gala as a screenwriter, in collaboration with the Spanish-born, naturalized Mexican Luis Alcoriza. The film, *Presagio* (*Presage*), directed by Luis Alcoriza, won a special mention and was released the following year. Alcoriza, whose work as a director is widely recognized, both in his own right and for collaborating with Luis Buñuel, is today remembered for *Presagio* and *Mecánica Nacional* (*National Mechanics*). Alcoriza died in 1992 in Cuernavaca, Mexico.

In 1975, García Márquez's long-awaited novel, *The Autumn of the Patriarch,* was published. This was the first large fictional account since *One Hundred Years of Solitude* in 1967, almost eight years between publications. If it had ever been a concern that García Márquez was just a one-book wonder, this novel would change that. The plot, Raymond Williams wrote, is not developed in a consistent fashion; the anecdotes do not appear in chronological order, and they sometimes include such gross anachronisms as the presence of Christopher Columbus and U.S. Marines in the same scene. Nonetheless, he considers it a major book for both García Márquez and the contemporary Latin American novel.[22] García Márquez, on the other hand, has been quoted as saying that his writing of *The Autumn of the Patriarch* was influenced by music, Béla Bártok in particular, along with Caribbean popular music, and inspired by the popular language used in the Colombian Caribbean. García Márquez considers *The Autumn of the Patriarch* "most important from a literary point of view, one which might save me from oblivion."[23] By then his circumstances were the best he could possibly desire. His economic success and his fame allowed him to write in comfort, and even search for the appropriate places, and countries, where the novel could flow more easily. On top of that, he says this is the book he always wanted to write.

To better understand the long time span between *One Hundred Years of Solitude* (1967) and *The Autumn of the Patriarch* (1975), one must take into account the time it took him to write the latter. The writing of *The Autumn of the Patriarch* took him 17 years to finish. During that time, he had to abandon two versions before he found the tone and language of the one we read today.

The book was in no way comparable to *One Hundred Years of Solitude* and it was not readily accepted by critics or the reading public. In fact, to some it was rather disappointing. But he was not out to please the expectations of the critics or of his readership. The passage of time has proved that the reading public and the critics would come to favor *One Hundred Years of Solitude* over any other of his books, but *The Autumn of the Patriarch* is today considered a minor masterpiece, although the same is also said of *No One Writes to Colonel* and *Chronicle of a Death Foretold*. *The Autumn of the Patriarch* could easily be associated with any number of Latin American dictators, but the idea for the novel came to García Márquez when he was living in Venezuela. According to Apuleyo Mendoza, Gabo started to draft the novel when the feared, hated military dictator of Venezuela, General Marcos Pérez Jiménez, fled the country on January 23, 1958. García Márquez was 31 years old. At that time, he started to research the lives of dictators such as François Duvalier, the Haitian president who, after being elected president in 1957, declared himself president for life in 1964 and ruled the country until his death in 1971. He was a medical doctor, to whom Haitians referred as Papa Doc. Upon his death, he was succeeded by his son, Jean-Claude "Baby Doc" Duvalier.

The image of the dictator in *The Autumn of the Patriarch*, as the labyrinthine book was taking form, was influenced by these and other rulers, like Dr. José Gaspar de Francia, the first great dictator of Paraguay, often referred to as Dr. Francia or simply El Supremo (The Supreme One). But if the reader wished to conjure up the name of Fidel Castro as a projection within the novel, the analogy would be improbable, on one hand, because García Márquez was critical of the political system behind the dictator he criticizes, and on the other, because he himself made it clear that his model was primarily—although not exclusively—the Venezuelan dictator, Juan Vicente Gómez, who ruled the country from 1908 until his death in 1935. "My original intention," Gabo once said, "was to make a synthesis of all Latin American dictators, especially the Caribbean ones. However, Gomez's personality was so powerful and he exercised such an intense fascination over me that the patriarch does contain much more of him than any of the others."[24] So the book, in essence, may have as many interpretations as there are readers with possible interpretations of a dictator. The dictator in the novel "is a man who carries disorder in his bones and leaves a trail of devastation in his wake, even within his own privileged space."[25] This interpretation, when left open ended, can encompass Juan Vicente Gómez and all others mentioned above, plus those dictators who followed, rulers who come to mind but are not mentioned: dictators of the turn of the new millennium.

In 1976, García Márquez was not in the spotlight for publishing any fiction, but rather for something more fitting for a tabloid, due to the sensationalist nature of the episode. His once good friend, Peruvian writer Mario Vargas Llosa, slugged García Márquez in the face around Valentine's Day, at a cinema in Mexico City, where Gabo had returned to live after a long stay in Barcelona. The feud arose over accusations of betrayal and adultery on the part of Gabo. The incident, however, was almost totally unknown about. It was not until 31 years later, after more than three decades of not talking to one another, that the incident was made public. Some have speculated that the fight was over politics. However, there was a photographer, to whom García Márquez had gone to have his picture taken to show the black eye. In fact, there are two such photographs of Gabo, one in which he's sporting a smile. The Mexican photographer was quoted as saying, "The cause was a woman—specifically, Mr. Vargas Llosa's wife, whom Mr. García Márquez consoled during a difficult period in her marriage."[26] These outrageous, scandalous quarrels between writers are not uncommon, regardless of the circumstances. "As a literary showdown, Mario Vargas Llosa vs Gabriel García Márquez ranks with some of the most famous feuds, including Lillian Hellman vs Mary McCarthy, Vladimir Nabokov vs Edmund Wilson, and Norman Mailer vs Gore Vidal. (When the encounter between Mr. Mailer and Mr. Vidal turned physical, if not bloody, Mr. Vidal is said to have responded from the floor, 'Words fail Norman Mailer yet again.')"[27]

While the bad blood came and went almost unnoticed in the United States in 1976, the public at large had the opportunity to purchase the English translation of *The Autumn of the Patriarch*. The translator, Gregory Rabassa, was the same who had previously translated *One Hundred Years of Solitude*.

The same year, in literary supplements in newspapers in the Spanish-speaking world, García Márquez published two short stories, "El rastro de tu sangre en la nieve" ("The Trail of Your Blood in the Snow"), and "El verano feliz de la señora Forbes" ("Miss Forbes's Summer of Happiness"). Both stories deal with love and death; both turn the ordinary into the absurd. No magical realism like his earlier stories, but rather an inability to deal with what is commonplace, the mundane.

His career as a journalist took center stage. He wrote newspaper articles for *Alternativa*, his own magazine; the Cuban publication, *Revista Casa de las Américas*; the Colombian newspaper *El Espectador*; *The Washington Post* in the United States; and other newspapers and magazines elsewhere. These pieces were always oriented towards the left-wing revolutionary movements that were alive in the Spanish Americas, whether the Montoneros in Argentina or the Sandinistas in Nicaragua. Argentina was going through the dictatorship of General Jorge Rafael Videla, and Nicaragua was under the boot of the last of the Somoza family, a political dynasty whose rule had lasted for over three decades. As if repeating the cycles of names in *One Hundred Years of Solitude*, the Nicaraguan dictatorships by the Somoza family began with Anastasio Somoza García from 1937 to 1956, and ended with Anastasio Somoza Debayle in 1979. Upon Anastasio Somoza García's death (he was shot, and died in a Panamanian hospital a week later), his son, Luis Somoza Debayle, took office from 1957 to 1967 with the help of his younger brother, commander-in-chief of the National Guard. Before the end of this family dynasty's vile dictatorship, there was room for yet another Anastasio. This time it was Anastasio Somoza Debayle (known as Tachito), who ruled from 1967 to 1979. He fled the country in 1979, first to Miami and then to Paraguay, where he was shot to death in Asunción, capital of Paraguay, by a leftist guerrilla group led by Enrique Gorriaran Merlo.

In April of 1978, García Márquez wrote two short stories, "La luz es como el agua" ("Light Is Like Water"), and "Sólo vine a hablar por teléfono" ("I Only Came to Use the Phone"). In 1979, now 52 years old, he turned the short story "I Only Came to Use the Phone" into a screenplay, only this time, it was without any collaboration with the director. The film, directed by Mexican Jaime Humberto Hermosillo, was released as *María de mi corazón* (*Mary my Dearest*). The adaptation follows the plot of the short story, in which an ordinary telephone call suddenly turns into something absurd. María, the protagonist, hitches a ride on a bus transporting patients to a mental hospital, where she ends up unable to get out. All her attempts to prove she is sane lead everyone to believe she is insane, just like the others in the institution.

Other than the screenplay for the film, in 1979, García Márquez also wrote "María Dos Prazeres." The story was published some years later in English, without the title ever being translated, perhaps assuming that the Portuguese, *Prazeres*, is rather close to the Spanish *Placeres* and its English equivalent, "Pleasures." The plot of the short story centers on the life of a prostitute, María, whose only companion is her small dog.

Before the decade came to a close, García Márquez had begun writing *Chronicle of a Death Foretold*.

CODA

The 1970s, in the Spanish-speaking world, were difficult years. Politically, few countries were not experiencing turmoil and social unrest. The fall of democracy in Chile was perhaps the bloodiest of them all. García Márquez was sought after for answers to the problems, as opposed to questions about the crises. He, however, spent plenty of time giving answers about Cuba, and also about the Sandinistas in Nicaragua who, in the end, ousted the Somoza dynasty. He was almost as famous as Fidel Castro, but unlike Castro, far more people liked Gabo, as opposed to those who disliked him. Many people hated Castro.

If the 1970s were hard times for the Spanish Americas in general, for García Márquez they were trouble free. He was famous, healthy, and rich; or, as he says, "he was a poor man with money." There were awards and interviews; followers all over the world sought his autograph; his books were translated, and others were adapted to the cinema; and the material he had written in the 1950s and 1960s was now published. He went on to become a businessman, an entrepreneur, a wealthy man with homes in more than one country. His name as a writer was ubiquitous in the Western world and beyond. His re-entry into the United States, after 10 years of being banned, coincided with the great popularity of *One Hundred Years of Solitude* in America. Mario Vargas Llosa's doctoral dissertation, *Historia de un deicidio* (*Story of a Deicide*), and Luis Harss' *Into the Mainstream* were "the visas" readers needed to enter the appealing but difficult-to-handle magical realist world of his fiction. In spite of that, when the long-awaited new novel, *The Autumn of the Patriarch*, came out, the magician of words had changed his style so much that the codes the readers had earlier learned in order to understand his work no longer sufficed. Even skilled critics and academics had a tough time understanding it. Once again, readers around the world would have to struggle to follow the plot and make sense of the tyrannical main protagonist.

The Latin American literary phenomenon of the 1970s, however, was not based on García Márquez's work alone. By 1972, Rita Guibert had put into book form a number of interviews with Latin American writers who were directly or indirectly associated with García Márquez's success. Before we knew of him in the United States, we had learned about the Argentines Jorge Luis Borges and Julio Cortázar, the poets Pablo Neruda and Octavio Paz (both of whom are Nobel Laureates), and the Guatemalan Miguel Angel Asturias (also a Nobel Laureate) who, prior to García Márquez's dictatorship novel, had written *Mr. President*, in the same genre. Guibert's book, titled *Seven Voices: Seven Latin American Writers talk to Rita Guibert*, included Cuban Guillermo Cabrera Infante, to complete the seven. Great names were left out, however. Guibert was not making revisions, but rather paying attention to what was happening in the world of letters in the United States. The interview with Borges was from 1968, and Cortázar's from 1969. These Latin Americans were the avant-garde.

As we look back, the violence of the 1970s was not only difficult for the Spanish Americas. The worst part of it all is that the fighting we saw then seems as tumultuous as the first decade of the twenty-first century. The same was true for the rest of the free world. In the United States, for the first time, the National Guard opened fire on a college campus, killing 4 and wounding 11. The shooting took place at Kent State University in Kent, Ohio, on May 4, 1970. Two years later, the Olympic Games were tarnished with blood when the terrorist group Black September, a branch of the Palestinian Liberation Organization (PLO), invaded the Munich Olympic village, killing two Israeli athletes and taking seven hostage. The political divide in the United States became more accentuated. American troops were taken out of Vietnam in 1973, but President Nixon approved the invasion of Cambodia. He resigned in 1974. For the Spanish Americas, however, the killing of Salvador Allende in Chile, on September 11, 1973, turned the capital city of Santiago into a slaughterhouse and set the stage for a totalitarian government led by military juntas. Some dictators were killed; others fled the countries they plundered; and others, like General Francisco Franco of Spain, died in 1975. But with Pinochet in Chile, Videla in Argentina, and Castro in Cuba, the tradition was kept alive. So, to better understand *The Autumn of the Patriarch*, the reader must take a look at a continent that has been plagued by dictators, real characters that helped to shape the theme of the novel for Gabriel García Márquez, the Gabo many love and others love to dislike simply for being friends with Castro.

NOTES

1. Ernesto González Bermejo interviewed García Márquez in 1971. Gene H. Bell-Villada translated the interview and included it in his book *Conversations with Gabriel García Márquez* (see chap. 5, n. 7).

2. Bermejo, *Conversations*, ed. Bell-Villada, 3.

3. Ibid., 13.

4. Celestine Bohlen, "Heberto Padilla, 68, Cuban Poet, Is Dead," in *The New York Times*, September 28, 2000.

5. But for Heberto Padilla, getting out of Cuba, even with García Márquez's help, meant a 10-year wait. Angel Esteban Porras del Campo and Stephanie Panichelli, *Gabo and Fidel: Portrait of a Friendship*, trans. Diane Stockwell (Miami, FL: Planeta, 2005), 80.

6. Porras del Campo and Panichelli, *Gabo and Fidel*, 232.

7. "Artur Lundkvist, A Swedish Essayist, Author and Poet, 85," *New York Times*, http://query.nytimes.com/gst/fullpage.html?res=9D0CE5D81E3AF930A2 5751C1A967958260.com.

8. Rita Guibert, "Seven Voices: Seven Latin American Writers Talk to Rita Guibert," cited in *Conversations*, ed. Bell-Villada, 52–53.

9. Ibid., 57.

10. Ibid., 55.

11. "Chile Starts Chasing the Capitalists," *Time*, January 4, 1971. http://www.time.com/time/magazine/article/0,9171,942419-1,00.html.

12. "Chile: Owner of the Future," *Time*, July 26, 1971. http://www.time.com/time/magazine/article/0,9171,877026,00.html.

13. Pablo Neruda, the Nobel Prize in Literature 1971, "Banquet Speech." The Nobel Foundation. http://nobelprize.org/nobel_prizes/literature/laureates/1971/neruda-speech.html.

14. Arango, *Un ramo*, 339 (see chap. 2, n. 10). (The translation is mine; the original was written in Spanish.)

15. *Gabriel García Márquez*, dir. Aylett (see chap 4, n. 14).

16. Ibid.

17. Apuleyo Mendoza, *In Conversation*, 95 (see chap. 2, n. 2).

18. García Márquez, *Por la libre*, *Obra periodística 4*, 7–22 (see chap. 4, n. 1). (All translations for the quotes from this text are mine.)

19. Ibid., 20.

20. Ibid., 22.

21. Ibid., 22.

22. Raymond Williams, "The Autumn of the Patriarch," in *Gabriel García Márquez*, ed. Bloom, 147–68 (see chap. 5, n. 18).

23. Apuleyo Mendoza, *In Conversation*, 62 (see chap. 2, n. 2).

24. Ibid., 82.

25. Patricia Tobin, "The Deconstructionist Moment of García Márquez," in *Gabriel García Márquez*, ed. Bloom, 207 (see chap. 5, n. 18).

26. Rodrigo Moya, as quoted by Noam Cohen in "García Márquez's Shiner Ends its 31 Years of Quietude," *The New York Times*, March 29, 2007. http://www.nytimes.com/2007/03/29/books/29marq.html.

27. Ibid.

Chapter 7

THE NOBEL PRIZE, TELEVISION, AND MOVIES

> On a day like today, my master William Faulkner said, "I decline to accept the end of man." I would fall unworthy of standing in this place that was his, if I were not fully aware that the colossal tragedy he refused to recognize 32 years ago is now, for the first time since the beginning of humanity, nothing more than a simple scientific possibility.
>
> —*Gabriel García Márquez*, 1982 Nobel Prize in Literature acceptance speech

In 1980, at 53 years old, Gabriel García Márquez experienced the closing of his left-wing magazine *Alternativa* (*Alternative*), undoubtedly the most recognized liberal Colombian publication of the 1970s. The respect and high opinion *Alternativa* enjoyed was not only due to Gabo being one of its founders, along with Orlando Fals Borda and Enrique Santos Calderón, but because the publication represented an unconventional way of thinking and showcased a unique style of writing. It was the kind of counter journalism that gave voice to the constant problems of the populace and the ideals of the popular fronts vis-à-vis the Colombian government and the establishment. Some journalists and critics have stated that the magazine actually closed in 1977. They are partially right. The periodical ceased publication in 1977, but only for four months. During the first months of the year, Gabo's associates who were involved in running the publication were considering whether to make it a daily. A decision was made against the change, for monetary reasons. By May of 1977, however, all parties involved in the production of *Alternativa* had resolved to continue publishing the bi-weekly journal. García Márquez then wrote a piece for the periodical, stating, "The only new thing is that I no longer will be visible in every part of the publication. But every other week, I will be within the 'four walls,' writing my personal column and saying whatever I want, on my own terms."[1] To better understand the quote, the reader may well take into account the fact that the magazine was not supported by any political party or independent agency, foundation or otherwise. The content of every article was free of pressure from outside interests, and represented only that of the writers. *Alternativa* is still referred to today by researchers and historians interested in Gabriel García Márquez's public life.

In 1981, while living in Mexico City, García Márquez gave an interview to Peter H. Stone, which was later reprinted in 2007 in *The Paris Review Interviews, II*. According to Stone, in 1981, Gabo was "a solidly built man, only about five eight or nine in height, who looks like a good middleweight fighter—broad-chested, but perhaps a bit thin in the legs. His hair is dark and curly brown, and he wears a full mustache."[2] The passage of time had changed García Márquez's appearance, but the mustache Stone mentioned still frames Gabo's face now, in his early eighties. Stone's interview was conducted over the course of three afternoons in sessions of two hours each. Stone's skilled ability to pose finely tuned queries, combined with the opportunity to rethink what to ask the next afternoon, made this particular interview one to which many researchers refer.

The following year, Gabriel García Márquez would become a Nobel Laureate, and even more famous than he was for his books and his legendary charm. Stone wrote that García Márquez's English at the time was "quite good," but he preferred to speak Spanish. Gabo's two sons helped Stone with the interpretation in the interview. Rodrigo, the oldest, was then 22, and Gonzalo, the younger, was 19. Rodrigo attended Harvard University, where he studied medieval history, so his English must have been excellent, and helpful. The publication of *The Paris Review Interviews, II*, includes a sample page of García Márquez's own corrections of *The Autumn of the Patriarch*'s manuscript, first published in 1975. It is interesting, indeed, to see his handwriting. After reading so much about him, booklovers start making accurate associations about his life and his sons. When Stone asked, "How did you start writing?" Gabo answered, "By drawing, by drawing cartoons. Before I could read or write, I used to draw comics at school and at home."[3] His younger son, Gonzalo, inherited his father's ability and became a graphic designer, with a BFA from the Parson School of Design in New York. Gonzalo's artistic work includes cover designs for books and magazines, paintings and drawings, and graphic design for films: *Nine Lives, A Little Princess*, and *Great Expectations*, among others.

Among the salient points of the interview is Gabo's acknowledgment of the reciprocal influence of journalism and fiction in his oeuvre, his strong dislike of theorists and critics, his great admiration for translators (having knowledge of both Italian and French, he would have liked to have translated Conrad and Saint Exupéry), and his sense of discipline when he says, "I think that I'm excessively demanding of myself and others because I cannot tolerate errors."[4] By then, 1981, he was writing from nine in the morning to two-thirty in the afternoon. He told Stone then that *One Hundred Years of Solitude* would never become a film. This is a statement that, in 2007, must have pleased his readers, considering the poor reception and negative reviews the film *Love in the Time of Cholera* received in the United States. Stone's interview took place a year prior to Gabo's Nobel Prize. Gabo thought receiving it would be a catastrophe, inasmuch as his fame would grow bigger. He ended his meeting with Stone by stating two facts: one, he wished he had a daughter, as well as his two sons; two, he was absolutely sure he was going to write the greatest book of his life in the coming years, but did not know when.[5] Other than a four-volume publication of his journalism work, he also published *Chronicle of a Death Foretold* in 1981, so this novel is not it. The English translation of *Chronicle of a Death Foretold* was published in 1983 in the United States.

Chronicle of a Death Foretold had an exceptional reception when it was first published. With publishing houses located in Spain, Argentina, Colombia, and Mexico, the novel had a print run of one million copies.[6] The usual first print for a book in the Spanish-speaking world, at that time, was between 5,000 and 30,000 copies. Unless another work surfaces in the new millennium, now almost at the end of its first decade, the book he was referring to during the *Paris Review* interview has to be *Love in the Time of Cholera*, first published in Spanish in 1985. A well-known critic and friend of Gabo wrote, "If *One Hundred Years of Solitude* had not secured the road to Stockholm for García Márquez to receive the Nobel Prize for Literature, *Love in the Time of Cholera* would have done so."[7] This opinion is shared by many others, even the casual reader. Based on his own statement to the *Paris Review* in 1981, *Cholera* may indeed be the greatest novel García Márquez has ever written, excluding the fact that academics and intellectuals alike would continue to call *One Hundred of Years of Solitude* his *magnum opus*.

The year 1981 was full of surprises for the Colombian-born writer whose popularity was already larger than life. However, not everything coming his way was pleasant. While the French government awarded him the French Legion of Honor Medal, and Gabo attended the presidential inauguration of his longtime friend, François Mitterrand, the

Colombian government ordered his arrest under the presidency of Julio César Turbay Ayala. At this time, he and his wife were living in his Bogotá apartment. Gabo was accused of collaborating with the Colombian counter-government revolutionary forces, known as M-19.

The year before, the M-19 had made headlines worldwide for taking over the embassy of the Dominican Republic in Colombia and taking diplomats from several countries hostage for over two months, including some from the United States, which was then under the presidency of Ronald Reagan. To the surprise of many in Colombia and abroad, Colombian President Turbay made concessions to the M-19 rebels, who fled free to Cuba. García Márquez had been suspected of financing the insurgents. Was he really providing monetary help to M-19, or was he presumed guilty by default, due to his friendship with Fidel Castro?

Before they were arrested, however, the writer and his wife sought and were granted political asylum at the Mexican embassy in Bogotá. The two had kept a house in Mexico City, where they had lived off and on since 1961. Faithful to his country of birth, on the other hand, García Márquez never took Mexican citizenship, even though his son Gonzalo was born there. They had resided in Mexico longer than any other country outside of Colombia.

In May 1982, he was invited to be a member of the International Cannes Film Festival jury. That year, the winners of the Golden Palm (official name, Palme D'Or) were *Missing* by Costa-Gavras, and *Yol* by Serif Gören. The poster was designed by none other than Federico Fellini, a canonical name in cinema. Also in May, the publication of García Márquez's conversations with his friend Plinio Apuleyo Mendoza appeared as *El olor de la guayaba* (*The Fragrance of Guava*). The print run was 200,000 copies. The first edition included personal pictures of him with his friends in the 1970s and 1980s, a photograph of him as a two-year-old, and one at 15. Another testimonial like the one above, also released in 1982, was *Viva Sandino* (*Long Live Sandino*). Published in Nicaragua, the book gives a biographical account of the life and revolutionary struggles of Augusto César Sandino (1895–1934). His legacy gave birth to the movement we came to know as Sandinista, short for Sandinista National Liberation Front.

Five months after the Cannes film festival, in October, the world press released the name of the year's winner for the Nobel Prize for Literature. It was Gabriel García Márquez, a 55-year-old short-story writer, novelist, journalist, and already world-famous Colombian who had now been recognized by the Swedish Nobel Foundation in Sweden as the winner of the Nobel Prize for Literature. A very young winner, undeniably, to the dismay of many writers, who in fact did not see him deserving of it, due

THE NOBEL PRIZE, TELEVISION, AND MOVIES 103

to his age and his rather small oeuvre, at the time. At that time, only the French (Algerian-born) writer Albert Camus had won the Nobel Prize for Literature at a younger age, 44. Camus won the prestigious prize in 1957. On October 21, 1982, the Spanish-speaking world, particularly the Colombians, was jubilant, literally in seventh heaven, thrilled. On the same day that the Nobel Prize news was announced, the Mexican government, under the presidency of José López Portillo, bestowed on García Márquez the Orden Mexicana del Aguila Azteca. Created in 1933, The Mexican Order of the Aguila Azteca, also known as the Aztec Eagle Medal, is the highest honor given to a foreign national. The Colombian government, on the other hand, which the year before had wanted his arrest but was now ruled by a new president, Belisario Betancur, wanted the prodigious Colombian son back in his native country.

Special publications of his books were immediately issued in Colombia and elsewhere. From all corners of the world, "the telegrapher's son from Aracataca" received calls of congratulation, whether from friends like Mitterrand in France and Castro in Cuba, or fellow writers like Camilo José Cela (who later won the Nobel Prize in 1989), and the 1968 Japanese Nobel Laureate Yasunari Kawabata. Guatemalan Miguel Angel Asturias, the 1967 Nobel laureate, was not in agreement with the Academy's decision, however. The nominees for the Nobel that year included names as varied as Doris Lessing, who at the time was already 62 years old (in 2007, however, at 87, she was awarded the prize). Gabo's friend Graham Greene was also a candidate. (In fact, Greene was a contender for the Nobel several times, never to win.) Acclaimed feminist Simone de Beauvoir was also an entrant, along with René Char and Henry Michaux. Above all, the Academy was debating whether to give it to Jorge Luis Borges, but García Márquez was the victor that year.

In the same way that the Mexican government celebrated Gabo's nomination for the Nobel with the Aztec Eagle Medal, the Cuban administration gave him the Felix Varela Medal, the highest honor for intellectual achievement. The friendship Gabriel García Márquez shares with Fidel Castro upsets many, but few pay attention to the familiarity and sympathy that the Cuban population, on the island, pays to the Colombian author. His celebrity status can be best measured by his book sales: "A print run of 130,000 copies of any book by García Márquez would completely sell out of the bookstores within 24 hours."[8]

The press release from the Academy was right: with his nomination, the Swedish Academy had not nominated an unknown writer, as is sometimes the case. The popularity of *One Hundred Years of Solitude* at that time, as is still the case today, was tumultuous and unprecedented.

But the poetic-sounding appeal of the novel's title was more than just poetry, as his Nobel lecture confirmed in December of that year, when he received the award. His lecture, like his novel, focused on the solitude of Latin America. His Nobel address was titled, "The Solitude of Latin America." Cleverly, as he closed the Nobel lecture, he inverted the order of events that end the 1967 novel. In *One Hundred Years of Solitude*, the reader comes to understand that "races condemned to one hundred years of solitude did not have a second opportunity on earth."[9] For the people of Macondo and their progeny, extermination is inevitable. But in the Nobel lecture, García Márquez subverts the tale and ends his talk, as if in crescendo, by saying, "Races condemned to one hundred years of solitude will have, at last and forever, a second opportunity on earth."[10] García Márquez wrote the Nobel acceptance speech in Cuba, days prior to the ceremony in Stockholm. He recorded it and listened to himself until he had it memorized. The recording took place at Fefe Diego's home. He "remembers that, since he [Gabo] was very shy and usually ill at ease at such formal proceedings, he had to try hard to overcome the crippling anxiety inherent in addressing such a large audience."[11]

When the speech was delivered, he did not wear the traditional formal tails that nearly all other male writers have worn when they came forward to receive the prize. On the occasion, as if he were more faithful to his regional roots, he wore a *liqui liqui,* the informal peasant garb discussed earlier, typical of northern Colombia (and the plains of Venezuela), whose long-sleeved shirt is the same color as the slacks. The traditional *liqui liqui* colors are white, black, or brown. On the biggest night for any writer being recognized for his oeuvre, on December 10, 1982, García Márquez wore a white *liqui liqui*. "He carried a yellow rose, a flower that symbolizes luck, and casts off evil spirits in people, objects, and situations, and inspires him to write."[12] Faithful to his roots, he also took with him some of his best friends: the Zuleta brothers and Rafael Escalona, Alvaro Mutis, and friends of his youth, Alfonso Fuenmayor and German Vargas. "Forty close friends accompanied him, along with a troupe of Caribbean musicians and dancers. The Queen of Sweden went up with him to accept the prize, following tradition. Fidel Castro sent a very special gift: 1,500 bottles of Cuban rum to share with his friends that day."[13] The number of bottles of rum in the quotation seems like hyperbole, compared to the way the anecdotes published by *El País* recounted the 1982 events. According to them, it was a case of Cuban rum. They in turn referred to the Swedish press, stating that the Colombian Nobel laureate taught the Swedes how to party, because the celebration did without the protocol of pomp and circumstance. He broke away from the formal dress code, and the music played was Caribbean rhythms (*vallenatos*) and drums. *El País* adds a note that somehow characterizes García Márquez in the eyes of his readers, his sense of sincere humility. To him, the mere fact that he had won the Nobel stimulates new generations of writers. If he, a man of modest means, without the heritage of a big family name, who had not attended a famous university, was able to win the Nobel, then many others could do the same.[14] Back in Colombia, approximately 25 million celebrated his triumph. The president of the country at that time, Belisario Betancur, said, "Great men are like Gabo" ("Los grandes son como Gabo").

The year 1982 must have seemed like an avalanche of great moments, places, and people for Gabriel García Márquez, his wife Mercedes, and sons Rodrigo and Gonzalo, who were then in their early twenties. Rodrigo was 24, and Gonzalo had turned 20.

And when the year came to an end, he rang in the New Year, 1983, in Havana with his friend, Fidel Castro. His yearning to be away from the spotlight, to enjoy life far removed from the obligations fame brings, was multiplied due to his new status as a Nobel Laureate. Colombians, in fact, refer to him as "Our Nobel," when not simply calling him "Gabo."

His will to help bring change in the political affairs of Central America and Colombia brought him closer to the turmoil experienced in the region. In February, he met with the leader of the M-19, Jaime Bateman, one of Colombia's main leftist groups. Bateman was the principal commander of military operations for the group. García Márquez's role was to help establish a dialogue to bring peace between the paramilitary and the government of President Belisario Betancur. Bateman, however, died soon thereafter, in a plane crash while flying to Panama on April 28, 1983. On July 27, 1983, the Nobel Laureate published a newspaper article he simply titled "Bateman." "We met outside Colombia," he wrote, "with the consent of the President." He saw Bateman as prudent and astute. Bateman's only mistake, he adds, was flying in a light aircraft with a single engine with an inexperienced pilot lost in a storm. To Gabo, no foul play was connected with Bateman's death.[15] No conspiracy could be proved, but it was certainly a mysterious death. The small plane was a Piper PA-28 with the Colombian license plate number HK 2139P. The pilot was Antonio Escobar Bravo.

In 1983, Gabo returned to Aracataca after receiving the Nobel Prize the year before. His visit was brief. He walked along some of the streets, but being as superstitious as he is, refused to walk inside the house where he was born. Although the house was designated a national monument, from 1982, it was abandoned and neglected until 2007, when work to rebuild it began.

In 1983, he published the third volume of his journalist work, a compilation by Jacques Gilard, *Obra Periodística 3: De Europa y América* (*Journalism, Volume 3: From Europe and America*). Volume 2, *Entre Cachacos* (*Among Cachacos*), was published in 1982, and Volume 1, *Textos Costeños* (*Coastal Writings*), was published in 1981. All three books were compiled by Jacques Gilard. The three volumes comprise Garcia Marquez's journalism up to 1960. The journalistic volumes that followed were published without Gilard's participation.

In May of 1983, Ruy Guerra, a respected Brazilian filmmaker, released the film *Eréndira*, shown at the Cannes Film Festival that year, when William Styron was the president of the jury. Martin Scorsese was a contestant with the film *The King of Comedy*. Directed by Sohohei Imamura, *Narayama Bushiko* was selected as best film. The poster for the festival was designed by the legendary Akira Kurosawa, considered a Japanese giant of twentieth-century cinema. Kurosawa was trained as a painter. As a filmmaker and screenplay writer, one of his most famous films is 1954's *Seven Samurai*. Among the many world film awards he received, he won the Oscar four times. His films are more revered in the Western world than in his native Japan.

Based on a short story by García Márquez, *Eréndira* was yet one more attempt at adapting Gabo's literary work to the cinema. Ruy Guerra has either directed or produced several other works written by García Márquez: in 1988, *Fable of the Beautiful Pigeon Fancier* (*Fábula de la bella palomera*); in 1992, "I Rent Myself to Dream" ("Me alquilo para sonar"), a segment of a TV mini-series of six episodes; and in 2004, *In Evil Hour* (*La mala hora*).

By 1983, García Márquez's work had become some kind of a popular literary cult to which almost everyone belonged. He gave a seminal interview for *Playboy* magazine, and *Time* reviewed *One Hundred Years of Solitude* and *Chronicle of a Death Foretold*. In Barcelona, the novelist Oscar Collazos published *García Márquez, la soledad y la gloria: su vida y su obra* (*García Márquez, Solitude and Glory: His Life and Works*). When García Márquez was not busy writing, many others were writing about him: books, journal articles, reviews, magazines, and comics, specials on television, films, and interviews; and every so often, tributes. "Even before his 1982 Nobel Prize, writing about García Márquez had become a 'growth industry.' He is a brand name, an industry of sorts. Proliferation was inevitable, given the Colombian novelist's sudden metamorphosis as a public institution and world event. There's his phenomenal global fame, with translations of his oeuvre into 37 languages (including Greek, Catalan, and Farsi)."[16]

THE NOBEL PRIZE, TELEVISION, AND MOVIES

Among the many journalistic articles he selected for *Volume 5* of his work as a columnist for the year of 1984, two entries help define him. One is about the art of writing; the other is about Julio Cortázar (1914–1984), a close friend. In the former, he sees himself as a writer who is destined to better the world we live in, not as a writer who is destined to better his bank account. The newspaper article about writing was titled "How a Novel is Written." The commentary has an anecdote worthy of mention. He remembers telling Jorge Gaitán Durán, in 1955, that he had nothing to give him to publish before his trip to Europe that year. As discussed in Chapter 3, this was Gabo's first trip to Europe. Gaitán Durán had come to see him off, but wanted something for publication as well. García Márquez was literally packing. He was going to take drafts of what he considered worth taking, and the rest of his writing was in the trash can. From the wastebasket, Gaitán Durán picked out the short story "Monologue of Isabel Watching it Rain in Macondo." Gabo adds, "That is how one of my best received short stories by critics and, above all, the readers, was recovered."[17] In the piece about Julio Cortázar, Gabo reminisces about going to Prague with him and Carlos Fuentes. The admiration for Cortázar flows as genuinely as the newspaper article, titled "The Argentine Everyone Loved." To him, Cortázar "was the most impressive person he had the chance to meet."[18] The article, in fact, reads like an elegy. Julio Cortázar's death from leukemia on February 6, 1984, was a great loss for his family and friends, but it was also a great loss for the world of letters in general, and particularly immense for Latin American writing. His body is buried in the Montparnasse Cemetery, in Paris.

In 1985, the Association of Colombian Journalists in Bogotá unanimously awarded García Márquez the 40 Años Prize. On the silver screen, moviegoers got a chance to see the remake of his motion picture *A Time to Die* (*Tiempo de morir*). The first version of it had been released as a western in 1966, under the direction of Arturo Ripstein. The 1985 adaptation was directed by Jorge Alí Triana, with García Márquez as producer and screenplay writer. His son, Rodrigo García, collaborated as camera operator. The dialogue, as was the case in the 1966 film, was written by Carlos Fuentes. The book industry published his complete works in Barcelona, and before the year was over, *Love in the Time of Cholera* had been printed throughout the Spanish-speaking world.

Although the plot is about love at first sight, based on the love story of the author's parents, the narrative is intricate, experimental, and not always easy to follow. After reading the novel, one comes to understand that the story could readily have started in chapter two. As is typical of a movie plot, the novel starts *in media res*. *Love in the Time of Cholera* was an intentional return to nineteenth-century realism, and the outright fantasy we associate with García Márquez is absent.[19]

As mentioned above, his parents' love story served as the basis for the novel. Readers of *Love in the Time of Cholera* may remember that Florentino Ariza is a young, poor telegrapher who falls in love with pretty, upper-class Fermina Daza, dazzling indeed, and firm in her decisions. She, Fermina Daza, is sent away by her father to forget Florentino Ariza. In real life, Colonel Nicolás Ricardo Márquez Mejía sent away his daughter, Luisa Santiaga. Both in the novel and in real life, the telegrapher finds a way to communicate (by telegram) with his beloved. The novel, however, gives readers a love triangle in which the heroine marries a well-born medical doctor. The analogies with García Márquez's parents are many. The abovementioned love triangle, on the other hand, is totally fictionalized, as is the development that Florentino waits 51 years, 9 months, and 4 days to vow his eternal love for Fermina again—right after Fermina's husband dies. Some critics see *Love in the Time of Cholera*, although questionably, as superior to *One Hundred Years of Solitude*. Carlos R. Rodríguez, a friend of García Márquez and a well-known literary critic, wrote that if *One Hundred Years of Solitude* had not secured the road to Stockholm for García Márquez to receive the Nobel Prize in literature, *Love in the Time of Cholera* would have.[20] The absolute flight of the imagination of *One Hundred Years of Solitude*, often referred to as magical realism, is gone, but the ability to create and recreate the imagination is not. *The New York Times* book review said, "He writes with impassioned control, out of a maniacal serenity: the Garcimarquesian voice we have come to recognize from the other fiction has matured, found and developed new resources, been brought to a level where it can at once be classical and familiar, opalescent and pure, able to praise and curse, laugh and cry, fabulate and sing and, when called upon, take off and soar."[21] Like many of García Márquez's works, *Love in the Time of Cholera* was adapted to the cinema. Its reception was rather halfhearted and, in the United States, often not favorable. The comments on the film adaptation of the novel are in Chapter 9 of this book.

In 1986, his will to bring peace to the Spanish Americas led him to work with Chilean Miguel Littín, a movie and TV director who was exiled to Mexico right after the 1973 Chilean coup d'état. The two produced a TV series to depict the repression Chileans were undergoing during the Pinochet regime. Gabo's collaboration with Littín, however, was not new. In 1979, the Chilean filmmaker had directed *La viuda de Montiel* (*Montiel's Widow*), a picture based on García Márquez's short story of the same name. The movie's cast included Geraldine Chaplin (daughter of Charlie Chaplin) as a leading actress. The year after, the film was released with English subtitles. The screenplay adaptation was written by Littín and the Mexican novelist and short-story writer, José Agustín. García Márquez, on the other hand, published *La aventura clandestina de Miguel Littín en Chile*. The publication was simultaneously printed in Bogotá, Buenos Aires, Barcelona, and Madrid. The English translation, *Clandestine in Chile: The Adventures of Miguel Littín*, was released the year after the original. Unlike his most important works, *Clandestine in Chile* was not translated by Rabassa or Grossman, the leading translators from Spanish to English in the United States for García Márquez's works. The book, whether due to the translation or its structure, did not receive favorable reviews. The small volume is the account of six weeks of Littín's undercover visit to Chile in 1985, during the repressive Pinochet regime.

After the TV experiment with Miguel Littín, in May of 1987, Gabo witnessed the film adaptation of his short novel, *Chronicle of a Death Foretold*. Francesco Rossi wrote the screen version and directed the film. The movie was shown at the 1987 Cannes Film Festival, where Rossi earned a Golden Palm nomination as best director. The film selected, however, *Under Satan's Sun*, was by the French director, Maurice Pialat. Of the members of the jury that year, the president was French actor Yves Montand and American novelist Norman Mailer (1923–2007).

While in Mexico, Gabo finished writing *Love's Diatribe against a Seated Man* (*Diatriba de amor contra un hombre sentado*), which is, to date, the only play ever written by García Márquez. The play opened in Buenos Aires, Argentina, in August of 1988. This is the same city where his fame as novelist had begun in 1967, with the publication of *One Hundred Years of Solitude*. This time the reviews were mixed, and often less than generous: Mr. García Márquez's 90-minute, one-woman play, *Diatribe of Love against a Seated Man*, was dismissed as "a superficial, repetitive and tedious melodrama" by the reviewer for *La Nación*, probably the most influential Argentine newspaper for theater and culture. By contrast, the mass-circulation daily *Clarín* called it a "beautiful" work, "provocative, charged with poetic ceremony, with vitality."[22] The author himself did not attend the opening night, but his wife, Mercedes, did. Later the same year, the play opened in Cuba, Mexico, and other countries, where the ticket sales were strong. The play resurfaced again in 2007 in several Italian cities where the Italians celebrated García Márquez's 80th birthday.

1988 was definitely an experimental year for the Nobel Laureate. Other than the play mentioned above, he insisted on making TV programs. The project titled *Dangerous Loves* (*Amores Difíciles*) was written by García Márquez for Spanish television, but eventually the TV series ended up as six individual films, all dealing with both love and death. He selected the directors for each of the six films and collaborated on all six screenplays. The films were *Letters from the Park*, *Miracle in Rome*, *The Summer of Miss Forbes*, *The Fable of the Beautiful Pigeon-Fancier*, *I'm the One You're Looking For*, and *Happy Sunday*. His son, Rodrigo García, worked as director of photography for *The Summer of Miss Forbes*. Both the TV project in its original form and the film adaptations are testimony of the wise marketing "industry" of García Márquez. None of the six films, however, enjoyed wide distribution at the box office. As a TV miniseries, however, *Miracle in Rome* won the prestigious Golden Nymph Award at the Monte-Carlo TV Festival in Monaco in 1989.

At the beginning of 1989, García Márquez published *The General in His Labyrinth*, a controversial historical novel about the last days in the life of Simón Bolívar. The publication in Spanish, as *El general en su laberinto*, was typical of most of his works. The book was simultaneously distributed in Spain, Colombia, Argentina, Mexico, and Cuba. The storyline follows the steps of the last trip the great Latin American Liberator took, in complete solitude, to his lonely death. García Márquez's friend, Alvaro Mutis, is credited as the originator of the idea. Once the novel was finished, Gabo dedicated it to Mutis. García Márquez was tactful enough never to refer to the historical character in any way other than "the general." The protagonist's last trip is up the Magdalena River, the same river that played a central role in *Love in the Time of Cholera*. This is the same river that García Márquez remembers as the steamboats' idyllic traveling route in the last part of the nineteenth century and first two decades of the twentieth century, in the Colombian Caribbean. The English translation came out the following year. The translator extraordinaire this time was Edith Grossman. The book review in *The New York Times* observed the controversial reception the novel got in Spanish. "Instead of Bolívar the legendary Liberator of South America, the reader comes away with a portrait of a conflicted and highly disillusioned man—a portrait that has already engendered considerable controversy in Latin America, where critics have objected to seeing their hero portrayed with feet of clay. Like the author's earlier heroes, this Bolívar is a disillusioned idealist, a dreamer torn between martyrdom and hedonistic pleasure, prodigal with women and warmly paternal with his men in arms." The critic, however, seems to contradict himself. The hero, Bolívar, he writes, is "like the author's earlier heroes." And then he closes the article by stating this, "Whereas his earlier novels created legends that inspired wonder and amazement in the reader, *The General in His Labyrinth* provides only

THE NOBEL PRIZE, TELEVISION, AND MOVIES 111

artfully embroidered facts stolen from the encyclopedia—history only halfway alchemized into art."[23]

In essence, by the mid-1980s, any of García Márquez's publications would be measured above all against both *One Hundred Years of Solitude* and *Love in the Time of Cholera*—and, to a lesser degree, compared to *No One Writes to the Colonel* and *Chronicle of a Death Foretold*.

CODA

The 1980s in the Spanish-speaking world were as difficult as the 1970s. Politically, Central America continued to face civil wars, and all forms of social unrest. The guerrillas and the drug cartels of Colombia turned the country upside down. Chile, unable to reestablish democratic elections, was still ruled by Pinochet. García Márquez, as in the 1970s, was sought after for answers. The pen is mightier than the sword, cries the adage, but the Nobel Laureate could do very little to alleviate the ongoing problems of the guerrillas in Colombia. His meeting with Jaime Bateman Cayón, founder and leader of the 19th of April guerrilla movement, better known as M-19, was an act of goodwill and nothing more. Years after Bateman died, in 1985, the M-19 stormed the Colombian Palace of Justice in Bogotá and executed 100 people, including 11 judges who were being held hostage.

While García Márquez kept his residence in Mexico City and traveled around the world, his desire to bring peace to Colombia has always been one of his foremost social and political interests. His interests, however, are so many that a serious aficionado can spend years learning about the most famous Latin American writer of modern times. In 1986, when nearly everyone was fascinated with the fact that Halley's Comet was once again visible within the solar system, Gabo was at the Vatican, meeting with Pope John Paul II. His visit with the Holy Father, born Karol Jósef Wojtyła, was to appeal for help on behalf of thousands of Argentines missing without a trace: young men, women, and newborn babies. However, little or nothing was gained from Gabo's meeting with the Pope.[24]

The fame he enjoyed in the 1970s and 1980s was unimaginable. He was everywhere. His earlier books continued to be reprinted and all new editions had second and third and fourth reprints, faster than any other Latin American writer. The name García Márquez was indeed an industry. His name as a writer was ubiquitous, and his skill as a writer was taken to television and the theater, adding to his passion for the visual arts. By 1989, at age 62, his wealth and his health were at their peak.

As it was with *The Autumn of the Patriarch* in the 1970s, Gabo, the magician of words, had tried something totally new for his readership and dared to publish the controversial novel *The General in His Labyrinth*.

Once again, readers around the world had a chance to judge him from a new perspective. To many, his treatment of the great Latin American *Liberator* was not pleasing.

As we look back to the 1980s, we cannot escape the turbulence. Pope John Paul II survived an assassination attempt in 1981. That same year, Gabo attended the inauguration of French President Mitterrand. During 1982, Argentina and Great Britain went to war over the Falkland Islands, the same year that García Márquez won the Nobel Prize for Literature. The violence that Latin America was experiencing was everywhere. Indira Gandhi was assassinated by two of her own bodyguards in 1984. The riots soon after resulted in the killing of over 2,000 Sikhs. *Love in the Time of Cholera* was published in 1985, the year Mikhail Gorbachev became the leader of the Soviet Union. García Márquez met with the Soviet head of state two years later. Just as thousands of Berliners took part in bringing down the Berlin Wall, in 1989, Chileans came forward to vote and elected Patricio Aylwin as president. Gabo's wish to have Pinochet removed from government had now become a reality. The elections took place in December, and the Chilean dictator moved out of La Casa de la Moneda (Chile's presidential palace) at the beginning of 1990.

The 1980s brought an awareness of Latin America and its peoples to larger numbers of Americans, who continued to cultivate a strong interest in the region and its writers. Argentine novelist Manuel Puig's novel, *Kiss of the Spider Woman* (*El beso de la mujer araña*), was adapted to film in 1985. The reception of the motion picture, that same year, was worthy of an Academy Award to William Hurt for his role as leading actor in the screen adaptation. Chilean writer Isabel Allende won global recognition with her debut novel, *The House of the Spirits* (1982). The film of the same name starred Meryl Streep, Glenn Close, Jeremy Irons, and Antonio Banderas, among other stars. Then came *Like Water for Chocolate* (1989) by Mexican writer Laura Esquivel. Both the novel and the film adaptation enjoyed larger success than the *House of the Spirits*. Allende and Esquivel were both influenced by García Márquez's magical realism. The 1980s Latin American phenomenon was a worldwide sensation, and García Márquez was the most talked-about name.

NOTES

1. Gabriel García Márquez, *Notas de prensa: Obra periodística 5 (1961–1984)* (Barcelona: Mondadori, 1991), 20. (The translation is mine.)

2. Peter H. Stone in *The Paris Review Interviews, II* (New York: Picador, 2007), 178.

THE NOBEL PRIZE, TELEVISION, AND MOVIES   113

3. Ibid., 183.

4. Ibid., 195.

5. Ibid., 206.

6. Pelayo, *Gabriel García Márquez,* 111 (see chap. 2, n. 3).

7. Carlos R. Rodríguez, "El amor y el cólera en tiempos de García Márquez," in *Repertorio crítico sobre Gabriel García Márquez,* ed. Juan Gustavo Cobo Borda, Vol. 2 (Bogotá: Instituto Caro y Cuervo, 1995), 239–44.

8. Porras del Campo and Panichelli, *Gabo and Fidel,* 242 (see chap. 6, n. 5).

9. García Márquez, *One Hundred Years of Solitude,* 448 (see chap. 3, n. 12)

10. *Nobel Lectures, Literature 1981–1990,* Editor-in-Charge Tore Frängsmyr, Editor Sture Allén (World Scientific Co., Singapore, 1993). http://nobelprize.org/nobel_prizes/literature/laureates/1982/marquez-lecture-e.html.

11. Porras del Campo and Panichelli, *Gabo and Fidel,* 247 (see chap. 6, n. 5).

12. Ibid., 250.

13. Ibid., 250.

14. "Anecdotas de un premio anunciado," *El Pais,* October 21, 2007. http://www.elpais.com.co/historico/oct212007/VIVIR/anecdotas.html.

15. García Márquez, *Notas de prensa: Obra periodística 5,* 524–27. (The translation is mine.)

16. Gene H. Bell-Villada, *NOVEL: A Forum on Fiction* 18, no. 3. (Spring, 1985), 281–284. http://www.jstor.org/stable/1345796.

17. García Márquez, *Notas de prensa: Obra periodística 5,* 607.

18. Ibid., 614.

19. Bell-Villada, *García Márquez,* 191 (see chap. 2, n. 1).

20. As cited in Pelayo, *Gabriel García Márquez,* 135 (see chap. 2, n. 3).

21. Thomas Pynchon, "The Heart's Eternal Vow," review of *Love in the Time of Cholera,* by Gabriel García Márquez, *The New York Times,* April 10, 1988. http://www.nytimes.com/books/97/05/18/reviews/pynchon-cholera.html.

22. Shirley Christian, "García Márquez's First Play Gets Mixed Reviews," *New York Times,* August 25, 1988. http://query.nytimes.com/gst/fullpage.html?res=940DEEDD163EF936A1575BC0A96E948260.

23. Michiko Kakutani, "The Human behind the Heroic Pose," review of *The General in His Labyrinth* by Gabriel García Márquez, *The New York Times,* September 11, 1990. http://query.nytimes.com/gst/fullpage.html?res=9C0CE2DA143AF932A2575AC0A966958260

24. García Márquez, *Por la libre: Obra periodística 4,* 277–82 (see chap. 4, n. 1).

Chapter 8

JOURNALISM, PILGRIMS, AND DEMONS

> The more persuasive stories in "Strange Pilgrims" unfold delicately, like complicated origami constructions, to delineate a character's entire life. Each of these tales is written from the vantage point of old age, and each of them possesses a tone of melancholy wisdom reminiscent of "Love in the Time of Cholera."
>
> —Michiko Kakutani, New York Times

The 1990s were a breath of fresh air around the world. Free elections were held in Nicaragua, but to the dismay of scores of people, the Sandinistas lost against Violetta Chamorro. In South Africa, Nelson Mandela was freed in 1990 after 27 years of imprisonment. In 1994, participating in the first multiracial election, Mandela was elected president of South Africa. In Europe, East and West Germany were officially reunited, ending the separation that had endured since the end of World War II.

In the world of letters, Mexican Octavio Paz won the Nobel Prize for Literature, and García Márquez's controversial novel, *The General in His Labyrinth*, was published in English (see Chapter 7). In America, the Pulitzer Prize was awarded to Oscar Hijuelos for *The Mambo Kings Play Songs of Love*.

As a filmmaker and member of the New Latin American Cinema, in 1990, García Márquez traveled to Japan to attend a Latin American Film Festival. En route to Japan, he made a stop in New York City to meet with three-time Academy Award-winning director, Woody Allen, whom Gabo admires. The trip to Japan would allow Gabo to talk with Japanese master film director Akira Kurosawa, whose film *Dreams* was released in the same year. If anyone could take García Márquez's ambitious, experimental, and complex novel *The Autumn of the Patriarch* to the big screen, Kurosawa could have. He had made film adaptations of literary works by Shakespeare, Dostoevsky, Gorky, Tolstoy, and contemporary writers Ed McBain and Georges Simenon. Kurosawa wanted to direct *The Autumn of the Patriarch* with a Japanese medieval setting. The project, unfortunately, never took off. Kurosawa died on September 6, 1998.

In Colombia, peace was not in sight, and the violence experienced in the 1980s continued to escalate to larger proportions. In the Colombian political arena of 1990, Gabo declined to run for a post in the National Assembly, where he was invited to participate. His desire to never hold an official political post was firm and unchangeable. The year after, however, he decided to live in Colombia, but kept his homes elsewhere. In 1990, in Mexico, where he has lived longer than in any other country, he co-wrote the TV script *El espejo de dos lunas* (*The Two-Way Mirror*) with Mexican Susana Cato, a journalist and scriptwriter for radio and television. The mirror as a recurring theme in García Márquez's work goes back as early as 1949, when he wrote the short story "Dialogue with the Mirror," compiled in *Eyes of a Blue Dog*. In *The Two-Way Mirror,* the antique mirror placed in the bride's room before her wedding shows a handsome nineteenth-century revolutionary soldier. It is evident that they can both see each other. The magic realist, romantic TV drama was produced in Mexico. Two other similar projects, also recorded in Mexico, were produced the following year. Gabo co-wrote *Contigo en la distancia* (*Far Apart; also translated Far Away*) with the Cuban novelist, screenwriter, and poet, Eliseo Alberto. The genre here is also a recurring one: the epistolary. An unsatisfied married woman receives a letter, sent some 20 years earlier from an ardent lover who wanted her to run away with him. The TV programs were conceived as a trilogy bearing the title *Don't Fool with Love* (*Con el amor no se juega*). The third program, *Ladrón de sábado* (*Saturday Night Thief*), was co-written by the Nobel Prize winner and Mexican Consuelo Garrido, screen and scriptwriter for television and radio. In *Saturday Night Thief,* also a romantic story in which the absurd plays an important part, a burglar is caught inside a middle-aged woman's house. The homeowner, a radio celebrity, falls in love with the intruder. The robber falls in love with her when he realizes she is his favorite radio star. *The Two-Way Mirror* and *Saturday Night Thief* were directed by Mexican Carlos García Agraz, and *Far Apart* by Cuban Tomás Gutiérrez Alea.

Although Gabo has written only one play, *Diatribe of Love against a Seated Man,* theater companies have adapted his work. Play adaptations of his novels have become routine in certain circles. The 1990 opening play at the Festival Latino of Theater in New York was a play based on the novel *Chronicle of a Death Foretold*. A reviewer for *The New York Times* wrote, "In his attempted distillation of the novel, Mr. Tavora has eliminated characters and compressed incidents while following the central line of the narrative. Momentarily projecting Angela and her husband, Bayardo, as figures in the future, he misses the principal point of the story in the book. The abandoned bride has persisted in her ardor for her absent husband for 17 years, sending him almost 2,000 letters, none of which he has opened." The reviewer did not like the adaptation and went on to say, "The most damaging of the director's decisions is the removal of the author as character, giving some of his comments to a priest and others. It is through the language and memory of García Márquez as active participant that one receives the most vivid emanations, and also those occasional moments of grotesque humor."[1] Having to adapt from one genre to another is always a difficult task, even more so when the original is by García Márquez. The same theatrical group that did the play in New York City presented it in Manizales, Colombia, in 1991.

For the XIII International Theater Festival of Manizales, there were two adaptations of García Márquez's works. From Spain, there was a presentation of *Chronicle of a Death Foretold*, by La Escuadra de Sevilla Group, and from Colombia, a theatrical group presented *Memoria y olvido de Ursula Iguarán* (*Memory and Forgetfulness of Ursula Iguarán*). A good portion of the adaptations to theater is done at colleges and universities, whether in the United States, the Spanish-speaking world, or elsewhere. The Manizales International Theater Festival had theater companies from Spain, Colombia, Chile, Argentina, Peru, Mexico, Costa Rica, and Brazil.

1991 was also the year that Gabo published *Volume 5* of his journalism work. A must-read for the García Márquez scholar and the aficionado alike, the book covers a rather long time period: 1961 to 1984. The volume reads almost as a memoir. It starts with a piece he wrote in 1961 about Ernest Hemingway's suicide. No other comment pertaining to the 1960s appears, except one in which he reflects upon being a writer. Interestingly enough, his opinion encompassed his view of the Nobel Prize, how much or how little writers earn, and whether writers will be remembered for their writing. Perhaps tongue in cheek, the closing of the article is in accord with its "Misfortunes of a Book Writer" ("Desventuras de un escritor de libros"). He ends the article by maintaining, "[Writing] is some kind of a deformation, which explains rather well the social outrage of so many men and women committing suicide out of hunger, wanting to do something that, in the end, to be honest, is worthless."[2] There is anger and frustration in this piece. It is evident that he did not know what was about to happen to his writing career one year later, with the publication in Argentina of *One Hundred Years of Solitude*.

By 1992, García Márquez's health was failing. His many years as a chain-smoker were taking their toll. In May, he underwent lung surgery to have a tumor removed. The operation was a success, but there was more to come as the decade elapsed. He was a 63-year-old with many projects and ambitions to fulfill. In a special issue of *Time* magazine, published in Los Angeles in October, to the question "What should mankind aim to accomplish in the coming decades?", he answered that the only new thing we can possibly attempt to save humanity in the twenty-first century is to have women take control of the world.[3] He seemed convinced men would be incapable of stopping the degradation of the environment and the end of humanity in the new millennium. He reasoned that men are unable to put aside their own personal interests.[4] His opinion, at that time, was reinforced by the strong female characters he had developed in his fiction, and the affirming answers regarding women in his many interviews. Historically, women have been at the forefront at times, controlling their worlds. One cannot ignore queens Cleopatra in Egypt, Isabella of Castile, Elizabeth I of England, and Catherine the Great of Russia, among others. The rule of Prime Minister Margaret Thatcher, during modern times, is yet another case that cannot escape our memory.

Strange Pilgrims (*Doce cuentos peregrinos*), a spellbinding book of 12 short stories, was published in 1992. Of all of his fictional books, this was the first ever to take place outside Colombia. All the short stories are set in Europe. Plots, however, revolve around Latin Americans either living or traveling in Europe. The first edition was published simultaneously in Argentina, Spain, Mexico, and Colombia. Edith Grossman's English translation was published the following year. The publication in Spanish coincided with the release of Ruy Guerra's film *I Sell My Dreams* (*Me alquilo para soñar*), which is, in fact, one of the 12 short stories in *Strange Pilgrims*. Inspired by García Márquez's own dream, in which he attends his own funeral, the storyline is of particular interest because his long-time friend, Pablo Neruda, is developed within the story as a fictional character. While the book of short stories, *Strange Pilgrims*, and the film *Me alquilo para soñar* were both released in 1992, the tale itself was written in March of 1980. Along with the book and the film, García Márquez must have been pleased to see that *Eréndira* underwent a musical adaptation as a chamber opera by music professor Violeta Dinescu. The libretto was by the composer, but follows Gabo's writing of the long short story. The Romanian-born Dinescu has been an Executive Board member of the International League of Women Composers since 1985.

Difficult or not, García Márquez's fiction continued to be adapted to different genres. In 1992, the Repertorio Español Theater in New York successfully adapted *Eréndira* as *La Cándida Eréndira*, under the direction of Jorge Alí Triana, founder of Teatro Popular in Bogotá. The theater review by the *New York Times* spoke highly of the theater version, unlike the previous adaptation, in 1990, of *Chronicle of a Death Foretold*. "At times, the elegant Gramercy Arts Theater seems about to burst from the sweeping grandeur and exciting energy of this play; its successful compression into such a small space is testimony to the skills of everyone involved, especially the 16 members of the Repertorio Español, who make all of the gritty, sometimes spectral, characters in this hallucinatory tale vivid, harsh and strangely beautiful."[5] *Eréndira* had seen a film adaptation, an opera treatment, and a theatrical version. The film adaptation, however, had been done a decade earlier (see Chapter 7).

1992 was a significant year for the Spanish-speaking world, because it was the 500th anniversary of the discovery of the New World. Among the many books, films, and TV specials that surfaced, Carlos Fuentes' *The Buried Mirror: Reflections on Spain and the New World* was among the most popular in the United States. In film, the most breathtaking was *1492: Conquest of Paradise*, starring Gérard Depardieu as Columbus, and Sigourney Weaver as Queen Isabella I. There were both large- and small-scale celebrations and publications throughout the Spanish Americas and Spain alike. In December, the University of Zaragoza, Spain, organized a congress at which more than 400 specialists participated in a discussion on *One Hundred Years of Solitude*. The congress was appropriately titled "500 Years of Solitude." According to many, and García Márquez in particular, one of the reasons for the state of affairs in the development of the Spanish Americas is the solitude and isolation this part of the hemisphere has endured through the ages. The celebrations of 1992 were to commemorate the 500 years of the discovery; the Zaragoza congress, however, celebrated the 25th anniversary of the publication of *One Hundred Years of Solitude*.

In 1993, García Márquez was awarded an honorary degree from the Autonomous University of Santo Domingo in the Dominican Republic. Later, he attended the III Zócalo Book Fair in Mexico City, one of the most important book events in Mexico. He became involved in a campaign in Colombia to protect the rights of authorship. The Institute Caro and Cuervo, a highly regarded university-styled Colombian institution involved in scientific research, higher education, and publication, named him an honorary member. In the political arena, he voiced his opinion about the drug treaties between the United States and Colombia. In a newspaper article, he recounted 11 years of effort between the two governments and pointed out that the results "are high-scale delinquency, blind terrorism, an industry of kidnappings, generalized corruption, and all of the above in an atmosphere of unprecedented violence."[6] His concern was as valid as any morally mindful citizen of Colombia, the United States, or any other country. In 1993, the drug culture and its side effects were completely out of control. His firsthand knowledge of this problem was going to surface in his writing with the publication, three years later, of the beyond-belief events in the shocking book *News of a Kidnapping*. It was in October of 1993 when the book began to take shape, after the victim of abduction, Maruja Pachón, and her husband, asked Gabo to write about her six-month-long kidnapping experience.

By October of 1994, his lifelong passion for journalism had led to the creation of La Fundación para un Nuevo Periodismo Iberoamericano (FNPI). The New Iberian-American Journalism Foundation is a nonprofit organization with headquarters in Cartagena de Indias, Colombia. García Márquez's vision in creating the foundation was to promote hands-on workshops and seminars where young journalists learn the craft from selected senior reporters, press officers, and columnists. The fruition of his vision was possible with the help of his younger brother, Jaime García Márquez, an engineer and the Foundation's vice-president. Jaime Abello Banfi, an integral part of the organization, is the executive director of the institution. Abello Banfi, a lawyer, had a strong background in the TV and film industries. An additional influential name in launching the journalist foundation was the Argentine novelist, short-story writer, essayist, journalist, and scholar Tomás Eloy Martínez, a close and longtime friend of García Márquez. Located within the historical walled city of Cartagena, where Gabo keeps a house that is referred to by tourist guides as "the house of the poet," the journalist institution has offices, a library, and two meeting rooms, which bear the names of two important names in the developmental stages of García Márquez's journalistic career: Alvaro Cepeda Samudio (1926–1972) and Clemente Manuel Zavala (1921–1963). Alvaro Cepeda was a member of the Barranquilla Group. Cepeda Samudio was so dear to García Márquez that his name (simply as Alvaro) appears in *One Hundred Years of Solitude* in the last part of the novel. Once again, always faithful to his long-time friends, Gabo was honoring him by naming a room after him. Clemente Manuel Zavala, on the other hand, was a mentor to García Márquez when Gabo was an apprentice at Cartagena's *El Universal* daily. They met in 1948. The FNPI is sponsored by private foundations and the United Nations Organization for Education, Science and Culture (UNESCO—Organización de las Naciones Unidas para la Educación, la Ciencia y la Cultura).

As in 1993, at the Autonomous University of Santo Domingo in the Dominican Republic, in 1994, the University of Cadiz, Spain, awarded him an honorary degree (*honoris causa*). In that year he published the novel *Of Love and Other Demons* (*Del amor y otros demonios*), an intricate story of love that takes place during Colombian colonial times in Cartagena. In the plot, the protagonist, a 12-year-old girl named Sierva María de Todos los Angeles, is bitten by a rabid dog. The Spanish publication of the book was distributed simultaneously in Spain, Argentina, Mexico, and Colombia. The English version was published the following year. A synopsis of the book reads, "Young Sierva Maria [of All Angels] speaks of strange dreams and stranger premonitions (a vision of snow on the Caribbean coast, and a cluster of magical grapes that contain the secret of her death), and she is soon hustled off to a local convent. There, the nuns not only blame her for bewitching the livestock and polluting the water, but also subject her to all manner of cruel and unusual punishments. Suddenly, however, the man who has been appointed to act as Sierva Maria's exorcist, a learned priest named Cayetano DeLauro, will unexpectedly fall in love with her, a development that promises the possibility of redemption (and eternal damnation) for them both."[7] Hyperbole, the dream world, and the supernatural come together in the novel to recreate a fictional event in which the narrative voice is that of a journalist. Today, García Márquez's home in Cartagena is located right across from the old convent where the fictional events take place. He, in contrast, is supposed to have learned about the events in 1949, when he worked as a journalist for the city's daily, *El Universal*. The 1950 short story "Eyes of a Blue Dog," dealing with the dream world and unfulfilled desire within a couple, was turned into a short film in 1994. Gabo's film adaptation was both directed and adapted to the screen by Lorenzo Shapiro. Shapiro's film adaptation sets García Márquez's short story plot in NYC.

García Márquez's literary production in 1995 would have to wait until the following year. Meanwhile, however, Gabo's reading public enjoyed Gustavo Arango's publication, *Un ramo de no me olvides* (*A Forget-Me-Not Bouquet*). The book is an homage to García Márquez's first two years as a journalist (1948 and 1949), when the 20-year-old came to Cartagena. The book is not available in English translation (refer to Chapter 2 for a full description of his life during these years). Gabo's journalism in 1995 included a revealing piece about Federico Mayor, a Spaniard who was Chair of UNESCO at the time. In the article "The Insatiable Optimism of Federico," we read that the United States stepped out of the organization, a move that effectively translated to a 25% loss in the operational budget. Among the remaining contributors, the Soviet Union was one of the strongest, but their own economy was rather shaky, García Márquez argued. Without mentioning the sources, however, the article praises UNESCO Chair Federico Mayor, who managed to find contributors to support UNESCO's agenda.[8]

The violence experienced in the 1980s was considered terrorism in the 1990s. In a study on global terrorism, the U.S. State Department reported, "Twice during 1995, President Samper declared a 'state of internal commotion,' invoking exceptional measures because of increased violence nationwide and the assassination on November 2 of Conservative Party patriarch Alvaro Gómez Hurtado. On that date, President Samper announced that he was empowering the military, governors of the 32 departments (states), and all mayors to authorize the evacuation of civilians from municipalities to combat illegal armed groups, including the guerrilla organizations operating in Colombia."[9] The State Department's report, as an official publication, might not have reached all four corners of the world, but Gabo's publication of *News of a Kidnapping* in 1996 probably did. In all languages, the book starts with an acknowledgment of those who provided the Nobel Laureate with all facts and circumstances. His literariness, however, takes away some of the crudeness of what he calls "a biblical holocaust that has been consuming Colombia for more than twenty years."[10] The U.S. State Department put it more bluntly: "Colombia continued to be wracked by violence in 1995, suffering numerous terrorist bombings, murders, and kidnappings for ransom. Drug traffickers, leftist insurgents, paramilitary squads, and common criminals committed scores of crimes with impunity, killing their targets, as well as many innocent bystanders. Although most of the politically motivated violence was directed at local targets, Colombia recorded 76 international terrorist incidents during 1995; the highest number in Latin America and nearly twice the 41 such incidents in 1994."[11]

To keep his ties with the cinema, García Márquez's screenplay collaboration on Sophocles' *Oedipus the King* was released as *Edipo Alcalde* in 1996. Sophocles is an influential author in García Márquez's literary career, particularly in his early years. The film was directed by Jorge Alí Triana, a Colombian director, producer, actor, and writer familiar with Gabo's work (in 1985, he directed the remake of García Márquez's *A Time to Die*). Spanish actress Angela Molina won the Premio Fotograma de Plata (Silver Photogram Award) in Madrid, for best actress in her role of Jocasta (Oedipus' mother and wife).

In March of 1997, the International Film and Television Festival in Cartagena, Colombia, celebrated García Márquez's cinematic work and showed six of his screenplays; *Edipo Alcalde* (*Oedipus the King*) was one of them. The festival organizers wanted to celebrate Gabo's 70th birthday, his 50th anniversary as novelist, the 30th of the publication of *One Hundred Years of Solitude*, and the 15th as a Nobel Laureate. Gabo, however, did not attend the tribute. He celebrated his birthday in Mexico instead. This time, unlike his exile during the 1980s under suspicion of aiding the M-19, it was a self-imposed exile. He was saddened, disheartened, and sick of the lies and corruption of the Colombian government.[12] Dasso Saldívar published *El viaje a la semilla* (*The Journey to the Seed*), a 611-page biography (a large collection of photos, end notes, and index included) that unfolded the fine points in the creation of *One Hundred Years of Solitude*, revealing the historical and cultural components that surround the novel, as well as the family ties that breathe through the epic tale.

On April 7, 1997, García Márquez gave the opening speech at the First International Congress of the Spanish Language, celebrated in Zacatecas, Mexico. His address was followed by Camilo José Cela and Octavio Paz, both Nobel Prize winners, the former from Spain and the later from Mexico. After their presentations were King Juan Carlos I of Spain, and Mexican President Ernesto Zedillo. The International Congress of the Spanish Language takes place every three years in one of the many Spanish-speaking nations. The second was held in Valladolid, Spain; the third took place in Rosario, Argentina; and the fourth occurred in Cartagena de Indias, Colombia, in 2007, where the attendees paid tribute to Gabriel García Márquez for the 40th anniversary of the publication of *One Hundred Years of Solitude*, for his 25 years as a Nobel Laureate, and for his 80th birthday. Details of the celebration appear in the next chapter. Despite having once been denied entry to the United States, in September of 1997, García Márquez met with President Bill Clinton at the White House.

On Sunday, January 25, 1998, García Márquez was in Cuba. Pope John Paul II was making a pastoral visit to the Caribbean island at the same time. The papal address, which was more than three hours, was listened to by thousands of Cubans in Havana's Revolution Square. The televised mass showed Gabriel García Márquez sitting alongside his longtime friend, Fidel Castro—Jesuit-educated, and a former altar boy.

In April of the same year, Gabo was at Princeton University to run a literary workshop. Around that time, Gabo intended to meet with President Clinton at the Oval Office. García Márquez contacted Bill Richardson to arrange a private visit with President Clinton to discuss the Colombia situation. The meeting, however, did not take place. Meanwhile, when Kenneth W. Starr was investigating President Clinton, Gabo and other intellectuals wrote a letter of protest, calling Starr "a fanatical prosecutor with unlimited power." The letter, presented in Paris, was "signed by an international roster of writers, scholars, and actors, including Bishop Desmond Tutu, the Nobel Peace Prize winner from South Africa; Gabriel García Márquez and William Styron, Pulitzer-Prize winning authors; the actresses Emma Thompson and Lauren Bacall and the singer Jessye Norman."[13] *The New York Times* report added, "The statement, co-written by Jack Lang, the former minister of culture of France, is being faxed to movie stars and other prominent people around the world. Vanessa Redgrave said yesterday that she was raising money to have the letter printed in newspapers throughout the United States and the world."[14] Gabo's sympathy for and friendship with President Clinton has been no secret. His political involvement was obvious; the results of it were not. The Clinton-Lewinsky affair, if there was one, was more of a travesty than a political affair. The investigation against Clinton started in 1995, and by 1998, was still not over.

In 1998, García Márquez's wealth allowed him to become one of the owners, and Chair, of the editorial board of the Colombian magazine *Cambio* (*Change*). *Cambio*, which has enjoyed wide circulation from the start, in hard print as well as on the Internet, is a news magazine dealing with multiple subjects of interest, both local and international. Its main focus, however, is a strong emphasis on internal Colombian affairs: its economy, political matters, culture, and entertainment.

In 1998, Fidel Castro published a book of his memoirs as a child, youth, and his political involvement, titled *Fidel: My Early Years*. Gabo wrote the introductory essay, "A Personal Portrait of Fidel." Castro, García Márquez wrote, "is a man of austere ways and insatiable illusions, with an old-fashioned formal education, of cautious words and simple manners and incapable of conceiving any idea which is not out of the ordinary."[15]

His journalistic work keeps him active at all times. Even in 1999, 72-year-old García Márquez, despite his battle against lymphatic cancer, kept active. On January 24, 1999, he published the newspaper article "La fatiga del metal" ("Metal Fatigue") for the Madrid-based Spanish daily, *El País*. The article was both a remembrance of the first time he had met President Clinton in August of 1995, at a dinner get-together at William Styron's Martha's Vineyard summer home, and an expression of strong support for the President. The title of the article, as is typical of García Márquez, captured the image he wanted to communicate. "Metal fatigue" was his analogy for President Clinton as he, Gabo, perceived him at a White House dinner celebration, given for Colombian President Andrés Pastrana in September of 1998. Clinton was no longer the youthful, impartial, fair college graduate he had met in Martha's Vineyard, Gabo wrote, but more of an uncertain convict who had lost weight and could not hide, behind his professional smile, the same organic wearing-away that destroys airplanes: metal fatigue.[16] The prose and tone of the article show Clinton as a weary, "metal-fatigued" man who was persecuted by the fundamentalist ideals of Kenneth W. Starr and those behind him.

By the summer of 1999, García Márquez had enjoyed the success of having one more of his novels turned into a film. *No One Writes to the Colonel* (*El coronel no tiene quien le escriba*) was shown at the Cannes Film Festival. The movie director, Mexican Arturo Ripstein, was nominated for the Golden Palm Award. In Spain, the film adaptation was nominated for The Goya Award (comparable to the Oscar). The following year, the film was shown at the Sundance Film Festival in Utah, and it was then that Ripstein won the award for best director.

At this time, García Márquez's journalism work was compiled in an additional volume. The book, *Por la libre: Obra periodística 4 (1974–1995)*, included selected articles from 1974 to 1995. The volume, the title of which might be freely translated as *No Toll, Journalistic Work 4 (1974–1995)*, is not available in English. None of his work in journalism is available in English or any other language than Spanish.

That summer, after being hospitalized for physical exhaustion, García Márquez was treated for lymphatic cancer. Surrounded by myth, the rumors of his worsening health gave way to a popular hoax of worldwide circulation of a poem titled "The Puppet" ("La Marioneta"). Countless followers believed the poem was indeed García Márquez's farewell. It was not. Gabo, however, did not comment on it. The poem had been written by Mexican ventriloquist Johnny Welch, for his sidekick puppet, Don Mofles. García Márquez, in fact, was later photographed with the famous ventriloquist.[17]

CODA

For Latin America in general, with a few exceptions, the 1990s were less violent than the previous decades. Organized guerrilla movements continued in Colombia, Guatemala, and Peru, but in the rest of Latin America were not a threat to the social, political, and economic stability. Marxism was somehow discredited by the collapse of the Eastern European countries, but under Fidel Castro, Cuba stayed the course. Crime in Colombia was related more to the drug cartels than the counter-insurgent groups, although the later were as active as ever. The largest Colombian guerrilla group, the Revolutionary Armed Forces of Colombia (FARC), was often said to be involved in supporting the drug cartels. Kidnappings in Colombia and Mexico alone became a form of "industry." In the 1980s, Gabriel García Márquez tried to negotiate peace for Colombians by talking to Jaime Bateman Cayón, the leader of the 19th of April guerrilla movement, better known as M-19. In the 1990s, he wrote a book to denounce the escalating violence Colombia was undergoing, in *News of a Kidnapping*. Colombia and Peru continued to be a major problem in the region. Chile, on the other hand, held free elections and enjoyed a rather prosperous economy during the democratic government of presidents Patricio Alwin (1990–1993) and Eduardo Frei (1994–1999). In Mexico, President Ernesto Zedillo (1994–2000) was the last Mexican head of state whose political party, the Institutional Revolutionary Party (PRI), had ruled Mexico for 70 years without interruption. This apparent change of political power has lasted two terms. After President Vicente Fox, whose political party is called PAN (Partido de Acción Nacional [National Action Party]), one more member of PAN was elected to power in the controversial, contested 2006 election of President Felipe Calderón.

García Márquez, often consulted for answers, was invited to become part of the Colombian National Assembly, but continued to decline any and all such offers. Was he trapped in his own labyrinth? On the other hand, Peruvian Mario Vargas Llosa, an internationally known novelist, essayist, playwright, short-story writer, and considered one of the best writers in the Spanish language today, must have thought differently: in 1990, Vargas Llosa ran for Peru's presidency, only to be defeated by Alberto Fujimori. Does a man of letters have to get involved in politics, and hold government posts, as many Latin American writers have done? Whatever the answer, García Márquez kept himself disenfranchised from any political affiliation, but active in his own right. One cannot help seeing him as the conscience of Colombians, the one who could provide guidance for social change. All these people have always forgotten that he is a writer, a journalist, not a philosopher, and definitely not a professional politician. He might be able to address the problems, talk to national and international audiences, but no more than that.

Interestingly enough, with all the problems Colombia faced in the 1990s, a recurring question for the Nobel Laureate was always his relationship with Fidel Castro and the lack of democracy in Cuba. "At a conference for journalists held in 1996 in Colombia, García Márquez said: 'Fidel is one of the people I love most in the world.' 'A dictator,' someone said, and the writer replied that elections were not the only way to be democratic. Then a Venezuelan journalist asked why he served as an honorary aide to Castro. 'Because he is my friend,' García Márquez answered, adding that one should do everything for one's friends."[18]

If, in the 1980s, García Márquez sought asylum in Mexico, in the 1990s, he was self-exiled to Mexico, and declined to attend a ceremony in his honor in Cartagena in 1997. His love for Colombia, however, is unquestionable. He does much more for the country than the general public knows. Among his contributions in the 1990s was the creation of the abovementioned New Iberian-American Journalism Foundation for young journalists. As if everything were circular, as in *One Hundred Years of Solitude*, in the 1980s, he was at the Vatican to meet Pope John Paul II. In García Márquez's fiction, in the multilayered short story "Big Mama's Funeral" (1962), the Pope comes to Macondo to Big Mama's funeral; in 1986, Pope John Paul II visited Colombia. In the 1990s, García Márquez was in Cuba to listen the Pope's mass in Havana. His health, however, was no longer what it had been in the 1980s. The 1990s began to show the decay of a great writer who, at times, had scared his followers with the possibility that he might die. To the joy of millions around the globe, however, he continued thriving.

His life is complicated for being *who he is*, the most popular writer alive in the Spanish language. Yet, for almost 30 years, he could not get a visa to visit the United States. In 1990, Congress passed a bill that prohibits the Immigration and Naturalization Service from keeping individuals out of the country because of their ideology. The bill, however, leaves room for interpretation. In 1992, after landing in New York City from Paris, he and his wife were detained and interrogated for no reason other than his name. "Mr. García Márquez said his name had been put on the list of people to be excluded [from entry to the United States] when he worked as a correspondent for four months in 1961 for Prensa Latina, the Cuban news agency. He left the agency after the Bay of Pigs incident, when, he said, "The Communist characteristics of the Cuban revolution took over and they cleared out all the non-Communists." "I was a leftist liberal, but not a Communist," he said."[19]

NOTES

1. Mel Gussow, review of *Crónica de una muerte*, directed by Salvador Tavora, Festival Latino in New York, *New York Times*, August 3, 1990. http://query.nytimes.com/gst/fullpage.html?res=9C0CE2DB163BF930A3575BC0A966958260.

2. García Márquez, *Notas de prensa: Obra periodística 5*, 18 (see chap. 7, n. 1). (The translation is mine.)

3. Ibid., 303.

4. Ibid.

5. D.J.R. Bruckner, review of *The Innocent Eréndira and a Ghastly Grandma*, directed by Jorge Ali Triana, Gramercy Arts Theater, New York, *New York Times*, February 9, 1992. http://query.nytimes.com/gst/fullpage.html?res=9E0CE6D7103 AF93AA35751C0A964958260.

6. García Márquez, *Por la libre: Obra periodística 4*, 307 (see chap. 4, n. 1).

7. Michiko Kakutani, "Books of the Times; Magical Realism from 2 Cultures," *New York Times*, June 2, 1995. http://query.nytimes.com/gst/fullpage.html?res=9800E1DC1639F931A35755C0A963958260.

8. García Márquez, *Por la libre: Obra periodística 4*, 325–27 (see chap. 4, n. 1).

9. Office of the Coordinator for Counterterrorism, U.S. Department of State, "Patterns of Global Terrorism, 1995: Latin America Overview," Hellenic Resources Network, April 1996. http://www.hri.org/docs/USSD-Terror/95/latin.html.

10. Gabriel García Márquez, *News of a Kidnapping*, trans. Edith Grossman (New York: Alfred A. Knopf, 1997).

11. "Patterns of Global Terrorism, 1995."

12. See Cristina Fernandez, "Gabo se secuestra" ("Gabo Kidnaps Himself"), *El Mundo*. http://www.elmundo.es/papel/hemeroteca/1997/03/02/cronica/230279/html.

13. "The Testing of a President; Celebrities Call Starr a Fanatic and Inquisitor," *New York Times*, September 26, 1998. http://query.nytimes.com/gst/fullpage.html?res=9B04E0D71539F935A1575AC0A96E958260.

14. Ibid.

15. Gabriel García Márquez, *Fidel: My Early Years* (New York: Ocean Press, 1998), back cover.

16. The paraphrasing of the article is a free translation of mine. http://www.sololiteratura.com/ggm/marquezprincipal.htm.

17. http://elshowdejohnnywelch.com/curriculum.html.

18. Porras del Campo and Panichelli, *Gabo and Fidel*, 401 (see chap. 6, n. 5).

19. Nadine Brozan, "CHRONICLE," *New York Times*, September 18, 1992. http://query.nytimes.com/gst/fullpage.html?res=9E0CE2DE1338F93BA2575AC 0A964958260.

Chapter 9

THE NEW MILLENNIUM

Books are a part of man's prerogative;
In formal ink they thoughts and voices hold,
That we to them our *solitude* may give,
And make time present travel that of old.

—*Sir Thomas Overbury, in James Parr,* Don Quixote:
An Anatomy of Subversive Discourse; *emphasis mine*

He is the son of Aracataca's telegrapher, the man of Macondo, a master of the short story, one-of-a-kind journalist, the most-read Latin American novelist, a magician of words, a key essayist, the 1982 Nobel Prize winner, and one of the world's most fascinating authors in any language. He is also a movie critic, and a script and screenplay writer. Gabriel García Márquez now belongs to the ages.

The octogenarian Gabriel García Márquez spent the year of 2007 literally in the spotlight. No other author, dead or alive, had more worldwide attention that year than he. Not even J. K. Rowling, whose popularity and book sales are unimaginable, or Doris Lessing, who received the Nobel Prize in Literature that year. In 2007, no writer enjoyed more popularity than the Colombian writer whose readers around the world, not just his close friends and family, now call simply "Gabo." J. K. Rowling dominated the headlines during the months of July and October with her new book, *Harry Potter and the Deathly Hallows,* and a new film, *Harry Potter and the Order of the Phoenix.* Yet, Nobel Laureate Lessing was merely a reference, who came and went almost unnoticed by most readers. Gabriel García Márquez, however, was in the limelight nearly the whole year.

From March 26 through 29, 2007, Colombia was the host country for the IV International Congress of the Spanish Language. The theme of the Congress, "The Present and Future of the Spanish Language: Unity amongst Diversity," attracted world personalities from all walks of life: presidents, the King and Queen of Spain, scholars, and many of Gabriel García Márquez's friends. According to the Cervantes Institute, today Spanish is spoken by more than 400 million people, making it the fourth most-spoken language after Chinese, English, and Hindi. Among the attendees were two hundred delegates representing all the Spanish-speaking nations. There were experts from countries other than Spanish-speaking nations, over 1,200 scientists, businessmen, writers, journalists, philosophers, professors, Hispanists, filmmakers, artists, linguists, sociologists, historians, politicians, architects, and publishers, members of the Language Academies and the Cervantes Institute, plus a large number of students from Colombian universities.[1] The Congress, however, on behalf of the 22 language academies of the Spanish Language, was dedicated to Gabriel García Márquez, to thank him for his oeuvre, to celebrate his 80th birthday, the 40th anniversary of the publication of *One Hundred Years of Solitude*, and his 25th anniversary as a Nobel Laureate. His *magnum opus*, *One Hundred Years of Solitude*, as Argentine Tomás Eloy Martinez described it, opened all doors and windows of our imagination in Spanish. It enriched and continues to enrich our worldview, and lastingly influences writers of other cultures and languages.[2] Carlos Fuentes reminisced about how he met Gabo in 1962, a friendship that has lasted for over four decades. The Mexican novelist was one of the first to compare *One Hundred Years of Solitude* to Cervantes' *Don Quixote*. Today the comparison is not new, but 40 years ago, it was. In a letter written to Julio Cortázar, Fuentes wrote, "I just finished reading *One Hundred Years of Solitude*: an exciting and sad chronicle, prose full of life with liberating imagination. I feel invigorated after reading this book, as if I had just shaken the hands of all my friends. I have just read the Latin American Quixote—a Quixote captured between the jungle and the mountains, without the flat dry land, a cloistered Quixote who must invent the world from within his four tumbled walls. What a brilliant re-creation of the universe, invented, and reinvented! What a prodigious image of existence, as if in Cervantes' style, turned into literary discourse, in a continuous passage from the real to the divine and the imaginary."[3] The International Congress of the Spanish Language, three days in length, is the biggest international event of its kind. This newborn tradition is 10 years old and takes place every 4 years.

When it was time for Gabriel García Márquez to address the assemblage at the opening ceremony in Cartagena, his words were of gratitude for such a significant event. Not in his wildest dreams could he have imagined that his 1967 novel, One Hundred Years of Solitude, would ever have a printing of a million copies. "To think that one million people [in Spanish] could read something written in the solitude of my room, with the 28 letters of the alphabet and two fingers as my total arsenal, under any circumstances, would have been madness." Today, he continued, "the language academies do it both for a novel that has been read by 50 million people already, and for an insomniac artisan like me who never ceases to be surprised by everything that has happened."[4]

The celebrations began 20 days earlier in March, in Aracataca, the town where the Nobel Laureate was born. The mayor of the town, Pedro Javier Sánchez Rueda, and the townspeople organized a military parade, a special Roman Catholic mass and 80 fireworks set off at 5:00 A.M. to celebrate the author's 80th birthday. This was the town's biggest event since the banana fever of the early 1920s had ended, as the New York Times put it: "But the most painful absence on Tuesday was that of Gabriel García Márquez, the native son for whom Aracataca was the inspiration for Macondo, the fictional setting for his epic novel, One Hundred Years of Solitude."[5] The rumor was that he was either in Cuba with his friend Fidel Castro, or at his Mexico City residence. The belated visit to his boyhood town took place on Tuesday, May 30, 2007. He and his wife, Mercedes Barcha, arrived in a vintage train called the Yellow Train of Macondo. The train ride began in Santa Marta, a coastal city and capital of the Magdalena Department, and progressed to Aracataca (Macondo), where the townspeople, journalists, and fans welcomed the town's favorite son. He toured the municipality for no more than an hour and a half and then left by bus with the entourage that had arrived with him by train. The train-project is one that Magdalena Department hopes will help the town's economy, by carrying hundreds of literary pilgrims.

As 2007 came to an end, the 80-year-old Gabriel García Márquez seemed to have a burst of energy. He was literally on and off airplanes as if he were reliving his younger years. It was as if his fight with lymphatic cancer were completely over. In November, he attended the opening ceremony of the 21st edition of the weeklong International Book Fair in Guadalajara, Mexico. Colombia, his country of birth, was honored, and Colombian author Alvaro Mutis received a special tribute throughout the week. Although Colombia has a rich literary heritage, it has a rather low level of literacy.

On November 16, with great expectation throughout the United States, the film adaptation of his novel, Love in the Time of Cholera, opened at movie theaters nationwide. The screen adaptation was done by Academy Award winner Ronald Harwood, who is best known for the Holocaust film, *The Pianist* (for which he won the Oscar in 2002), and the film adaptation of *Oliver Twist* (2005); both pictures were directed by Roman Polanski. The South African-born Ronald Harwood has an impressive career in literature. Among several other honors, he was made a Fellow of the Royal Society of Literature in 1974; President of English PEN (poets, playwrights, essayists, editors, and novelists), 1989–1993; and President of International PEN, 1993–1997. The director of *Love in the Time of Cholera*, however, was Mike Newell. Mr. Newell's work as film and television director is rather extensive, but to date, he has not won any significant awards. His work as director prior to *Love in the Time of Cholera* was 2005's *Harry Potter and the Goblet of Fire*. The soundtrack for *Love in the Time of Cholera* includes songs by Colombian-born singer/songwriter Shakira, who has won two Grammys and eight Latin Grammys. The cast, led by Javier Bardem as Florentino Ariza, Benjamin Bratt as Dr. Juvenal Urbino, and Giovanna Mezzogiorno as Fermina Daza, all praised the hospitality of the people of Colombia, where the forty-five-million-dollar movie was filmed.

The film critics, however, were obsessed with the greatness of the novel and considered the film inferior to it. Writing for *The New Yorker*, David Denby was prompt to make an analogy with Dante and his obsession with Beatrice before relating the film to another film. "He [Mike Newell] doesn't paint with the camera; he doesn't seize on certain visual motifs, as he should, and turn them into the equivalent of a lover's devotion to fetishes. He's a realist handling comically extravagant material, and he does little more than competently frame a mixed set of performances." But not all is lost, Denby adds: "It's a well-crafted, handsome period piece, and pleasant to watch."[6]

On Wednesday, December 5, the 80-year-old García Márquez arrived at José Martí International Airport in Havana to attend Havana's 29th New Latin American Film Festival. His presence at the event was as president and one of the founders of the celebration. The gala coincided with the 40th anniversary of the death of legendary Ernesto Che Guevara, member of the July 26 Movement and instrumental in the triumph of the 1959 Cuban Revolution. Che Guevara was killed in Bolivia in 1967. Among other celebrities attending the film festival were two famous Latin actors, Spaniard Javier Bardem and Mexican Gael García Bernal. The former is best known for his roles in *Before Night Falls* (2000) and the 2007 films *Love in the Time of Cholera* and *No Country for Old Men*.[7] His presence at the festival, however, was not related to any of the above films, but rather as producer of the film *Invisibles*. Gael García Bernal, on the other hand, was at the film festival as a debutant movie director. Famous in the United States for his most recent roles in *Babel* (2006) and *The Motorcycle Diaries* (2004), his directorial view was for the film *Deficit*. The festival, which ran through December 14, opened with *Redacted*, a film by Brian De Palma that caused a great deal of controversy in the United States. The motion picture, shown at several film festivals, has in fact been redacted due to its subject (anti-Iraq War), and De Palma wants the film to be shown uncensored. De Palma had won the Silver Lion prize as best director at the Venice Film Festival, but he could not attend the Cuban Fête because the U.S. State Department denied his visa. About 500 films were shown, with a tribute and special presentations: the former for Luis Buñuel; the latter for Fritz Lang, whose film *The Spiders* was restored and shown. The film fest closed on December 14 at the Theater Karl Marx in Havana, with a speech delivered by Alfredo Guevara. The film to close the festival was *Earth (Tierra)*, a British-German co-produced documentary.

Seven years earlier, at the turn of the new millennium, García Márquez found himself recuperating from lymphatic cancer. Typical of García Márquez's approach to life, he saw it as a stroke of luck. Similar to the popular Buddhist saying, "through the cracks, the light comes in," he found time to be by himself and began writing the first of his three-volume memoirs. His treatment for the lymphoma lasted for over a year. The book, *Living to Tell the Tale*, was published first in Spanish, in 2002, as *Vivir para contarla*. The English translation, by Edith Grossman, appeared in 2003. There were many reviews soon after the book was published. Most of them stated that the writing style of the memoir, reminiscent of his fiction, traced the chronological Colombian historical facts, the family affairs that helped to shape his writing, and his literary influences. *Living to Tell the Tale*, wrote one of the reviewers, is "the first volume of a planned autobiographical trilogy. But its most powerful sections read like one of his mesmerizing novels, transporting the reader to a Latin America haunted by the ghosts of history and shaped by the exigencies of its daunting geography, by its heat and jungles and febrile light. The book provides as memorable a portrait of a young writer's apprenticeship as the one William Styron gave us in *Sophie's Choice*, even as it illuminates the alchemy Mr. García Márquez acquired from masters like Faulkner and Joyce and Borges and later used to transform family stories and firsthand experiences into fecund myths of his own."[8] The upcoming two volumes are underway. The second one is supposed to cover his life as a writer after 1955, where *Living to Tell the Tale* ends, and up to the publication of *One Hundred Years of Solitude* in 1967. The third and last volume is alleged to cover his friendships, some of which are with world leaders like Fidel Castro, Françoise Mitterrand, Bill Clinton, and Omar Torrijos, and with writers like Pablo Neruda, Carlos Fuentes, Julio Cortázar, Alvaro Mutis, Graham Greene, and others. Then, of course, there are those friends of his youth and humble beginnings who most likely will not be ignored. Some of these friends are depicted in this book (see Chapter 10).

His self-imposed isolation and solitude were due both to his medical condition and his will to write. He was diagnosed with lymphatic cancer in the summer of 1999. When he was finally seen in public, in 2000, it was for the inauguration of Mexican president Vicente Fox. García Márquez was seen in the company of Cuban President Fidel Castro, and U.S. Secretary of State Madeleine Albright. As mentioned earlier, Mexico City is where he has lived longer than anywhere else, and Mexicans think of Gabo as one of them. Moreover, Mexico is the only country in the region that never broke relations with Cuba, something imposed by Washington on all other Spanish-speaking nations during the 1960s, after the triumph of the Cuban revolution in 1959.

In 2001, his youngest brother, Gabriel Eligio García Márquez, published an important work tracing the ins and outs of the writing of *One Hundred Years of Solitude*. The book, printed in Spanish, was titled *Tras las claves de Melquíades: Historia de Cien años de soledad* (*In Search of Melquíades' Secrets: The History of One Hundred Years of Solitude*). The same year, Rubén Pelayo published his text, in English, *Gabriel García Márquez: A Critical Companion*. The former was a personal and detailed look at the production of what is without question the most important book written by García Márquez. The latter was an educational text that provides an accessible explanation of the Nobel Laureate's most representative works, short stories and novels, prior to the new millennium. In 2001, one of García Márquez's best friends of all time, Colombian Alvaro Mutis, was awarded the Cervantes Award. To celebrate the event, the Madrid-based newspaper *El País*, the largest daily newspaper in Spain, published an article García Márquez had written eight years earlier, in 1993, when the Colombian government paid tribute to Alvaro Mutis on the occasion of his 70th birthday. In the article, "Homage to a Friend," we gain insights into both authors, for they have known each other since 1949, and have cultivated the friendship ever since. It is worth noting that it was Mutis who introduced García Márquez to the Mexican writer Juan Rulfo. The latter, according to critics, became one of the influences on Gabriel García Márquez's writing style.[9] Mutis and García Márquez's friendship is both long and legendary. Alvaro Mutis was the first to read the manuscript when *One Hundred of Years of Solitude* was finished and ready to be sent to Buenos Aires for publication. While a copy of the first edition in English of *One Hundred Years of Solitude* can sell for a modest three thousand dollars, in September of 2001, when the galley proofs of the original, the 1967 edition by *Sudamericana,* were auctioned in Barcelona, the opening price was ninety-five million pesetas, approximately half a million dollars. Prior to the September auction of the galleys, in July, García Márquez himself published an article in *El País* newspaper titled "La odisea literaria de un manuscrito" ("The Literary Odyssey of a Manuscript"). In it he included many known details about the writing of *One Hundred Years of Solitude* (see Chapter 5). What is new, however, was the revelation that he had given the only existent galleys of the novel to filmmaker and dear friend Luis Alcoriza and his wife, Janet. He dedicated the galley proofs to them: "From the friend who loves you most in this world" ("Del amigo que más los quiere en este mundo"), and signed it "Gabo." The inscription was signed in 1967. The Alcorizas kept the galley proofs for years. Eighteen years later, however, at yet another gathering at the Alcorizas', someone said the galleys were worth a large amount of money. Gabo adds in his newspaper account that Luis Alcoriza stood up and, in theatrical fashion, exclaimed, "Well, I would rather die than sell this jewel signed by a friend!" ("¡Pues yo prefiero morirme antes que vender esta joya dedicada por un amigo!") It was then that Gabo, seeing the manuscript again after all this time, wrote on it "confirmed," "1985," and signed again as Gabo. The newspaper article recounts that Alcoriza died in 1992, at 71 years old, without ever selling the galley proofs; his wife, Janet, died six years later. Their heir, Hector Delgado, was responsible for the auction.[10] The required minimum bid was so high that no one bid on the proofs.

Although the luck of the galley proofs, and Alcoriza's sole heir, did not have a happy ending, the rights to *Living to Tell the Tale* were astounding. Rumor has it the rights were sold for ninety million dollars. Bear in mind that whether true or false, not the whole amount went to the author. However, 2003 was another "fever year" for Gabo in the English-speaking world. Many readers do not realize that the content of *Living to Tell the Tale* is not fiction, but fact. This, of course, was the same reaction many readers had when reading *News of a Kidnapping.* Fiction and reality, more and more, continue to confuse García Márquez's readers in any language, even though *Living to Tell the Tale* was on the *New York Times* "Reader's Choice" list of 2003 as one of three nonfiction books.

In 2004, García Márquez's popularity in the United States increased many times over when Oprah Winfrey included *One Hundred Years of Solitude* as her book club choice for the month of January 2004. Oprah's

Book Club is unquestionably the most watched and the richest in the United States, and, one must add, a rather serious approach to books for a popular TV show. As Caryn James wrote, regarding the way the acclaimed novel was dealt with on Oprah's TV show: "There are features like 'Understanding Gabo's Masterpiece' and 'Gabo and Faulkner,' an interactive family tree to keep the characters straight, and a section in which a college professor answers readers' questions weekly."[11] James' review is accurate, pointing out that the success of the novel (and Oprah's Book Club) with the reading public is based on how carefully the work is presented, for the work itself can always be intimidating and not easy to follow: "As beautiful and accessible as it is, such a sprawling novel can also be intimidating and confusing. It runs 448 pages in the paperback with the 'Oprah' sticker; time is fluid, and ghosts appear; there are so many Aurelianos and José Arcadios that it's no wonder readers need an Oprah to guide them. Extending her television personality to the Web, she takes readers by the hand and leads them through features that seem enthusiastic and not—that dreaded word—educational."[12] While we popularized *One Hundred Years of Solitude* in the United States at the start of 2004, this time by way of television, before the year ended, we had learned that after 15 years of refusing to sell the rights for his 1985 novel, *Love in the Time of Cholera*, García Márquez had finally changed his mind. The love triangle story of the fictional Florentino Ariza, Fermina Daza, and Juvenal Urbino, loosely based on the author's parents' love story, was headed to the big screen. Scott Steindorff, movie and television producer, is said to have been so persistent in seeking the rights that García Márquez finally accepted to make a deal and sold him the rights for $1 million for the film adaptation. Other than his Florentino-like, relentless determination—insisting for over three years—Steindorff had experience in producing film adaptations from books. In 2003, Steindorff produced *The Human Stain*, the film adaptation of Philip Roth's novel by the same title, with a very impressive cast, including, among others, Anthony Hopkins, Nicole Kidman, Ed Harris, and Gary Sinise. The screenplay adaptation, as mentioned earlier, was done by Ronald Harwood, who won an Oscar for his 2002 film script for *The Pianist*. The 2004 Spanish publication of *Memories of My Melancholy Whores* (*Memoria de mis putas tristes*) provoked all types of reactions, as is the case with anything published by García Márquez. There were those who saw it as an irresponsible piece, dealing with child abuse, and even as a stimulus for violence against women. There were those who criticized it as sensationalist, and as a sheer commercial stunt. No fiction by the Nobel Prize winner had been published in 10 years, since the publication of the young, female protagonist named Sierva María de Todos los Angeles who is bitten by a rabid dog in *Of Love and Other Demons* (see

Chapter 8). After the enormous sales of *Living to Tale the Tale* (nonfiction), the first print of *Memories of My Melancholy Whores* sold a million copies in Spanish alone. The title itself is shocking; the plot is scandalous. Was the novella worth waiting for? While the individual reader has the last word, one can always look at it as a literary text and find that "the plot shows no rough edges or cracks, the characters are portrayed with superb irony. If one pays attention to style, one cannot help noting the lexical precision and the craftsmanship in the treatment of expressions. García Márquez continues to be the best writer in the Spanish language today. The precision with which he uses the lexicon, the tone and gleaming characteristic of his prose have no model; it's all his own."[13] In the world of cinema, the movie *In Evil Hour*, homonymous with García Márquez's 1961 novel, was released in 2004. Directed by Ruy Guerra, the film won nominations at the Brazilia Festival of Brazilian Cinema in Brazilia, the Cinema Brazil Grand Prize in Rio de Janeiro, and the San Sebastián International Film Festival, in San Sebastián, Spain, but only won an award at the Havana Film Festival, known as the Festival of New Latin American Cinema, for best cinematography.

In 2005, as mentioned above, the English translation of *Memories of My Melancholy Whores* made headlines for Gabriel García Márquez. However, Rodrigo García Barcha, his oldest son, also had top billing in his own right. Normally known as Rodrigo García, he cannot be seen as the alter ego or the shadow of his Nobel-Prize-winning father simply because of his love for the cinema. He is doing what his father never did: direct. But like his father, he also writes screenplays. In 2005, he wrote and directed the film *Nine Lives*. He lives in Los Angeles, with his wife and two daughters, and during an interview in Hollywood, he made an interesting comment about himself as the son of García Márquez: "My father's legacy has daunted me. I did not want to be the mediocre writer son of a famous writer." He added, "So, I did not write."[14] But, in fact, he does. He does not write literary fiction, but he writes fiction for the big screen. Not necessarily the same, but writing, by any means. The following year, at 79 years old, Gabriel García Márquez had the privilege of seeing one more adaptation of his work, this time a dance production of his previously adapted short story, "A Very Old Man with Enormous Wings." The dance adaptation was directed by Hiroshi Koike, and had its United States premiere at the Japan Society in New York City. Hiroshi Koike is well known for his avant-garde dance-theater adaptations of literary works such as *The Three Sisters* by Chekhov.

In 2006, just before his 80th birthday celebrations, García Márquez teamed up with his longtime friend, Fernando Birri, co-founder with García Márquez of the International School of Cinema, Television and Video in San Antonio de los Baños, in Cuba, and released the documentary *ZA 05. The Old and the New* (*ZA 05. Lo viejo y lo nuevo*). García Márquez wrote the script in collaboration with Birri, Julio García Espinoza, and Orlando Senna. The documentary is a filmed tribute to screenwriter Cesare Zavattini (1902–1989). Zavattini is remembered as the leading figure of the Italian neorealist film movement. He was also a poet, painter, and novelist. As a screenwriter, he worked with celebrated directors Vittorio de Sica, Michelangelo Antonioni, Federico Fellini, and Luchino Visconti, to name just four.

CODA

There was no point in explaining that the new millennium would not start until the year 2001. The arrival of the year 2000 was celebrated all over the globe. In 2000, Gabriel García Márquez, like thousands of people in the United States, Cuba, and elsewhere, got involved in what was ultimately called the "Battle for Elián," the question of "extradition" of a six-year-old freedom boat survivor en route to Florida. Gabo wrote an article that was a combination of politics, journalism, and anecdotal literature, accurately titled "Shipwreck on Dry Land." The turn of events had more of a political overtone. In the end, Elián was returned to his biological father, Juan Miguel González, in Cuba. The whole affair seemed more like a montage from a virtual reality show.

The terrorist attacks of September 11, 2001, on the World Trade Center and the Pentagon changed the way we live today. Osama bin Laden and al-Qaeda remain at large. "Bioterrorism" became a familiar word in the vocabulary of the general public, and Saddam Hussein a target and focus of American foreign policy. In the Spanish-speaking world, the economy in South America was worsening in Argentina. In Venezuela, students and members of the middle classes organized massive protests against President Hugo Chávez, but he remained extremely popular among the poor. The armed conflicts of Colombia, on the other hand, have continued to escalate. Alvaro Uribe, a lawyer, was elected Colombian President in May. His promise to fight the drug cartels and the revolutionary armed forces, the paramilitary, was echoed immediately. During his inauguration, the Presidential Palace suffered a grenade attack and 14 were killed in a nearby neighborhood. The Revolutionary Armed Forces of Colombia (FARC) were presumed responsible. The Colombian Diaspora found displaced civilians, fearful of guerrilla abuses, fleeing to Ecuador, Panama, Venezuela, Costa Rica, Mexico, Spain, the United States, and other countries. What will ever end the violence in Colombia? The new millennium confirmed that the conflict is an ongoing, multifaceted problem that involves countries other than Colombia and its four main guerrilla groups: the Revolutionary Armed Forces of Colombia (FARC), the National Liberation Army (ELN), the Popular Liberation Army (EPL), and M-19 (April 19 Movement). Interestingly enough, the latter has become a Colombian political party, recognized by the electorate.

In Aracataca, where Gabriel García Márquez was born, the townspeople rejected a proposal to change the town's name to Macondo to honor the Nobel Prize winner. It was not, however, an outright rejection of the referendum. True, there were not enough votes in favor, but the abstentions were larger than those who voted in favor. Those who voted to support the name change were fewer than the expected 7,400 votes required. According to a newspaper article, "Despite a campaign to whip up support, Mayor Pedro Sánchez did not have the backing needed for the name change, which he said would have brought tourism to this down-at-the-heels town of 53,000 in Colombia's northern banana-growing country."[15] My own visit to Aracataca in July of 2007, however, showed large road signs reading "Aracata-Macondo" as we entered the town to see the house where Gabriel García Márquez was born, the telegraph office where his father worked, the downtown church of San José of Aracataca, the Montessori School where he learned to read, the railroad station, the main street (Calle del Camellón), the few wooden houses with zinc rooftops still standing, the cemetery, and the Aracataca river that gives its name to the town.

NOTES

1. Congresos internacionales de la lengua española, homepage: http://congresodelalengua.es/cartagena/default.htm.

2. http://congresodelalengua.es/cartagena/inauguracion/default.htm.

3. Carlos Fuentes, "Para darle nombre a America," Homenaje a Gabriel García Márquez ("Homage to Gabriel García Márquez"), Congresos Internacionales de la lengua española. http://congresodelalengua.es/cartagena/homenaje/fuentes_carlos.htm.

4. Gabriel García Márquez, "Agradecimiento," Homenaje a Gabriel García Márquez ("Homage to Gabriel García Márquez"), Congresos Internacionales de la lengua española. http://congresodelalengua.es/cartagena/homenaje/garcia_marquez_gabriel.htm.

5. Simon Romero, "The Town's Biggest Event since the Banana Fever Ended," *New York Times*, March 7, 2007. http://nytimes.com/2007/03/07/world/americas/07marquez.html.

6. David Denby, review of *Love in the Time of Cholera*, directed by Mike Newell, *The New Yorker* (New York: November 27, 2007), 104–5.

7. At the Oscars ceremony in February 2008, Javier Bardem won the Oscar for his role as best supporting actor in *No Country for Old Men*.

8. Michiko Kakutani, "Books of the Times: A Family Haunted by the Ghosts of History," review of *Living to Tell the Tale* by Gabriel García Márquez, *The New York Times*, November 11, 2003. http://query.nytimes.com/gst/fullpage.html?res=9504E2DF1E39F932A25752C1A9659C8B63.

9. Gabriel García Márquez, "Homenaje al amigo," *El País*, December 16, 2001. http://www.elpais.com/articulo/cultura/homenaje/amigo/elpepicul/20011216elpepicul_1/Tes.

10. Gabriel García Márquez, "La odisea literaria de un manuscrito," Sololiteratura.com, July 15, 2001. http://www.sololiteratura.com/ggm/marquezlaodisea.htm.

11. Caryn James, "CRITIC'S NOTEBOOK; Online Book Clubs as Lit 101 Fun," *The New York Times*, March 12, 2004. http://query.nytimes.com/gst/fullpage.html?res=9B0CE6DE133EF931A25750C0A9629C8B63&partner=rssnyt&emc=rss.

12. Ibid.

13. Joaquín Marco, "Memoria de mis putas tristes." http://sololiteratura.com/ggm/marquezjoaquin.htm. (The translation is mine.) Joaquín Marco is a well-known author, editor, and essayist whose work is available in Spanish and Catalan. Among his many contributions, his introduction to *One Hundred Years of Solitude*, in Spanish for Austral Collection, is paramount for the García Márquez reader.

14. Monica Corcoran, "Rodrigo García. All About Eves," *New York Times*, October 9, 2005. http://www.nytimes.com/2005/10/09/fashion/sundaystyles/09NITE.html.

15. "Birthplace of 'Magic Realism' Wonders What's in a Name," *New York Times*, June 26, 2006. http://www.nytimes.com/2006/06/26/world/americas/26macondo.html.

Chapter 10

THE READINGS AND THE FRIENDSHIPS

> Aristotle says that there are three kinds of friendship: friendship out of interest or usefulness, friendship out of pleasure, and "perfect friendship, that of good men of similar virtue, because each equally desires the good for the other."
>
> —*Octavio Paz*, The Double Flame, Love and Eroticism

Gabriel García Márquez has captured the attention of readers around the world as a magical realist. Some booklovers see him as synonymous with the term. He, however, is in the company of well-established Latin American writers like Alejo Carpentier from Cuba and Miguel Angel Asturias from Guatemala, who were writing in this style before he did, and whose works were not unfamiliar to García Márquez. They too wrote of a reality where the separation between the rational and the irrational was blurred, and their work is also considered magic realism.

As a child, García Márquez did not enjoy the idyllic experience of having a parent who would read to him before going to bed. Nevertheless, one of his greatest recollections is his first contact with the written word as a five-year-old. As a result of an argument with a bystander, while at a circus tent in town, his maternal grandfather, Colonel Ricardo Márquez Iguarán, gave him a dictionary. "This book [his grandfather told him] not only knows everything, but it is also the only one that is never wrong."[1] The impact of such a gift, we know now, was immeasurable. His grandfather was then the most important person in his life. It is no wonder that scholars like Joaquín Marco have said, "If one pays attention to style, one cannot help but note the lexical precision and the craftsmanship in the treatment of expressions. García Márquez continues to be the best writer in the Spanish language today. The precision with which he uses the lexicon, the tone and gleaming characteristic of his prose have no model; it's all his own."[2] Carlos Fuentes summarized the above quote when he said García Márquez's writing is "a prose full of life with liberating imagination."[3]

During García Márquez's childhood, he started to read school assignments under the direction of teacher Rosa Elena Fergusson. Poetry interested him most, all through his childhood and teenage years. At the Colegio San José, a boarding school in Barranquilla, he began writing poetry. His poetry reading continued at the Liceo Nacional of Zipaquira, yet another boarding school, where he wrote sonnets under the pseudonym Javier Garcés. It was here, as a teenager, that his interest in Marxism and left-wing leanings began. He read Friedrich Engels' *The Origin of the Family, Private Property, and the State*, became familiar with the writing of Karl Marx, but also read William Shakespeare, Sigmund Freud, Saint John of the Cross, and Jules Verne's *Twenty Thousand Leagues under the Sea* and *Around the World in Eighty Days*. He would read anything he could: short stories by Mark Twain, *The Magic Mountain* by the 1929 Nobel Prize winner Thomas Mann, or *The Man in the Iron Mask* by Alexandre Dumas. During these years, Dumas' *The Count of Monte Cristo* was one of García Márquez's favorite books. He read the works of Rubén Darío, José Martí, Pablo Neruda, and other poets, novelists, short-story writers, and essayists, under the guidance of his teacher, Carlos Calderón Hermida, who encouraged García Márquez to write.

Although seldom mentioned, his readings included work prescribed by the Colombian Ministry of Education: the canon of classical Spanish readings and selected texts from different periods of Spanish and universal letters. Among many others was Colombia's own José Eustasio Rivera, author of *The Vortex*; *The Literary Experience*, by Mexican poet and essayist Alfonso Reyes; novels by Venezuelan Rómulo Gallegos; and works by Garcilazo de la Vega, Francisco de Quevedo, Lope de Vega, Juan Ramon Jiménez, and Federico García Lorca. In his spare time, he came into contact with the sensuous poetry of French poet Paul Valéry. When he finished high school, he was awarded what he considered an unforgettable book: *Lives of Famous Philosophers*, by Diogenes Laercio. While his love for literature was intrinsic to his persona, algebra and mathematics were of least interest to him.

When he enrolled in college, at 20 years old, his readings and friendships reached a new level. It was as if his friends from high school had vanished. Their images and names flicker in and out of his memoir, *Living to Tale the Tale*. Once in college, he read Franz Kafka's *The Metamorphosis* and met Camilo Torres Restrepo. Reading Kafka would trigger his ambition to write, and, according to many critics, would influence his writing. This influence is most visible in the short stories compiled in his book *Eyes of a Blue Dog*. *The Metamorphosis* affected him because of the strong connection he felt with the stories he had heard from his grandmother during his childhood. Camilo Torres, who later became a priest and a member of the National Liberation Army (ELN), was one of the first of the lifelong friends he would make at a young age. Their solid friendship led García Márquez to ask Camilo Torres to baptize his firstborn son, Rodrigo.

After the Czech-born Franz Kafka, whose novels depict the alienation of mankind, García Márquez began to move from reading poetry to reading novels. It was around this time that his literary fascination embraced the Russians, Fyodor Dostoyevsky and Leo Tolstoy, among other authors dealing with the theme of the double. This theme is visible throughout García Márquez's oeuvre. Dostoyevsky's ability to write about the divided self in novels like *The Double* or *The Poor Folk* must have sparked García Márquez's desire to experiment with the subject. Both Dostoyevsky and Tolstoy are considered among the most influential writers of the Western world. They are considered the best Russian novelists of all time. Imagine García Márquez reading Tolstoy's *War and Peace* and *Anna Karenina* while a freshman in college, and it is easy to picture the 20-year-old Colombian not having time to read the assignments for his law courses.

His literary thirst, his desire to be conversant with his friends and acquaintances, drove him to read Flaubert and Stendhal. Gustave Flaubert's masterpiece, *Madame Bovary*, was a self-imposed obligatory reading, as was Stendhal's *The Red and the Black*. It was then, García Márquez wrote in *Living to Tell the Tale*, that he started to read the Argentines Jorge Luis Borges, Felisberto Hernández, and Julio Cortázar, and the English writers Aldous Huxley, D. H. Lawrence, and Graham Greene. The latter was to become his friend at a time when Gabriel García Márquez was more famous than Graham Greene ever was. Greene, nevertheless, was influential in García Márquez's depiction of the Caribbean dictator in his novel *The Autumn of the Patriarch*. While the theme of "the double," for García Márquez, can be traced as far back as his readings of Dostoyevsky, Borges also wrote and developed the theme to perfection. As a 20-year-old, in 1947, reading the abovementioned authors must have been challenging for García Márquez. But in spite of this, he read James Joyce's *Ulysses* and *Finnegans Wake*. All titles were in translation, of course. The only language he spoke then was Spanish. With the passage of time and having lived in Europe, he learned Italian and French, and is also conversant in English.

In the 1940s, in Latin America, poetry was still at the forefront in the world of letters. The leading authors were Vicente Huidobro and Pablo Neruda, both from Chile, but there were others, like Peruvian poet César Vallejo and Cuban Nicolás Guillén. In the mid-1950s, while García Márquez was living in Paris, he became friends with Nicolás Guillén and, years later, in the 1970s, with Pablo Neruda. His friendship with Neruda, 1971 Nobel Prize winner, became legendary as they traveled together. Neruda would introduce Gabo to people of great power in the world of politics, art, and letters. One of them was President François Mitterrand. Neruda brought them together at a dinner party at Neruda's home in Paris, years before Mitterrand became president. Pablo Neruda was then ambassador for Chile to France under the government of President Salvador Allende. Gabo's friendship with Mitterrand lasted through the years. When Mitterrand was inaugurated as French President in 1981, Gabo and his wife, Mercedes, were special guests. His friendship with heads of state other than Mitterrand and Castro included Salvador Allende and Omar Torrijos, and years later, President Bill Clinton. That friendship began in the summer of 1995, at William Styron's summer home in Martha's Vineyard.

As a freshman in college, in 1947, his voracious reading would lead to absenteeism and eventually to dropping out of school without completing his sophomore year. That year, however, his close friend Camilo Torres introduced him to journalist Plinio Apuleyo Mendoza. The friendship with Apuleyo Mendoza would not only stand the test of time, but also lead García Márquez to find a lifelong passion for journalism. Years later, the young friends would confirm the strength of their friendship when Father Camilo Torres baptized García Márquez's son, Rodrigo, and Apuleyo Mendoza became the baby's godfather.

The following year, in Cartagena, García Márquez landed his first job as a journalist when he was hired to write for *El Universal*. What García Márquez found in Clemente Manuel Zabala, in 1948 at *El Universal*, was more of a mentorship than a friendship, although the two were not mutually exclusive. Zabala was the first to read and edit all the original drafts of *Leaf Storm*.[4] From his work at *El Universal*, we know that he had, in fact, read Aldous Huxley's *Brave New World* and *Point Counter Point*, that he was familiar with the Irish dramatist George Bernard Shaw, and had read some of the works of William Faulkner: *As I lay Dying*, *The Sound and the Fury*, and *Light of August*. In the same category as Clemente Manuel Zabala—boss and friend at *El Universal* and another important figure Gabo met and with whom he remained friends—was Víctor Nieto Núñez. The latter celebrated García Márquez's 80th birthday in 2007, at the Cartagena International Film Festival, with a tribute to the Nobel-Prize winning author. Víctor Nieto Núñez is the director of the festival.

Gabo's newspaper commentaries in *El Universal*, in 1949, confirmed his familiarity with the writings of the Americans Edgar Allan Poe, Nathaniel Hawthorne's *House of the Seven Gables*, and *Moby Dick* by Herman Melville. He was also familiar with the English essayist Thomas De Quincy, and the detective stories of Americans Willard Huntington Wright—better known by his pseudonym S. S. Van Dine—and Ellery Queen, pseudonym of Frederic Dannay.

In Barranquilla, Colombia, at the end of 1949, he met two mentors and friends who would affect his life forever: José Felix Fuenmayor and Ramón Vinyes (the Wise Catalan who is referenced in *One Hundred Years of Solitude*). Along with Vinyes, there were three other seminal friends with whom he would retain close ties forever: Alvaro Zepeda Zamudio, Germán Vargas, and Alfonso Fuenmayor (son of José Felix Fuenmayor). In literary circles, these friends are referred to as the Barranquilla Group. These were friends with a much more ample literary formation than García Márquez and helped shape his literary worldviews. Their meeting places were two bars, Bar Happy, and The Cave (La Cueva). In 2004, The Cave reopened as a museum, restaurant, and cultural center in Barranquilla.

It was there that his friends provided the young García Márquez with copies of *A Journal of the Plague Year* by Daniel Defoe, and *The Counterfeiters* by the 1947 Nobel Prize winner, André Gide. Alvaro Zepeda gave him Virginia Woolf's *Mrs. Dalloway* as a gift. No longer attending law school, García Márquez's voracious reading included works by John Dos Passos, Ernest Hemingway, John Steinbeck, and Erskine Caldwell. Influenced by his reading of Virginia Woolf's *Mrs. Dalloway*, while he was working for the Barranquilla newspaper *El Heraldo* and spending his time drinking rum with friends at The Cave, García Márquez signed his journalist work with the name "Septimus."

His reading around this time included Arthur Rimbaud, Paul Verlaine, Alain Fournier, and American novelist Truman Capote. Fournier's only novel, *The Grand Meaulnes*, became one of Gabo's favorite books. In high school, he had read Homer's epic poems, the *Iliad* and the *Odyssey*. On the other hand, influenced by the members of the Barranquilla Group, he took a strong and special interest in reading Sophocles' *Antigone* and *Oedipus the King*. In the early 1950s, the two friends who helped García Márquez expand his scattered literary foundation were indeed members of the Barranquilla Group: Alfonso Fuenmayor and German Vargas.

Ramón Vinyes had died in 1952. To honor the memory of Ramón Vinyes, "The Wise Catalan," an auditorium bearing his name is being built at the back of the House-Museum where Gabriel García Márquez was born. His literary readings, on the other hand, were complemented with his readings and reviews about film during 1953 and 1954.

The following year, a 28-year-old García Márquez left for Europe for the first time. He traveled to Switzerland and then moved to Italy. He lived in Rome for a short time. It was enough time, however, to study film at the Centro Sperimentale di Cinematografia, where he forged a lasting friendship with Argentine Fernando Birri. Fernando Birri is co-founder with García Márquez of the International School of Cinema, Television, and Video in San Antonio de los Baños, in Cuba. Birri has worked with Gabo on many film projects and adaptations.

In 1955, García Márquez traveled to Poland and Czechoslovakia, and then moved from Rome to Paris. Once in Paris, he found himself unemployed. His friends from the Barranquilla Group sent him money from time to time, and Apuleyo Mendoza gave him the opportunity to write, from Paris, for *Elite* magazine in Caracas. Apuleyo Mendoza was the editor in chief of the magazine. It was in the company of Apuleyo Mendoza and his sister, Soledad, that Gabo made the trip he published as *90 Days behind the Iron Curtain*.

Plinio Apuleyo Mendoza is among the friends Gabo made in his early years and the one who helped him the most during the two and half years of García Márquez's first stay in Europe. Plinio has witnessed the passage of time through the new millennium. He is among the few friends still left from the late 1940s and 1950s. His friendship with Gabo might be legendary, but when García Márquez married Mercedes Barcha on Friday, March 21, 1958, Plinio Apuleyo Mendoza was not at the wedding.

García Márquez came to live in Mexico City in July of 1961. He was a relatively unknown writer, married, and the father of a two-year-old son. His good luck, once again, upon arrival, was having a friend as close as Colombian writer Alvaro Mutis, who was then living in the Mexican megalopolis. The two had been friends since Gabo was 20 years old, over 60 years ago. Mutis introduced García Márquez to Carlos Fuentes the following year. Fuentes was, at that time, one of the movers and shakers of culture in Mexico, both in cinema and literature. Gabriel García Márquez could not have hoped for a better entrance into the Mexican milieu of arts and letters. Carlos Fuentes, as he recalled in the tribute speech he gave in Cartagena, at the IV International Congress of the Spanish Language in 2007, had already read García Márquez's first novel, *Leaf Storm*. Their friendship started right there and then, in 1962, in Mexico City. As

Carlos Fuentes had put it, their friendship began "with the instantaneity of the eternal."[5] The friendship Gabo had with Carlos Fuentes and Alvaro Mutis would lead him to many other friendships and, eventually, to the fulfillment of García Márquez's ambition of making films and writing without having to hold down a different kind of job. Carlos Fuentes was also directly responsible for García Márquez's reception in the English-speaking world, before *One Hundred Years of Solitude* was published in English in 1970.

Among the friends and acquaintances Gabo met through Carlos Fuentes and Alvaro Mutis are Juan Rulfo, Manuel Barbachano, Carlos Monsiváis, José Emilio Pacheco, Elena Poniatowska, Homero Aridjis, and Luis Buñuel, among many others. Carlos Fuentes has remained one of Gabriel García Márquez's closest friends. Fuentes, along with Juan Rulfo and Manuel Barbachano, were influential in García Márquez's ambition to make films during the 1960s in Mexico. García Márquez's talent was recognized by his Mexican friends, but their power and connections accelerated Gabo's success. Among the many memorable events that took place in Mexico City, where García Márquez still keeps a house and spends more time than anywhere else, were the birth of his second son, Gonzalo, and the writing of *One Hundred Years of Solitude*.

Before 1967 was over, the year when *One Hundred Years of Solitude* was published, García Márquez had met Peruvian writer and essayist Mario Vargas Llosa. They met in Venezuela, at an International Congress where Vargas Llosa was awarded the Rómulo Gallegos Prize for his novel *The Green House*. By 1971, Vargas Llosa's friendship with García Márquez was showcased in Vargas Llosa's book *The Story of a Deicide* (*Historia de un deicidio*), considered one of the most complete works about Gabriel García Márquez and *One Hundred Years of Solitude*. The book, in fact, was Vargas Llosa's doctoral dissertation. Both García Márquez and his wife, Mercedes, provided Vargas Llosa with personal information for the book. Theirs was a friendship that became newsworthy around the globe in 2007, when García Márquez turned 80 years old, but the reason for this was not pleasant. Thirty-one years earlier, in 1976, the two had had a feud over accusations of betrayal and adultery on the part of Gabo.

When Gabo lived in Barcelona, American writer William Kennedy visited him in his apartment. Kennedy's interview (see Chapter 5) confirms some of the authors mentioned above, but also adds new ones: Polish-born English novelist Joseph Conrad, Greek biographer Plutarch, Austrian poet, essayist, and short-story writer Stefan Zweig, Scottish novelist A. J. Cronin (in full, Archibald Joseph Cronin), François Rabelais, and British author Frederick Forsyth. When asked about his influences, García

Márquez mentioned Graham Greene and William Faulkner as foremost. We can add that Sophocles is also an influential and visible influence in his work, particularly in the apprenticeship years and up to 1967.

During the 1970s, García Márquez was almost as famous as Fidel Castro. Their friendship, however, reached the limelight in 1971, in part due to the Padilla Affair (see Chapter 6). Their friendship has been questioned by many, some of García Márquez's friends included. He, nevertheless, continued his closeness with the Cuban dictator who, in February of 2008, stepped down after 49 years as head of state. Throughout the 1980s and 1990s, the two were photographed at all sorts of public functions. It is obvious that García Márquez sees Fidel Castro as a friend. He sees him as a whole person, not just as a politician and head of state. An example of this can be found in the introduction García Márquez wrote for a book Castro published, called *Fidel: My Early Years*. Fidel Castro, he said, "is a man of austere ways and insatiable illusions, with an old-fashioned formal education, of cautious words and simple manners and incapable of conceiving any idea which is not out of the ordinary."[6] (For more on their friendship, see Chapter 8.)

When Gabriel García Márquez was in Stockholm in 1982 to receive the Nobel Prize, 40 of his close friends accompanied him. Other than Alvaro Mutis, Alfonso Fuenmayor, and Germán Vargas (mentioned earlier in the chapter), his longtime friend, "vallenato" musician Rafael Escalona, attended the Nobel celebration with him. Escalona later wrote a song to honor García Márquez, titled "Estocolmo" ("Stockholm").

A friend for whom García Márquez felt special affection was Julio Cortázar. The two traveled together, along with Carlos Fuentes, and spent quality time in Barcelona, Paris, and other European cities. He once wrote that Julio Cortázar "was the most impressive person I had the chance to meet."[7] While Cortázar did not work on any special projects with Gabo, his longtime friend Tomás Eloy Martínez did. He helped García Márquez launch the New Iberian-American Journalism Foundation in 1994, headquartered in Cartagena, Colombia. Faithful to his long-time friends, Gabo gave two reading rooms of the journalistic institution the names Alvaro Cepeda Samudio (1926–1972) and Clemente Manuel Zabala (1921–1963). Alvaro Cepeda was a member of the Barranquilla Group. Clemente Manuel Zabala, on the other hand, was a mentor for García Márquez while Gabo was an apprentice at Cartagena's *El Universal* daily newspaper.

He has many more friends than those listed here; there are those he has done business with and with whom he kept ties, but are seldom reported. There are those who are not necessarily in the political arena or whose names would be unrecognizable to the average reader. Two of these friends were filmmaker Luis Alcoriza and his wife, Janet. He gave them the only existing galleys of *One Hundred Years of Solitude*. The inscription he wrote reads: "From the friend who loves you most in this world ["Del amigo que más los quiere en este mundo], Gabo." The dedication was signed in 1967.

NOTES

1. García Márquez, *Living to Tell the Tale*, 90 (see chap. 1, n. 1).
2. Marco, "Memoria de mis putas tristes" (see chap. 9, n. 14). (The translation of the quote is mine.)
3. Fuentes, "Para darle nombre a America" ("Homage to Gabriel García Márquez") (see chap. 9, n. 4).
4. Arango, *Un ramo*, 107–6 (see chap. 2, n. 10).
5. Fuentes, "Para darle nombre a America" ("Homage to Gabriel García Márquez") (see chap. 9, n. 4). http://congresodelalengua.es/cartagena/homenaje/carlos_fuentes.htm.
6. García Márquez, *Fidel: My Early Years*, back cover (see chap. 8, n. 15).
7. García Márquez, *Notas de prensa: Obra periodística 5*, 607 (see chap. 7, n. 1).

SELECTED BIBLIOGRAPHY

WORKS BY GABRIEL GARCÍA MÁRQUEZ
(IN ENGLISH TRANSLATION AND WORKS CITED
FROM HIS JOURNALISM COLLECTION)

No One Writes to the Colonel and Other Stories. Translated by J. S. Bernstein. New York: Harper & Row, 1968.

One Hundred Years of Solitude. Translated by Gregory Rabassa. New York: Perennial Classics, 1998.

Leaf Storm and Other Stories. Translated by Gregory Rabassa. New York: Harper & Row, 1972.

Cuando era feliz e indocumentado. Barcelona: Plaza & Janés, 1975.

The Autumn of the Patriarch. Translated by Gregory Rabassa. New York: Harper & Row, 1976.

De viaje por los países socialistas: 90 días en la "Cortina de hierro." Colombia: Ediciones Macondo, 1978.

Innocent Eréndira and Other Stories. Translated by Gregory Rabassa. New York: Harper & Row, 1978.

In Evil Hour. Translated by Gregory Rabassa. New York: Harper & Row, 1979. New York: Harper Perennial, 1991.

Obra periodística 2, Entre Cachacos. Compiled by Jacques Gilard. Bogotá, Colombia: Editorial Norma, 1982.

Chronicle of a Death Foretold. Translated by Gregory Rabassa. New York: Knopf, 1983.

Obra periodística 3, De Europa y América. Compiled by Jacques Gilard. Bogotá, Colombia: Editorial Norma, 1983.

Collected Stories. Translated by Gregory Rabassa and J. S. Bernstein. New York: Harper Perennial, 1999.
The Story of a Shipwrecked Sailor. Translated by Randolph Hogan. New York: Knopf, 1986.
Clandestine in Chile. The Adventures of Miguel Littín. Translated by Asa Zatz. New York: Henry Holt, 1987.
Love in the Time of Cholera. Translated by Edith Grossman. New York: Knopf, 1988. New York: Knopf, 1997.
"The Solitude of Latin America (Nobel Lecture, 1982)." Translated by Marina Castañeda. *Gabriel García Márquez and the Power of Fiction*. Edited by Julio Ortega. The Texas Pan American Series. Austin: University of Texas, 1988.
Collected Novellas: Leaf Storm, No One Writes to the Colonel, Chronicle of a Death Foretold. Translated by Gregory Rabassa and J. S. Bernstein. New York: HarperCollins, 1990. New York: Perennial Classics, 1999.
The General in His Labyrinth. Translated by Edith Grossman. London: Jonathan Cape, 1991.
Notas de prensa: Obra periodística 5 (1961–1984). Barcelona: Mondadori, 1991.
The World of Marquez: A Photographic Exploration of Macondo. Text by Gabriel García Márquez. Photographs by Hannes Wallrafen. London: Ryan Publishing, 1992.
Strange Pilgrims. Translated by Edith Grossman. New York: Knopf, 1993. New York: Penguin Books, 1994.
Of Love and Other Demons. Translated by Edith Grossman. New York: Knopf, 1995. New York: Penguin Books, 1996.
Obra periodística 1, Textos Costeños. Compiled by Jacques Gilard. Bogotá, Colombia: Editorial Norma, 1997.
News of a Kidnapping. Translated by Edith Grossman. New York: Knopf, 1997. New York: Penguin Books, 1998.
Por la libre, Obra periodística 4 (1974–1995). Colombia: Editorial Norma, 1999.
Living to Tell the Tale. Translated by Edith Grossman. New York: Alfred A. Knopf, 2003.

SPANISH-LANGUAGE WORKS BY GABRIEL GARCÍA MARQUÉZ

La Hojarasca. Bogotá: Organización Continental de los Festivales del Libro, 1960.
Funerales de la Mamá Grande. Xalapa: Universidad Veracruzana, 1962.
El coronel no tiene quien le escriba. México: Ediciones Era, 1963.
Cien años de soledad. Buenos Aires: Editorial Sudamericana, 1967.
La mala hora. México: Ediciones Era, 1967.

La increíble y triste historia de la cándida Eréndira y de su abuela desalmada. Buenos Aires: Editorial Sudamericana, 1972.
Cuando era feliz e indocumentado. Barcelona: Plaza & Janés, 1975.
El otoño del patriarca. Buenos Aires: Editorial Sudamericana, 1975.
Todos los cuentos de Gabriel García Márquez. La Habana: Casa de las Américas, 1977.
De viaje por los países socialistas: 90 días en la "Cortina de hierro." Colombia: Ediciones Macondo, 1978.
Relato de un naúfrago, que estuvo diez días a la deriva en una balsa. Barcelona: Tusquets, 1979.
El olor de la guayaba: conversaciones con Plinio Apuleyo Mendoza. Bogotá: Editorial La Oveja Negra, 1982.
Obra periodística 2, Entre Cachacos. Bogotá: Editorial Norma, 1982.
Obra periodística 3, De Europa y América. Bogotá: Editorial Norma, 1983.
El amor en los tiempos del cólera. Barcelona: Bruguera, 1985.
La aventura de Miguel Littín, clandestino en Chile. Buenos Aires: Editorial Sudamericana, 1986.
El General en su laberinto. Colombia: Editorial La Oveja Negra, 1989.
Notas de prensa: Obra periodística 5 (1961–1984). Barcelona: Mondadori, 1991.
Del amor y otros demonios. Barcelona: Mondadori, 1992.
Doce cuentos peregrinos. Buenos Aires: Editorial Sudamericana, 1992.
Diatriba de amor contra un hombre sentado. Barcelona: Grijalbo, 1995.
Noticia de un secuestro. Barcelona: Mondadori, 1996.
Obra periodística 1, Textos Costeños. Bogotá: Editorial Norma, 1997.
Por la libre, Obra periodística 4. Bogotá: Editorial Norma, 1999.
Vivir para contarla. Barcelona: Mondadori, 2002.
Memorias de mis putas tristes. Barcelona: Mondadori, 2004.

BIOGRAPHICAL INFORMATION AND INTERVIEWS

Anderson, John Lee. "The Power of García Márquez." *The New Yorker,* September 27, 1999.
Apuleyo Mendoza, Plinio. *In Conversation with Gabriel García Márquez: The Fragrance of Guava.* Translated by Ann Wright. London: Verso, 1983.
———. *Aquellos tiempos con Gabo.* Barcelona: Plaza & Janés, 2000.
Arango, Gustavo. *Un ramo de no me olvides: Gabriel García Márquez en El Universal.* Cartagena, Colombia: El Universal, 1995.
Baldwin, Stanley. *Gabriel García Márquez: His Life and Works.* New York: Spark Notes, 2003.

Bell-Villada, Gene H. *García Márquez: The Man and His Work*. Chapel Hill, North Carolina: University of North Carolina Press, 1990.

———. Ed. *Conversations with Gabriel García Márquez*. Jackson, Mississippi: University Press of Mississippi, 2006.

Gabriel García Márquez: Tales beyond Solitude. Videocassette. Directed by Holly Aylett and produced by Sylvia Stevens. London: Luna Films Limited, 1989.

Guibert, Rita. "Gabriel García Márquez." *Seven Voices: Seven Latin American Writers Talk to Rita Guibert*. Trans. Frances Partridge. New York: Random House, 1973.

Saldívar, Dasso. *El viaje a la semilla: la biografía*. Madrid: Santillana, 1977.

Simons, Marlise. "A Talk with Gabriel García Márquez." *Gabriel García Márquez. A Study of the Short Fiction*. Ed. Harley D. Oberhelman. Boston: Twayne Publishers, 1991.

———. "The Best Years of His Life: An Interview with Gabriel García Márquez." *New York Times Book Review*, 11 April 1988.

Vargas Llosa, Mario. *García Márquez: Historia de un deicidio*. Barcelona, Spain: Barral, 1971.

SUGGESTIONS FOR FURTHER READING AND WORKS CITED

Bell, Michael. *Gabriel García Márquez: Solitude and Solidarity—Modern Novelist*. New York: St. Martin's Press, 1993.

Bell-Villada, Gene H. *NOVEL: A Forum on Fiction* 18, no. 3. (Spring 1985): 281–284. http://www.jstor.org/stable/1345796.

Bloom, Harold, ed. *Gabriel García Márquez: Modern Critical Views*. New York: Chelsea House Publishers, 1989.

Bohlen, Celestine. "Heberto Padilla, 68, Cuban Poet, Is Dead." *The New York Times*, September 28, 2000.

Bodtorf Clark, Gloria Jeanne. *A Synergy of Styles: Art and Artifact in Gabriel García Márquez*. New York: UP of America, 1999.

Canfield, Martha L. *Gabriel García Márquez*. Bogotá: Procultura, 1991.

Christian, Shirley. "García Márquez's First Play Gets Mixed Reviews." *New York Times*, August 25, 1988. http://query.nytimes.com/gst/fullpage.html?res=9 40DEEDD163EF936A1575BC0A96E948260.

Cobo Borda, Juan Gustavo. *Para llegar a García Márquez*. Bogotá, Colombia: Ediciones Temas de Hoy, 1997.

———. *Repertorio crítico sobre Gabriel García Márquez*. Vol. 2. Bogotá: Instituto Caro y Cuervo, 1995.

———. *Para que mis amigos me quieran más—: homenaje a Gabriel García Márquez*. Bogotá: Siglo del Hombre, 1992.

Denby, David. Review of *Love in the Time of Cholera*, directed by Mike Newell. *The New Yorker*. New York: November 27, 2007.

Fuentes, Carlos. "Para darle nombre a America", Homenaje a Gabriel García Márquez, Congresos Internacionales de la lengua española. http://congresodelalengua.es/cartagena/homenaje/carlos_fuentes.htm.

———. *Gabriel García Márquez and the Invention of America*. Liverpool: Liverpool UP, 1987.

Gabriel García Márquez: Magic and Reality, videocassette. Directed by Ana Cristina Navarro and produced by Harold Mantell. Princeton, NJ: Films for the Humanities, Inc., 1981.

García Márquez, Gabriel Eligio. *Tras las claves de Melquiades: historia de Cien años de soledad*. Colombia: Editorial Norma, 2001.

González, Aníbal. "Translation and the Novel: *One Hundred Years of Solitude*." In *Gabriel García Márquez: Modern Critical Views*, ed. Harold Bloom. New York: Chelsea House Publishers, 1989.

Gussow, Mel. Review of *Crónica de una muerte*, directed by Salvador Tavora, Festival Latino in New York. *New York Times*, August 3, 1990. http://query.nytimes.com/gst/fullpage.html?res=9C0CE2DB163BF930A3575BC0A966958260.

Harss, Luis, and Barbara Dohmann. *Into the Mainstream: Conversations with Latin American Writers*. New York: Harper & Row, 1966.

James, Caryn. "CRITIC'S NOTEBOOK; Online Book Clubs as Lit 101 Fun." *New York Times*, March 1, 2004. http://query.nytimes.com/gst/fullpage.html?res=9B0CE6DE133EF931A25750C0A9629C8B63&partner=rssnyt&emc=rss.

Janes, Regina. *One Hundred Years of Solitude: Modes of Reading*. Boston: Twayne Publishers, 1991.

Kafka, Franz. *The Complete Stories*. Edited by Nahum N. Glatzer and translated by Willa and Edwin Muir. New York: Schocken Books, 1971.

Kakutani, Michiko. "Books of the Times; A Family Haunted by the Ghosts of History." Review of *Living to Tell the Tale*, by Gabriel García Márquez. *New York Times*, November 11, 2003. http://query.nytimes.com/gst/fullpage.html?res=9504E2DF1E39F932A25752C1A9659C8B63.

———. "Books of the Times; Magical Realism from 2 Cultures." *New York Times*. June 2, 1995. http://query.nytimes.com/gst/fullpage.html?res=9800E1DC1639F931A35755C0A.

———. "Books of the Times; The Human behind the Heroic Pose." Review of *The General in His Labyrinth*, by Gabriel García Márquez. *New York Times*, September 11, 1990. http://query.nytimes.com/gst/fullpage.html?res=9C0CE2DA143AF932A2575AC0A966958260.

Marco, Joaquín. *Memoria de mis putas tristes*. http://sololiteratura.com/ggm/marquezjoaquin.htm.

McNerney, Katheleen. *Understanding Gabriel García Márquez*. University of South Carolina Press, 1989.
Ortega, Julio. *Gabriel García Márquez and the Powers of Fiction*. Austin: UT Press, 1988.
Parr, James. *Don Quijote: An Anatomy of Subversive Discourse*. Newark, Delaware: Juan de la Cuesta, 1988.
Paz, Octavio. *The Double Flame, Love and Eroticism*. Translated by Helen Lane. New York: Harcourt Brace & Company, 1995.
Pelayo, Rubén. *Gabriel García Márquez: A Critical Companion*. Westport, CT: Greenwood Press, 2001.
Porras del Campo, Angel Esteban and Stephanie Panichelli. Translated by Diane Stockwell. *Gabo and Fidel: Portrait of a Friendship*. Miami, FL: Planeta, 2005.
Pynchon, Thomas. "The Heart's Eternal Vow." Review of *Love in the Time of Cholera*, by Gabriel García Márquez. *New York Times*, April 10, 1988. http://www.nytimes.com/books/97/05/18/reviews/pynchon-cholera.html.
Solanet, Mariana and Bergandi, Hector L. *García Márquez para principiantes*. Argentina: Era Naciente RSL, 1999.
Stone, Peter H. *Latin American Writers at Work, The Paris Review*. Edited by George Plimpton, 2003.
———. *The Paris Review Interviews, II*. New York: Picador, 2007.
Wood, Michael. *Gabriel García Márquez: One Hundred Years of Solitude*. Cambridge: Cambridge University Press, 1990.

INTERNET SOURCES

García Márquez, Gabriel. Home page. http://www.themodernworld.com/gabo/.
García Márquez, Gabriel. "The Solitude of Latin America." Nobel Lecture. December 8, 1982 *Nobel Lectures, Literature 1981–1990*. Editor-in-Charge Tore Frängsmyr. Editor Sture Allén. World Scientific Co., Singapore, 1993. http://www.nobelprize.org/nobel_prizes/literature/laureates/1982/marquez-lecture-e.html.
García Márquez, Gabriel. "Agradecimiento, Homenaje a Gabriel García Márquez." Congresos Internacionales de la lengua española. http://www.congresodelalengua.es/cartagena/homenaje/garcia_marquez_gabriel.html.
Centro Virtual Cervantes. http://www.cvc.cervantes.es/ACTCULT/garcia_marquez/cronologia.html.
http://www.themodernworld.com/gabo/gabo_films_movies.html.

INDEX

Allende, Isabel, 4, 112
Apuleyo Mendoza, Plinio, 7, 20, 38, 41, 49, 68, 83, 102, 144, 146
Aracataca, 1–13, 20, 25, 32, 55, 70, 85, 103, 105, 129, 131
Asturias, Miguel Angel, 9, 66, 96, 103, 142
Autumn of the Patriarch, The, 74–75, 92–94, 96–97, 100, 111, 116, 143

Barranquilla, 7, 15, 24, 28, 38, 41, 142, 145
Bell-Villada, Gene H., 7, 16, 24
Big Mama's Funeral, 37, 39, 58, 64, 73, 127
"Blackman, the Good Vendor of Miracles," 75
Bloom, Harold, 71
"Blue Lobster, The," 34
Bogotazo, 16, 21, 25, 28
Boom, 66, 84
Borges, Jorge Luis, 17, 19, 66, 71, 73, 82, 96, 103, 143
Buñuel, Luis, 35, 60, 91, 133, 147

Carpentier, Alejo, 9, 66, 141
Cartagena, 9, 21, 23, 27–28, 32, 70, 79, 87, 120, 123, 127, 130, 144, 148
Castro, Fidel, 43–44, 49, 68–69, 78, 83, 85, 93, 95, 102, 104–5, 123, 125, 131, 148
Cervantes, 4, 81, 130, 134
Chronicle of a Death Foretold, 3, 22, 93, 95, 101, 106, 109, 111, 117, 119
Clandestine in Chile, 22, 109
Colonel Nicolás Ricardo Márquez Mejía, 1, 32, 108
Cortázar, Julio, 4, 65–66, 71, 73, 82–83, 96, 107, 130, 134, 143, 148

"Dangerous Loves," 110
Dante, 4, 132
"Dialogue with the Mirror," 24, 116
Don Quixote, 4, 68, 79, 129–30
"Don't Fool with Love," 116
Dos Passos, John, 25, 146
Dostoyevsky, Fyodor, 19, 143

INDEX

Eréndira, 22, 55, 75, 88–89, 106, 118
"Eva Is Inside Her Cat," 19
"Eyes of a Blue Dog," 116, 121, 143

Flaubert, Gustave, 19, 71, 143
Fragrance of Guava, The, 7, 40, 102
Fuenmayor, Alfonso, 25, 27, 33, 104, 145, 148
Fuenmayor, José Félix, 24–25, 27, 145
Fuentes, Carlos, 4, 52, 54, 58, 60, 65–67, 71, 78–79, 82–83, 85, 87, 107, 119, 130, 142, 146–48

Gaitán, Jorge Eliécer, 20, 25, 50, 56
García Lorca, Federico, 4, 142
García Márquez, Gabriel: early years, 3–6, 8–10; education, 15–16, 20–23, 31; family life, 44–45, 51; marriage, 42; Nobel Prize, 99
General in His Labyrinth, The, 110–11, 115
González Bermejo, Ernesto, 81–82
Guajira, La, 3
Guevara, Ernesto (Che), 43, 49, 51, 85, 132–33

"Handsomest Drowned Man in the World, The," 75–76
Hemingway, Ernest, 22, 25–27, 52, 117, 145
Huidobro, Vicente, 18, 20, 144

In Evil Hour, 21, 39, 55–57, 59, 64, 73, 106, 137
"I Only Came to Use the Phone," 95

"I Sell My Dreams," 118
Journey to the Seed, The, 123
Joyce, James, 19, 72, 143

Kafka, Franz, 16–17, 143

"Last Voyage of the Ghost Ship, The," 75
Leaf Storm, 3, 11, 22, 28, 35, 44–45, 64–66, 73, 87, 144, 146
"Light Is Like Water," 95
Living to Tell the Tale, 6–7, 9, 16–17, 25, 41, 68, 133, 135, 143
Love in the Time of Cholera, 3, 8, 101, 107–8, 110–13, 131–32, 136
"Love's Diatribe against a Seated Man," 109

Magic realism, 141
"María Dos Prazeres," 95
Masetti, Jorge Ricardo, 44, 49–50
Memories of My Melancholy Whores, 22, 136–37
Mistral, Gabriela, 26, 40
Mitterrand, Françoise, 84–85, 101, 103, 112, 134, 144
"Monologue of Isabel Watching It Rain in Macondo," 10–11, 28, 107
"Montiel's Widow," 21, 41, 109

Neruda, Pablo, 4, 6, 19, 26, 82, 84, 86, 96, 118, 134, 142, 144
News of a Kidnapping, 22, 120, 122, 126, 135
Nobel Prize, 12, 17, 19, 25–27, 78, 84, 100, 104, 108, 111
No One Writes to the Colonel, 21, 39, 46, 56–57, 59, 64–67, 70–71, 73, 111, 125

INDEX

Of Love and Other Demons, 23, 121, 136
One Hundred Years of Solitude, 2, 3, 6, 11, 13, 25, 42, 49, 54–56, 59, 63–64, 67, 69, 70–71, 75, 78, 81, 87, 92, 94, 101, 103–4, 108, 111, 118, 120, 123
Onetti, Juan Carlos, 66

Padilla Affair, 83–85, 148
Paz, Octavio, 4, 19, 54, 83–84, 87, 96, 115, 123
Pelayo, Rubén, 134
Pinochet, Augusto, 6, 74, 89, 97, 108, 111–12
Poe, Edgar Allan, 23–24, 145
Porrúa, Francisco, 67

Riohacha, 3
Roh, Franz, 9
Rojas Pinilla, Gustavo, 29, 34, 39, 44, 57
Rulfo, Juan, 52, 58, 60, 66, 82, 134, 147

"Saturday Night Thief," 116
"Sea of Lost Time, The," 54–55, 57
Shakespeare, 4, 116, 142
Steinbeck, John, 25, 145
Stendhal, 19, 143
"Story of a Deicide," 78, 96, 147

"Story of a Shipwrecked Sailor, The," 22, 81
Strange Pilgrims, 10, 118

"There Are No Thieves in This Town," 58, 60
Third Resignation, The, 17–19, 46
Thousand Days War, 1–2
"Time to Die, A," 59, 107, 22
Tolstoy, Leo, 19, 143
Torres, Camilo, 17, 20, 45, 143–44
"Tuesday Siesta," 11
"Two Way Mirror, The," 116

United Fruit Company, 2, 11
Uribe, Rafael, 1

Vallejo, Cesar, 19, 144
Vargas Llosa, Mario, 4, 41, 51, 66, 71–72, 78, 83–84, 87, 93–94, 96, 126, 147
"Very Old Man with Enormous Wings, A," 38, 75–76, 137
Vinyes, Ramón, 24–25, 28, 145–46

Walsh, Rodolfo, 45, 49–50
"Winter Time," 28
Woolf, Virginia, 24–26, 73, 145

Zalamea Borda, Eduardo, 18, 45
Zepeda Zamudio, Alvaro, 25, 145

About the Author

RUBEN PELAYO, Ph.D., is Professor of twentieth-century Latin American literature at Southern Connecticut State University in New Haven, CT. He is the author of *Gabriel García Márquez: A Critical Companion* (Greenwood Press, 2001), and co-author of *La voz: A Practical Approach for Understanding Spanish Phonetics and Mastering Pronunciation* (2007). His essay publications include poststructuralist and linguistic studies, literary criticism, and the merging of genres. Professor Pelayo has presented his research both nationally and internationally.